FAMILY HEIRLOOM RECIPES

from the
Illinois State Fair

FAMILY HEIRLOOM RECIPES

from the
Illinois State Fair

Compiled by Greater Midwest Foodways Alliance

Catherine Lambrecht, Editor

Greater Midwest Foodways Press

Family Heirloom Recipes from the Illinois State Fair

This book presents the Greater Midwest Foodways Alliance's inaugural compilation of Family Heirloom Recipes from the Illinois State Fair in honor of the Illinois Bicentennial. It showcases family heirloom recipes entered in annual contests at Midwestern state fairs. Contestants enter their best scratch family heirloom recipe suitable for a family or community dinner. The recipe should have originated 50 years ago or earlier.

Copyright © 2018 by the Greater Midwest Foodways Alliance

All Rights Reserved.
Editor: Catherine Lambrecht
Design and Layout: R&J Pro

Library of Congress Control Number: 2019901755

ISBN-13: 978-1-950403-00-4 (Softcover)
ISBN-13: 978-1-950403-01-1 (eBook)

Except as permitted under the United States Copyright Act of 1976, no part of this publication may be reproduced in any manner whatsoever without prior written permission of the author, except in the case of brief quotations embodied in critical articles and reviews.

Cover page: *From An Illustrated Atlas, Geographical, Statistical, And Historical, Of The United States And The Adjacent Countries.* By Thomas G. Bradford. Boston: Weeks, Jordan, And Company. New York: Wiley And Putnam. This map was provided by courtesy of George Ritzlin Antique Maps and Prints.

This map was issued in 1838 after the end of the Black Hawk War, when the Native Americans were driven across the Mississippi River and settlers poured into the fertile lands of Illinois. Counties are named and indicated in contrasting shades, and rivers, lakes, and towns are precisely depicted. This was a period of great growth, with the matching development of railroad transportation throughout Illinois.

Table of Contents

Acknowledgments
vii

Introduction
1

**1.
Breakfast Foods**
7

**2.
Soups**
35

**3.
Salads**
55

**4.
Main Dishes**
87

**5.
Vegetables**
157

**6.
Desserts**

Cakes
185

Candies and Cookies
203

Pies
225

Varied Desserts
249

**7.
More Good Food**
277

Recipe Index
297

Acknowledgements

Thank you to the Illinois State Fair and to Billye Griswold, Superintendent and John Griswold, Assistant Superintendent of the Culinary Competitions.

Thank you to The Spice House (TheSpiceHouse.com) for their sponsorship of prize money and spices. Pampered Chef provided prizes to our winning contestants for a few seasons. Corvus Blue LLC also provided funding.

Thank you to our judges: Peter Engler, Julianne Glatz, Gina Hunter, Bruce Kraig, Barbara Kuck, Catherine Lambrecht, Ashley Meyer, Victoria Moré, Aggie 'The Tomato Lady' Nehmzow, Jennifer Worrell and Jeanne Zasadil.

Thank you to the founding board of Greater Midwest Foodways Alliance who grasped this idea immediately and supported it: Bruce Kraig, President, Catherine Lambrecht, Vice-President, Gerri Rounds, Secretary, Jeanne Zasadil, Treasurer, Wanda Bain, Eleanor Hanson, Christopher Koetke, Barbara Kuck and Kantha Shelke.

Thank you for thoughtful contributions to this book: Susan Brewer, Peter Engler, Debbie Fandrei, Gary Fine, Michael Gebert, Stephanie Kowalyk, Barbara Kuck, Kathleen Leable, Joe McFarland, Yvonne Maffei, Deb Silberstein, Jeff Stern and Nancy Webster.

Photographs by Peter Engler, Barbara Kuck, Catherine Lambrecht and Victoria Moré (2012).

Cover: Illinois map was produced by Bradford in 1838 provided by courtesy of George Ritzlin Antique Maps and Prints.

We are very grateful to the people who contributed their family's recipes and stories to our Family Heirloom Recipes contest at the Illinois State Fair from 2009 to 2018:

Carmen Arnberger
Grandma's Beef and Noodles

Kitsy Amrheim
Best Strawberry Pie Ever
Grandma's Cobbler
Grandmother Mohr's Pasta Salad
Nanny's Mother's Applesauce
Zwieback Pie

Jackie Bales
Ruth's Pasta Salad

Nancy Bathurst
Grandma's Black Walnut Fudge

Margaret Baucom
The Kenny Family's Irish Soda Bread

Caroline M. Becker
Kluski (Potato Dumplings) with Round Steak and Gravy

Christine Beckman
Grandmother Wierman's Mashed Potato Salad

Denise Bollman
Grandma Guth's Stuffed Cabbage Rolls with Sauerkraut

Carlene Carter
Tomato Soup

Elizabeth Carter
Great-Great Grandma Rouch's Brown Sugar Cookies

Linda D. Cifuentes
Bublanina (Coffeecake)
Cherry Cake, Grandma's Birthday Cake
Houby (Mushrooms)
Kidney Bean Salad
Ox Tail Soup
Ptacki (Rolled Round Steak)
Souffle de Zanahoria (Carrot Souffle)
Stuffed Peppers
Svestkove Knedlicky (Fruit Dumplings)

Florence M. Cook
Grandma Cook's Disappearing Baked Beans

Darlene Crider
Apple Dumplings
Chicken and Noodles
Potato Soup with Rivels
Grandma Rouch's Sweet Legacy Sugar Cookies

Liz Drake
Rhubarb Roll Up

Rob Dunbar
Mint Drink

Pam Elliott
Dueling Potato Salads

Mary Gillespie
Beans N'Such

Kimberli Yount Goodner
Spring Wild Greens

Barbara (Luchtefeld) Hopgood
Prune Cake

Jill Jackson
Great-Grandma's German Potato Salad

Dennis Kirby
Bacon, Potato, Cheese Casserole
Cottage Cheese Breakfast Pie/Dessert

Brazilla Leonard
Sarah Leonard's Family Fruit Cake

Gail Long
Grandmother's Gingerbread Cake

Michael Marchizza
Polenta with Meat Sauce
Religieuse (French Pastry)

Carol Meadows
Barbecue Sauce
Grandma Bushon's Blackberry Dumplings
Aunt Pearl's Chicken and Dumplings
Grandma Daniel's Spicy Peach Pie

Earl Meadows
Grandma's Old Fashioned Blackberry Bubble

Grace Meadows
Date Nut Pudding

Mary Joan Miller
Upside Down Cake

Betty Moser
Old Fashioned Baked Rice Pudding
Pfeffernusse Cookies

Marilyn Okon
1-2-3-4 Cake
Lima Beans in Tomato Sauce

Cindy Petriw
Tomato Cabbage

Pamela Lynn Sage
Chocolate Sour Cream Pound Cake

Janie Saner
Grandma Delong's Meatloaf

Jeanne Schultheis
Great-Grandma's German Potato Salad

Jone Schumacher
Buelah's Chicken Salad
Family Sweet Corn
Grandmother Nickel's Donuts
Grandmommy's (My) Fudge Tarts
Grandmother's Meringue Shells
Grandmother's Raspberry Sauce
Molasses Cut-Out Cookies
Mother's Day Strawberry Rhubarb Salad
Old Fashion Oven Fried Chicken

Crystal R. Smith
Grandma Cook's Disappearing Baked Beans

Paul L. Smith
My Family's Recipe for Date Nut Pudding

Deborah Steele
Saltibarsciai (Cold Beet Soup)

Dianna M. Wara
Great Grandma's Pasties
Potica (Breakfast Bread)
Sugar Pie

Amy Wendling
Grandma's Rhubarb Dessert

Amy Wertheim
Aunt Lynd's Infamous Corn Pudding
Butterscotch Pie
Fried Sage – or Nature's "Potato Chips"
Great-Grandma's Meatloaf Cake
Old Version Beef 'n Noodles
Original Oyster Dressing
Peanut Brittle
Peixe a Lumbo (African Shrimp and Rice Stew)
Simple Asparagus Soup
Spargelsuppe – White Asparagus Soup
Today's Oyster Dressing
Updated Version Beef and Noodles

Introduction

I have always loved narratives which explain how we got to where we are today via small and mighty ideas, inventions and quirky personalities.

When I was 10 years old, I had the privilege to live with my German grandmother, Helen Lambrecht, for a few months. We always loved Sunday lunches with what I supposed was Oma's food fit for company. I was always curious how Oma ate every day. I soon learned every day was wonderful food. Leftover vegetables from dinner were repurposed as next day's lunch of soup, thanks to her Osterizer. Leftover pot roast was shredded and served over noodles with a gravy full of fresh mushrooms. Dessert was an apple cake with a generous dollop of Cool Whip. As much a whipped cream snob as I may be, Cool Whip is a bold exception because it reminds me of Oma.

My father remembered when his mother was learning to cook. Fortunately, I came along when Oma had a solid repertoire of reliable recipes and the skills to pull it off. There were the infrequently made dishes, which required a recipe card as a reminder. There were kitchen meals made without recipes due to repetition and experience, meals our family adores, though meals Oma might not serve to company.

Oma died unexpectedly a few months short of my 16th birthday. Our favorite dinners with Oma were those she never documented, because she just knew what to do. We almost never saw her cooking, because everything was ready when we arrived. She wanted to enjoy our company rather than fuss in the kitchen.

It took two years of trial and error to bring those dishes back to our family's table. Over time all these recipes we almost lost were written and distributed to everyone in the family. The experience of family favorites almost lost has been a hard-earned lesson I have shared often as a cautionary tale.

While living in Massachusetts in the mid-1960s, my mother joined Homemakers, an organization with strong ties to land grant university extension services. It influenced my later association with University of Illinois Extension as a master gardener and master food preserver. As part of my volunteer efforts, I was assigned to judge 4-H food competitions. Wishing for a similar experience, I competed at county and state fairs with a best of show and several champion rosettes as proof.

When Greater Midwest Foodways Alliance was kicking around for a project, I suggested sponsoring a family heirloom recipe contest at Midwestern state fairs. Contestants would enter their best scratch family heirloom recipe suitable for a family or community dinner. The recipe should have originated 50 years ago or earlier. Contestants would bring a prepared dish along with a history of who passed the recipe down to them, ethnicity, if relevant, number of years the recipe has been in their family and any interesting information about their recipe. The all-important history of the recipe would account for fully half the score, with execution and taste (40%) and display and appearance (10%) accounting for the other half.

This book offers an opportunity to follow the judging experience by providing the histories and recipes presented as submitted. Any editing was very light to correct a typo or missing period, though unique measurements, spellings and grammars were retained. A picture of the food taken as presented at the fair. The foods were sometimes submitted simply in their transport container, or more elaborately on the family's china with relevant props of family pictures, kitchen paraphernalia and their loved one's handwritten recipe.

None of these recipes have been tested or adapted. They are provided as presented to preserve their historical integrity. Some of these recipes originated when oven temperatures were difficult to regulate, or temperature was taken literally by hand: stick your hand in the oven chamber and count the seconds before your hand cannot tolerate it. When dealing with oven-baked goods, please use your best judgment as to whether the product has finished cooking in the time stated in the recipe.

Unlike many sponsored contests which rely on state fair-appointed judges, we send our members to judge the Family Heirloom Contest. This contest is unique because the final decision is not solely dependent on the recipe's execution. We weighted the history at 50% to emphasize it is a major consideration. Consequently, an excellent history can trump a recipe's execution, but an excellent dish with no history will never go far. We recognize participation would be greater if we dropped the requirement of a history, though it is a cost we can live with to achieve our goal of breathing new life into old recipes.

At the end of the state fair season, these recipes, histories and images are loaded to our website: www.GreaterMidwestFoodways.com. Over the holidays, there is usually a bump in traffic as people search for long lost recipes. The digital age provides great opportunities to explore, though the content is fragile if a website is no longer funded, or a virus wipes out a memory. Memorializing the precious content from this contest in a book reduces the opportunity for loss by spreading the word. If used book stores exist two hundred years from now, I can only hope someone gasps with recognition of a name or recipe in this book.

For the long haul the original histories and recipes will be archived. At this writing, we are in conversation with the University of Michigan Library Special Collections Research Center, concerning the possibility of placing these recipes and histories in the Janice Bluestein Longone Culinary Archives in Ann Arbor. This culinary archive is a mecca for researchers. We want to encourage the continued use and study of these Family Heirloom Recipes, because these recipes and their histories will live on as long as they are not forgotten.

If nothing else, should this book inspire you to document a family favorite recipe to share with loved ones, then we have accomplished our mission.

All the best,

Cathy

Catherine Lambrecht
October 20, 2018

Greater Midwest Foodways Alliance
FAMILY HEIRLOOM RECIPES

Illinois State Fair
2010

2010 Display

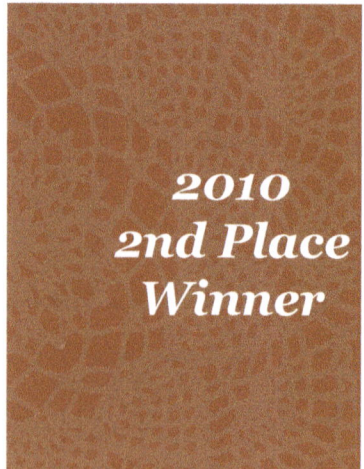

2010 2nd Place Winner

Breakfast Foods

The Kenny Family's Irish Soda Bread

Potica (Breakfast Bread)

Bacon, Potato, Cheese Casserole

Bublanina (Coffeecake)

Grandmother Nickel's Donuts

Grandma Buchon's Blackberry Dumplings

Cottage Cheese Breakfast Pie/Dessert

Contestant, 2014

The Kenny Family's Irish Soda Bread
Margaret Baucom, Scott Air Force Base, Illinois

This recipe has been part of my Irish heritage for over 90 years.

On August 5, 1922 my mother, Alice Kenny, departed County Leitrim Ireland at the age of five with her parents and three siblings. After an eight-day crossing, they arrived aboard the SS Belgic at the port of New York.

Growing up in Rye, New York I can remember watching my grandmother and mom prepare this humble recipe in our welcoming kitchen. After all the dry and wet ingredients were stirred together and combined, they placed the dough in a cast iron skillet. My mom would make a cross mark on top of the loaf a decoration symbolizing our Catholic roots.

After it was baked, we would sit together at the kitchen table and savor each slice with a pot of tea. My grandmother especially loved this tradition and made sure it would be continued in America.

It is now a custom that I have come to treasure. To this day, I enjoy having a cup of tea and Irish soda bread with my daughter.

Photo by Catherine Lambrecht

The Kenny Family's Irish Soda Bread
Margaret Baucom, Scott Air Force Base, Illinois

Ingredients:

4 cups of all-purpose flour
¼ cup of sugar
1 teaspoon of baking soda
1 teaspoon of baking powder
1 teaspoon of salt
4 teaspoons of caraway seeds
½ cup of unsalted butter cut into chunks
1½ cups of raisins
1 egg lightly beaten
1⅓ cups of sour milk (to sour milk stir in 1 tablespoon of fresh lemon juice and let stand for 5 minutes until thickened)

Directions:

Adjust an oven rack to the middle position and preheat the oven to 375-degrees Generously coat a 10½-inch cast-iron skillet using vegetable oil spray.

Combine flour, sugar, baking soda, baking powder, salt and caraway seeds. Cut in butter until mixture resembles coarse meal. Add raisins. Combine beaten egg and sour milk. Pour into mixture and combine until just moistened. Gather dough into a ball and press into prepared skillet. Using a knife, make a ¼-inch-deep cross over the dough. Bake in the preheated oven for 45 minutes. Let stand for 5 minutes, remove from skillet and serve warm with butter or jam.

Second Prize, 2009

Potica (Breakfast Bread)
Dianna M. Wara, Washington, Illinois

Oh my Gosh! I can remember walking into my grandma's kitchen on Christmas morning to the smell of this wonder breakfast meal.

Our traditional Christmas breakfast entree was this wonderful bread pronounced Poka-tiza. When it's served warm, like my grandma did for Christmas, the filling just oozed on the plate. YUMMY! Grandma also served the Pokatiza with orange juice and coffee for the adults. My grandfather was Croatian and depending on which region you lived, the pronunciation, shape and flavors could vary. My grandma explained that it was a special bread made for special events only. Christmas was the special event in which my family made this bread. My grandmother taught my mother how to make this bread many years after she married my dad. I remember asking

Photo by Peter Engler

my grandma why she waited so long to teach my mom this bread. As grandma explained to me, she wanted to make sure she (my mom) was a keeper. Once grandma figured out that mom was a "keeper," she taught her the recipe. I'm glad that mom passed the test! Actually, my mom has been a "keeper" for 47 years so far.

When we no longer went to grandma's for Christmas. My mom continued the family's traditional Christmas breakfast. When mom bakes the Pokatiza, she bakes it the day before Christmas. So, when we slice it on Christmas morning, the filling doesn't ooze anymore. But she taught us a trick to that. We just microwave the Pokatiza and we had the warm ooze of filling that we all know and love so much! And yes, she still serves it with orange juice and coffee. When my mom took over the baking of the Pokatiza, she decided to celebrate one other special day. That was on April 6th. That was the day that my mom and dad were married. It was another special day that was celebrated with the Pokatiza. My mom in later years taught me how to make the bread and tradition continues.

> My grandma explained that it was a special bread made for special events only.

I made this bread for you today, just as my mom does for our family. The walnuts that grandma used, were always picked from trees on her farm. My mom always uses walnuts that my dad has picked and cleaned from his farm. So, it is with great pride that I present this bread to you today, made from walnuts that my dad picked and clean, just for me.

Potica (Breakfast Bread)
Dianna M. Wara, Washington, Illinois

Photo by Peter Engler

Ingredients:

Dough
2 to 2½ cups all-purpose flour
1 package active dry yeast
⅓ cup milk
¼ cup butter
2 tablespoons sugar
½ teaspoon salt
2 eggs

Filling
3 cups black walnuts, small chopped
⅓ cup brown sugar
¼ cup honey
1 slightly beaten egg
3 tablespoons milk
½ teaspoon vanilla
¼ cup butter
1 teaspoon ground cinnamon

Directions:

1. In a bowl combine 1 cup of the flour and the yeast; set aside. In a saucepan heat the cup milk, butter, 2 tablespoons sugar, and salt just until warm (125–130 degrees F). Add to flour/yeast mixture. Then add 2 eggs. Beat with an electric mixer on low to medium speed for 30 seconds, scraping bowl. Beat on high speed for 3 minutes. Using a wooden spoon, stir in as much of the remaining flour as you can.

2. On a lightly floured surface, knead in enough of the remaining flour to make a moderately soft dough that is smooth and elastic (3 to 5 minutes total). Shape into a ball. Place dough in a greased bowl, turning once to grease surface. Cover and let rise in a warm place until double.

3. Meanwhile, for filling, mix walnuts, sugar, honey, remaining egg and milk and vanilla. Set aside.

4. Punch dough down. Cover and let rest 10 minutes. Grease two 9x5 loaf pans. On a lightly floured cloth, roll dough into a 15-inch square. Cover and let rest 10 minutes. Then roll dough into a 30×20-inch rectangle.

5. To assemble, cut dough lengthwise in half to form two 30×10-inch sheets. Spread the butter on top of both dough rectangles. Sprinkle the cinnamon on top. Spread walnut filling evenly on top of the dough, keeping to within 1 inch of the edges. Using the cloth as a guide, roll each rectangle up into a spiral, starting from a short side. Pinch seams and ends to seal. Place loaves, seam sides down, in the prepared pans. Mom and grandma would shape them like the letter "U" and then place it in the pan. Cover and let rise until nearly double (45 to 60 minutes).

6. Bake in a 325-degree F oven 45 to 50 minutes until bread sounds hollow when lightly tapped. If necessary, cover with foil the last 15 minutes of baking to prevent overbrowning. Remove from pans; cool. Makes 2 loaves.

First Prize, 2015

Bacon, Potato, Cheese Casserole
Dennis Kirby, Champaign, Illinois

There is a Season for Everything!

As an avid animal lover and growing up on a farm in the South, the Fall always troubled me. During the Spring time, we would have calves, chicks, ducklings, piglets, puppies, and kittens … on the farm. Spring was my favorite time of year. I would always be the one that would gravitate to the runts of the litter and try to save them, so they weren't left to die by the mother or culled by my father. It was a reality that runts seldom lived, but I always wanted to try.

Coming from a farming community, the reality was that, throughout the year, animals would have to be slaughtered for the family to sell and to eat. That realization didn't make things any easier for me. We always had spring pigs to sell to other farmers who didn't raise hogs. I would always "try" to hide the runt of the litter because I wanted to hand raise the runts myself. I knew deep in my heart that eventually the piglet would grow into a full-sized hog and would either be slaughtered or have to be sold. But

Photo by Peter Engler

that didn't keep me from trying my best to hide the little thing.

In Spring of 1969, I was still young and fairly naive around the farm. I am now 53 years old and my memory of this Spring is still clear in my head. Our sow had given birth to 14 piglets that spring. There happened to be two runts of that litter. My Dad explained to me that they needed to be culled because they probably wouldn't live anyways. Being a stubborn little man, I begged him to let me try and bottle feed them. One was a male and one was a female. I was only 8 or 9 at the time. I got permission from my school teacher to bring the piglets in to class each day, so I could bottle feed them. She thought it was a great idea to have the other students help bottle feed them and learn about them as the piglets grew. By the end of the school year, both of the piglets had survived with feedings every 2-3 hours around the clock while they were little. They were big enough to sell.

I did not realize that my dad had decided to keep the male or why. We kept the male and sold the female for $25.00. At that time $25.00 was a lot of money for us to have plus I knew that she would be used for breeding. I had no idea what was in store for Bart. I kept feeding Bart and he continued to get fatter.

October rolled around and my Father and Grandfather, Grandmother, and Mom sat me down and we had a long heart to heart talk. They explained that the first frost would soon be coming and that they were going to have to slaughter Bart. We couldn't afford to keep him over the winter. Feed was expensive even then. It had to be done. I was heartbroken. I ran from the room yelling and screaming absurdities that I knew better to even entertain in my head much less let them come out of my mouth. I cried for two weeks. School was back in session when the first frost hit that year. I knew that weekend would be Bart's last day. I asked a neighbor friend of mine if I could spend the weekend with them because I didn't want to be at the house when it happened.

When I got home late Sunday (I didn't go to Church that Sunday morning because I was even mad at God, or at least I thought I was then). The dinner table was set, and everyone was silent. You could hear the crickets underneath the porch outside chirping away, nothing but silence. Mom had made my favorite for dinner, fried chicken and potato salad. I just sat there with tears welling up in my eyes. I didn't say a word. I knew I would be in for a thrashing if I let out another round of "smart mouth" to my Mom and Dad. I didn't eat much that night. When it was time for me and my brother to go to bed, Daddy said, "I will be up in a few minutes to talk to you." My brother slept on the couch that night. I knew I was going to get it for not eating my dinner and for not going to Church that day. I waited in bed. I had put on two pair of pajamas and extra socks in preparation for my punishment.

> There is a season for everything, Son.
>
> There is a time to be born and a time to die.
>
> A time to reap, and a time to sow.
>
> There is even a time, Son, to be angry and a time to show compassion and understanding.

Daddy didn't even knock on the door. He walked right on in. He sat down on the edge of the bed. Neither of us said anything for about 5 minutes. Finally, he broke the silence. "You know, Son, we raise animals to sell and to have food for the winter. We have to make ends meet. You know that, right?" I told my Dad, "Yeah, I understand but I don't have to like it or watch it when it happens."

"No, you don't," he responded sternly. He said to me, in a low voice "There is a season for everything, Son." "There is a time to be born and a time to die." "A time to reap, and a time to sow." He then said something that I have told my own Son many times, "There is even a time, Son, to be angry and a time to show compassion and understanding." He got up and walked out of the room. I didn't understand his words at that time, but I felt at peace with everything right then.

The next morning, I came down to breakfast and there was a bacon, potato, cheese casserole on the table for breakfast. I knew in my heart that it was Bart that was on the table. I couldn't eat. I excused myself from the table and said I was going on to school. Mom looked at me and said, "Dennis, your Dad wants your help up at the hog shed." I stared and said, "Alright." I walked slowly to the hog shed and my Dad was waiting with hog slop and water. He looked at me and said that he had hurt his back slaughtering the hogs on Saturday when he slipped and fell (my Dad never slipped and fell, but I didn't say anything). I grabbed the feed and water and walked on up the hill to the hog pen. There was Bart! He wasn't dead. I didn't know then that Dad had used part of the money we had gotten for the sow and some of the money he and Mom had saved up for Christmas presents and bought a hog from another farmer to slaughter. My Dad had spared Bart.

Dad had walked up the hill behind me and was standing there smiling at me. "You realize this is your Christmas present and any piglets that he sires will be sold in the Spring to pay for the hog we bought to kill." I knew he was right, but my Dad had shown compassion and understanding to me, FOR ME. I ran to him and gave him a huge hug and thanked him. Even though I knew in my heart this would never happen again, I understood that sometimes we have to show understanding and compassion for others.

He said, "Come on, let's get back to the house. Your Mom made us breakfast, and we have to show her we like it and appreciate her getting up at 3 a.m. to fix it for us." That was the last time my Dad held my hand, but I remember it as well today as if it happened yesterday. That was the best Bacon, Potato, Cheese casserole I had ever eaten. I can't make it as well as my Mom but give it a try. It's simple and cheesy and loaded with bacon and potatoes. Be prepared to spend 2 and ½ hours for it to bake, but it's well worth the wait. It's great hot or cold.

Even though this recipe has been around in our family for many years it has recently resurfaced a fan favorite for family reunions.

Bacon, Potato, Cheese Casserole
Dennis Kirby, Champaign, Illinois

Photo by Peter Engler

Ingredients:

1½ lbs. of lean bacon
2 lbs. of potatoes, skin on
1 large onion
1½ lbs. of Colby Jack Cheese
¼ teaspoon salt each layer
¼ teaspoon pepper each layer

Directions:

Use a frying pan that can be put into a 350-degree oven.

Line the bottom and side of the pan with parchment paper or use 2 tablespoon lard to prevent from sticking.

Starting at the very center of the pan, line bacon strips side by side, alternating a little forward and a little back to prevent overlapping on the bottom of the pan.

Once this is done, thinly slice potatoes, and onions (ONLY ONE LAYER OF ONIONS) layering them on top of the bacon. Add a layer of cheese and then season with salt and pepper. Repeat the process (potatoes, cheese, salt and pepper) until you have about 4 to 6 layers.

Taking your time, fold the bacon over the top of the potatoes. Place a heavy lid on top of the casserole to prevent bacon from curling. Bake in a preheated 350-degree oven for about 2½ hours. Be sure to place a drip pan beneath the skillet to prevent bacon grease from splattering everywhere.

Remove from oven and drain as much grease as possible. Turn pan over onto a large plate to release casserole and remove parchment if used. Use a second plate to turn casserole over again. Sprinkle with a little more cheese. Cut in pie slices and serve warm as a main dish or allow to cool for a side dish! Top with sour cream, extra shredded cheese and green onions if desired! Enjoy! This dish has been around for many years and has only just recently resurfaced as a popular family gathering dish.

Third Prize, 2013

Bublanina (Coffeecake)
Linda D. Cifuentes, Mahomet, Illinois

*Bublanina is a Czech coffeecake.
This recipe was handed down to me from my mother
Helen Brezinsky Holas who got it from her Babi
(Czech for grandma) Philomena Sekera.*

My great-grandmother, Philomena, came to the United States in 1902 from Prague along with her husband and three children through Ellis Island. Philomena's middle child was my grandma Elizabeth Sekera Brezinsky. The family settled in Cicero which along with Berwyn was predominantly Czech community. This area featured bakeries, butcher shops, and flower shops where mostly Czech was spoken.

By the time my grandma Betty was married my great grandfather had passed away and Philomena; my great-grandma lived with her and her family which included the baby of that family; my mom Helen. Philomena was a great cook, and this was a good thing because grandma Betty was not. Philomena did most of the cooking and passed her love for cooking and her skill to her mom. I would like to think then my mom passed that down to me.

Bublanina was a summer staple that became a summer tradition. I remember when I was a little girl and my mom pulled out the old and worn cookie sheet, we knew it was time for Bublanina. I would sit at the table for what seemed like forever for the coveted cake to get into the oven. It seemed to take my mom forever to pit and cut those cherries. The waiting was soooo worth it!! I would grab a couple of slices right out of the pan and run to the living room to devour them. Being of chubby stature; then and now I always went back for more.

Bublanina has now become a tradition in my family–It isn't summer if you don't have Bublanina. Making this coffeecake also brings back happy memories from my childhood and of my mom, considering how far this recipe traveled it also reminds me of my family history.

Bublanina (Coffeecake)
Linda D. Cifuentes, Mahomet, Illinois

Ingredients:

1½ cups sugar
¾ cup butter
4 whole eggs
¼ tsp. lemon extract
1¾ cup flour
2 tsp baking powder
½ tsp salt
¼ cup milk
2 pounds Bing cherries; pitted and halved

Directions:

Cream sugar and butter. Add eggs one at a time and beat well after each addition. Sift dry ingredients and add alternately with milk. Add extract. Blend well. Pour batter on to a cookie sheet that has been greased and sprinkled with bread crumbs. place cherries over entire top of batter. Bake ½ hour in a 350F oven.

Photos by Catherine Lambrecht

Third Prize, 2009

Grandmother's Yeast Donuts
Jone Schumacher, Chapin, Illinois

Grandmother Nickel's Donuts

The folks living in the little village of Concord in the 1930's had most likely never had the delicacy of a donut until my grandmother, Sara Nickel, made them. My grandfather, Roy Nickel, produced Morgan-Scott Hybrid Corn and had a seed processing building outside Concord. My father and aunts tell me when Grandfather held an open-house field-day for his seed corn business, Grandmother made the donuts from scratch to serve the visiting farmers. Considering I awakened early in the morning to make one small batch of donuts for the fair, I wonder what time Grandmother rose to make the number needed to satisfy the hungry men. As a child, I do not remember the open house events, but I do recall the days Grandmother would make her unusual treat to take for morning breaks for the workers who

Photo by Peter Engler

did the hand grading and processing of the corn at the seed plant several times during the fall. I recall being thrilled when there were donuts "left over" to be enjoyed by the grandchildren for an after-school treat, although I now realize Grandmother made an amount to assure there would be some left over. Grandmother's donuts were the first and only donuts I recall eating as a child. I know donuts are very common and readily available today, but they were quite unusual, highly praised, and greatly looked forward to in the community of Concord.

I, like my grandmother, love to bake and experiment in the kitchen. It is special for me to now have my Grandmother's heirloom recipe as my aunt located it and gave me a photo copy in Grandmother's own handwriting. Since Grandmother did not have in her recipe exactly the sugar coating, feel special being able to update her recipe from my aunt's memory. Grandmother's recipe did not specify they type of fat used for frying, but my father was very sure she would have had their own rendered lard to use which he believes added to the flavor. Since most people today do not perform the many hours of hard farm labor which helped to metabolize the animal fat, I choose to update my use of Grandmother's recipe by choosing vegetable oil for health-conscious folks of modern day.

> I recall being thrilled when there were donuts "left over" to be enjoyed by the grandchildren

I hope someday, my grandchildren will recall with fond memories the wonderful treat of their grandmother's special homemade donuts I have made with love for them as much as I reminisce about my grandmother's donuts. Even more, I hope my grandmother's donut recipe will be handed down through the generations and that my daughters and granddaughters will have inherited our "culinary gene" to carry on the family donut tradition.

Grandmother's Yeast Donuts
Jone Schumacher, Chapin, Illinois

Ingredients:

½ cup butter
1½ cup milk, divided
½ cup sugar
2 teaspoons salt
2 packages dry active yeast
½ cup lukewarm water
2 eggs, beaten
7+ cups flour

Photo by Peter Engler

Directions:

Sprinkle the yeast over the lukewarm water. Let rest until bubbly.

Combine the butter, sugar and salt in large mixing bowl. Scald ¾ cup milk and pour over the sugar mixture. Stir until butter is melted. Stir in the remaining cold milk to cool mixture to lukewarm.

Stir in the yeast. Beat in the eggs.

Add flour gradually, stirring well until well blended. Continue to add flour until dough is stiff enough to turn out onto a floured board to knead.

Knead for 5 minutes until dough is smooth and elastic.

Place in greased large bowl and cover with a clean dish towel and let rest in warm draft-free area for about an hour until doubled.

Punch down and let rest a few minutes before rolling out.

On floured board with rolling pen, roll dough to large rectangle about ½ inch thick. Cut with round biscuit cutter and cut out center with smaller cutter. Placed on greased tray, cover and let rise until doubled.

Heat fat to 375 degrees. With large spatula, lift raised dough and slide into hot fat. Fry on for approximately 2-3 minutes until golden brown. Turn over to fry to golden brown on second side. Lift from fat and drain.

Grandmother did not specify in her recipe what her sugar cinnamon or powdered sugar glaze was exactly, so I researched through my aunts and my father and thus adapted as close to their memory as possible and made this addition to her recipe.

Glaze:

2 tablespoons melted butter
1½ cups powdered sugar
½ teaspoon vanilla
2-3 tablespoons milk

Sugar Cinnamon:

½ cup granulated sugar
1 teaspoon cinnamon

Combine ingredients of glaze and stir until well blended. Using a pastry brush, brush glaze on one side of warm donut; let set for a few minutes on wire rack. Brush the other side of donut and let rest to set.

Stir together the sugar and cinnamon. Place in small bowl. Place warm donut in to the sugar and turn to coat with the sugar.

Yield: 2 to 2½ dozen medium sized donuts

First Prize, 2010

Grandma Bushon's Blackberry Dumplings
Carol Meadows, Springfield, Illinois

Even though Grandma Buson could not read or write she was a great cook and made sure that her children learned to read, write, and cook.

y husband recalls one of his fondest memories as a child was going to Centralia to visit his grandma in the summer.

He tells of waking in the morning to the smell of fresh baked bread with honey from her bees. Picking blackberries along the side of the railroad tracks where they grew wild, bringing them back to the house where grandma would make a cobbler, pie or dumplings.

My husband tells that her mother (his great grandmother) died at an early age (around the turn of the century) and she along with her brothers and sisters were placed in an orphanage. While

Photo by Barbara Kuck

she was in the orphanage, she met the boy who would become her future husband. She ran away from that horrible place and worked for others.

She didn't go to school, nor did she learn to read and write though up until the time of her death this was her fondest wish. My husband would read articles that she clipped out of the newspaper and placed in a shoe box that she thought might be important or might mean something. She asked my husband if he would teach her the A, B, C's and how to read but she passed away before he was able to. To keep her recipes alive her daughters would write down the ingredients she used, and any other information needed to duplicate the recipe. Grandma's recipes are still prized by family members.

> She asked my husband if he would teach her the A, B, C's

She was deeply religious and believed everything had a purpose. In the summer you would find her in the garden picking the odd bug and turtles off the plants. If you asked her why she didn't just kill the bugs she would tell you, they were all God's creatures, and everything had a purpose. So, she would load bugs and turtles in a bucket and empty them in the ditch. The next day you would find her in the garden repeating the process.

Even though she could not read or write she was a great cook and made sure that her children learned to read, write, and cook. I obtained her recipe for Blackberry Dumplings from her daughter Lilly Ragan who in her own right was a fantastic cook. Grandfather Meadows died when the children were young during the great depression. She later married Grandfather Bushon. If you speak to family members about grandma, the stories they recall are filled with love and admiration.

Grandma Bushon's Blackberry Dumplings
Carol Meadows, Springfield, Illinois

Ingredients:

3 Cups Water
2 Bags Frozen Blackberries or 2 Quarts Wild Blackberries
1 Cup Sugar
½ Cup Packed Brown Sugar
¼ Teaspoon Cinnamon
⅛ Teaspoon Nutmeg
3 Tablespoons Soft Butter
1½ cups Flour
2 Teaspoons Baking Powder
¼ Teaspoon Salt
¾ Cup Milk

Photo by Barbara Kuck

Directions:

In a large no stick pan place blackberries, sugar, brown sugar, cinnamon, and nutmeg. Place over medium heat and cook until sugar dissolves and berries start to boil. Stir to make sure berries do not stick. In a bowl place soft butter, flour, baking powder, and salt. Blend together with a pastry blender. Add milk and mix well. Drop a spoon at a time into the boiling blackberries. Cover berries and dumplings and let cook for 15 minutes do not take the lid off the pan or the dumplings will fall. Turn off heat and remove lid.

Serve dumplings and berries (while berries are still hot) with vanilla ice cream. If you are in a hurry instead of making dumplings from scratch, you can also use the dumpling recipe on the Bisquick box.

First Prize, 2012

Cottage Cheese Breakfast Pie/Dessert
Dennis Kirby, Champaign, Illinois

Just reading the recipe card caused me to remember fondly my grandfather and my Mom ...

Looking back to my first day of school in September 1969, I remember my Mom had breakfast on the table and I was too excited about the idea of going to school to eat. Mom told me that she had a surprise for me when I got home. She hinted that it had something to do with an old recipe of my Grandmother's and was a favorite of my Grandfather's.

Now, my Mom knew, of her three boys, I was always willing to try anything new that there was to eat. I had a pretty good appetite and there wasn't much that I wouldn't eat. When I tried to get more information from her about what the surprise was, she just said that it was one of her favorite desserts when she was growing up on

Photo by Victoria Moré

the farm in Virginia. I was pretty excited about getting home that day to find out what Mom was hinting at.

After school that day, I rushed home as fast as my little legs would carry me. When I walked into the house, I smelled the most wonderful aromas coming from the kitchen-lemon, vanilla, and aromatic bitters. I hurried into the kitchen and found that Mom had already sliced a piece of pie for me and herself. Mom watched my face as I took my first bite. It was the most delicious thing I had ever tasted. Mom was smiling at me at the way my eyes closed as I savored the rich taste of the pie.

> My fondest memory of my Grandfather was him pulling me onto his lap when I was quite young and sharing pie and a glass of cold lemonade.

Recently, I came across the recipe for the pie while getting ready for a yard sale. Just reading the recipe card caused me to remember fondly my grandfather and my Mom (she passed away in October 1996).

With those memories came the idea that I needed to make the pie recipe for my own son and start another generation of memories that include this luscious dessert. After getting all the necessary ingredients together, I made the pie and served it to my son. He took one bite and another generation of cottage cheese pie lovers was born.

A little history of the family. My Mother was born deep in the foothills of Fries, Virginia. When she was seven years old, she was already cooking for her brothers and sisters and my grandparents.

My Grandfather, Clarence, was a sharecropper and very poor. His family had very little when they were growing up. He made his living by growing crops and milking cows for the land owner for whom he sharecropped. My Grandfather struggled to raise nine children, work acres of land, and maintain the family home during the Depression. To say the least, my Grandfather was not a sophisticated or cultured man, but he did love his family deeply.

My fondest memory of my Grandfather was him pulling me onto his lap when I was quite young and sharing pie and a glass of cold lemonade. He never showed a lot of affection but, like most men of that generation, he showed his love by the way he cared for his family and the smiles and warm expressions on his time-worn face.

My Grandfather passed away on Father's Day of 1969 after a second heart attack. I was devastated by the loss. I remember my Mom trying to console me by telling me she would make my Grandfather's favorite pie in his honor when we returned home that day. Seems that the pie was a family favorite, because four of the cottage cheese pies were waiting for us when we arrived home that had been brought over by thoughtful relatives and friends. The recipe evidently dates back to the 1890s and originated somewhere in Europe where cow milk was plentiful. It has been in our family since about the early 1900s.

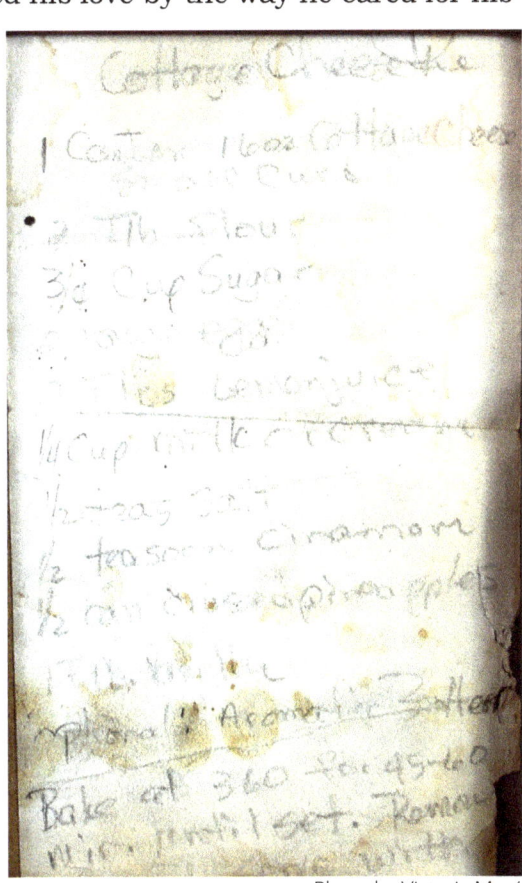

Photo by Victoria Moré

Cottage Cheese Breakfast Pie/Dessert
Dennis Kirby, Champaign, Illinois

Ingredients:

Filling:

1 Carton Small or Large Curd Cottage Cheese (16 oz.) Can be pureed for smooth creamy consistency
2 Tbsp. Flour
¾ Cup Sugar
3 Large Eggs Well Beaten
2 Tbsp. Lemon Juice
¼ Cup Milk or Cream
½ teaspoon salt
1½ teaspoon cinnamon
½ Can Crushed Pineapples (14.5 oz) drained. Discard juice except for 2 Tbsp. to add to filling for flavor
1 Tbsp. Vanilla

Optional: 1 teaspoon aromatic bitters

Pie Crust:

2½ cups all-purpose flour plus extra for rolling
1 cup unsalted butter (8 oz. or 2 sticks) (be sure the butter is very cold and cut ½-inch squares)
1 teaspoon salt
6-8 Tbsp. ice water

Directions:

Will make 2 crusts but you only need 1 for this pie. Do not over mix ingredients or crust will be tough. Roll out and put in a 9" or 10" pie tin. This pie bakes better in a tin pie plate compared to a glass pie plate.

Preheat oven to 425 degrees. Mix all ingredients together except for ½ teaspoon cinnamon. (If pureeing cottage cheese, do so for about 2 minutes). Add reserved pineapples into mixture. Sprinkle top with remaining cinnamon. Place on middle rack of preheated oven and bake for 5 minutes. Without opening oven reduce heat to 360-degrees and continue baking for 45-50 minutes until pie is set. Remove from oven and allow to cool for about 30 minutes. Great served warm or cold as a breakfast dish or as a main dessert. Serve with fresh berries or melon for a refreshing breakfast!

Photo by Victoria Moré

Greater Midwest Foodways Alliance
FAMILY HEIRLOOM RECIPES

Illinois State Fair
2011

Soups

Spargelsuppe (White Asparagus Soup)

—⟫◆⟪—

Simple Asparagus Soup

—⟫◆⟪—

Ox Tail Soup

—⟫◆⟪—

Potato Soup with Rivels

—⟫◆⟪—

Saltibarsciai (Cold Beet Soup)

—⟫◆⟪—

Tomato Soup

First Prize, 2016

Asparagus Soups
Amy Wertheim, Atlanta, Illinois

Like all good family feuds, this one goes back several generations, but it also has ties across an ocean, thru several countries and political unrest, as well as social economic levels. Its white vs green – and you get to help to decide once and for all, which color is the winner.

I'm sure you've heard the expression, dirt poor. Well that is what my mother's relatives were when they first came to America shortly after World War I. The real irony of their union is that neither of my great-grandparents knew one another when they boarded their ship transports in England and made their way here; but yet, they both ended up working on a rather large agriculture farm in central Iowa. My great-grandfather, Paul, was a field hand, learning the rules of the land and hog farming; my great-grandmother, Annetta, was a house maid and primary keeper of the owners' children, who could be quite unruly. It was the children's ill behavior that brought the two together one afternoon as the children "escaped" and hid from Annetta in the farm's asparagus patch. Oh, the damage they did, breaking off stalks and trampling them. Paul was the first to discover the little minks, and promptly returned them to the house, where Annetta took them quickly in hand, but the damage was done. And in the Midwest of the Unites States, there is but a small window of opportunity to have fresh green asparagus ... and now it was gone, literally trampled into the ground. Paul, not wanting to see Annetta in trouble, quickly released several cows and sounded the alarm; although the farmer and his wife were not happy with the damage done by the "cows", all was forgiven because those darn cows were always finding a way to get out and cause problems ...

The farmer & his family salvaged what they could, making the usual asparagus casseroles, pies, pickled varieties and soups to put up for the lauder for later meals and winter dinners. No one was ever the wiser for the children's involvement and Annetta soon looked at Paul in a whole new light, as her hero and someone who would protect her always. They were married

Photo by Peter Engler

soon after and moved to Emden, IL where a large population of Germans had chosen to settle. The town of Emden reminded Annetta of her home, Emden, Germany, and they soon were able save enough to purchase a small farm and start a family of their own. However, it wasn't too long before the original status of dirt poor took on a whole new meaning (see pic of two girls in the chicken yard). Times were hard entering in the middle 1930's and they struggled to keep their farm, raise a family and keep the children clothed. But the one constant on the farm, was the asparagus bed that Annetta lovingly tended, as this was the binding tie between her and Paul.

Nothing went to waste on the family farm, as the oldest daughter, Margaret, was in charge of the chickens …. After killing, plucking and cooking the chicken, the broth was always reserved for use in the special asparagus soup Annetta would make and preserve for those special family dinners. Every Thanksgiving and Christmas, Annetta would serve this special dish (see pic of two girls in front of dinner on dining table) and all couldn't wait to eat it – it truly was the highlight of the meal, as Paul would recount the story of the children/cows that brought them together thru the ruined asparagus patch.

SOUPS

On the other side of the ocean, life wasn't so difficult money-wise, but politically things couldn't be worse. My father's relatives had been encouraged for quite some time to leave Germany, even Europe, all together, but only the oldest boy, Elias, had made the journey to America many years prior. Those still in Germany soon were facing deportation to the camps and all but a very few would survive the war and Hitler. Elias was desperate for news of his family, but even his uncle in Vermont could offer no information or hope. It would seem, the entire family was gone; and he only had a handwritten volume of recipes and stories provided by his mother that she had given him before he left as his only link to the past. His new bride, Frances, tried to ease his pain by making many of the favorite recipes his mother had provided to him; his primary favorite being a Spargelsuppe, or white asparagus soup. White asparagus is quite common in Germany, but not so in the United States. But Frances would not be deterred; she ordered special shoots to grow to make sure to always have plenty of the vegetable on hand to make for Elias whenever he was feeling especially low.

> ... he only had a handwritten volume of recipes and stories provided by his mother ...

As inferred, my great-grandparents were on opposite political sides during the Great War, WWII. My mother's family were German and would receive Nazi propaganda sent to them from their relatives in the homeland which my great-grandmother would quickly bury in the back yard. America had changed their perspective, slightly, on others ... but their fear of discovery of supporting the Nazi party had primarily to do with the pink book my great-grandmother had to carry. She had not yet passed her citizenship test, and should anyone ask during the war, she had to immediately produce this as identification; she could have been taken and interned at any time for no reason. My father's relatives however were Jewish and well, as prior to the war and still after, they are the most persecuted entity in history ....

Many, many years passed, and each family raised their family, the second generation, to remember the past — relatives still living and those lost, their traditions and even the recipes that tied them to their homeland. But soon it came to pass, that the two family's lives would cross and become ever intertwined. The granddaughter of Annetta & Paul would fall in love and marry the grandson of Elias and Frances. All seemed to go well, until that first Thanksgiving ...

As the newlyweds attended their first big family dinner at Annetta & Paul's home, the traditional (green) asparagus soup was brought out and served. The granddaughter was excited to have her groom hear the love story of her grandparents ... but her groom was confused, why was the asparagus soup green? And it had strange flavor to it – asparagus soup should be white, have a "clean" ungreen taste and be served slightly cooled. The new bride was hurt that her groom wasn't enamored of the family's soup of honor, but she didn't really think much of it at the time, because well, she was in love.

The next Thanksgiving meal was at the grandparents of the groom; and yes, you guessed it, Spargelsuppe (white asparagus soup) was served. The groom was excited to share his family's tradition of serving Spargelsuppe with his new bride along with many of the other Jewish dishes, which were quite full of flavor, for you see the purpose of the Spargelsuppe is to clean and cleanses the palate for the next course. The bride was not enamored of this family's soup either ... but the groom was in love so although he noticed, he didn't seem to care.

Along about spring, both the groom and the bride began to get excited – each for the picking of the asparagus at their respective family farms. And again, each were surprised to find an asparagus patch of differing color, green & white. Well, the honeymoon although not quite over, was past its infancy and each made their feelings known, quite loudly and firmly as the story goes, about the oddness of the other's asparagus. The bride was especially upset because she was hoping to plant a bed of green asparagus at their new home – "absolutely not," declared the groom, "it is white or nothing." And so, they each planted their own asparagus beds, harvested and preserved them. They even took to including their children in growing of the asparagus (see man and young child preparing the soil for the new bed) ...

But as each year passed, and each family served their own version of the asparagus soup, the discussions would often lead to loud and terse conversations – the extended family often bringing in each other's heritage & religion, for you see even though it was now 30 years past the war, feelings still ran deep and strong. Both sides of the family would even try to bring the children into it though they wisely would never admit to liking one soup over the other ... and neither the bride nor the groom ever took a liking to the others soup. And neither ever made it for the other.

Now with the 4th generation joining in the preparation of the asparagus beds (see young boy with wheelbarrow) there is only one bed that remains .... The white asparagus isn't a hardy plant in this part of the world; it's more suited to the forests of Germany or the hills of Peru. The green asparagus bed however, planted in the middle 1930's, still thrives to this day. It's a thing of legends with any of the tenant farmers in the area with many wishing they could pick from the bed, but only family is allowed to gather from it – there's even one tenant that is referred to as "Asparagus Bob", because he is so persistent in trying to gather from it and being caught every year; but the rule stands – only family, never anyone else.

So, I invite you to enjoy the two soups; green is more of what people consider a true asparagus soup; the white is less "flavorful" but provides a clean, cleansing taste .... And we ask you to decide on which really is the better soup – and we won't tell, because the ensuing discussion is more than most would want to endure.

Spargelsuppe – White Asparagus Soup
Amy Wertheim, Atlanta, Illinois

Ingredients:

½ cup chopped white onion
2 tablespoons butter
1½ pounds white asparagus,
    peeled & cut into 2-inch pieces
6 cups chicken or vegetable broth
½ cup heavy whipping cream
salt and pepper to taste

Photo by Peter Engler

Directions:

Prepare the asparagus: white asparagus must be peeled, similar to a carrot to remove the woody flesh. Be sure and peel prior to cutting into 2-inch pieces. Reserve some tips for garnish. Set aside.

In a large soup pot, melt the butter over medium heat. Add the onions and sauté until soft, approximately 4 minutes. Add the asparagus (but not the tips) and continue to sauté until the asparagus and onion are tender, about 3-5 minutes. Add the broth and cook for 30 minutes until the asparagus is soft and pliable.

Remove the soup from the stove after it is done simmering & puree the soup until smooth and then return it to the pot. Add the heavy whipping cream salt and pepper to taste. If the soup has cooled too much, heat on high, stirring until the soup is as hot as you like. Serve with the reserved asparagus tips.

Note: This is not a big batch of soup – this recipe was for 4 people as it was served between courses to cleanse the palate; however, for a single course meal only, if there are other side dishes like bread and salad it would be enough. My grandparents were known to sometimes add a splash of white wine for a little kick (acidity).

Yield: Serves 2-4

Simple Asparagus Soup
Amy Wertheim, Atlanta, Illinois

Ingredients:

1 tablespoon butter
1-pound asparagus
2 tablespoons flour
⅛ teaspoon pepper
1 cup milk
1 teaspoon lemon juice
salt and pepper to taste
¾ cup onion, chopped
1 tablespoon butter
½ teaspoon salt
1¾ cup chicken or vegetable broth
½ cup plain yogurt*
¼ cup Parmesan cheese + some for garnish

Photo by Peter Engler

Directions:

Prepare the asparagus: snap off the woody ends. Chop off the tips and set aside. Chop the remainder into ¼ -inch pieces. Set aside.

In a large pot, melt the butter over medium heat. Add the onions and sauté for 2 minutes. Add the asparagus (but not the tips) and continue to sauté until the asparagus and onion are tender, about 3-5 minutes.

In a small bowl, combine flour, salt, and pepper. Using a wooden spoon, to move the veggies to the side of the pot. Melt 1 tablespoon butter on the clear side of the pot; add the flour mixture and whisk it together to make a paste while keeping the veggies on the other side of the pan. Cook the mixture for about a minute, then add the broth in small increments, whisking between each addition. Whisk out any lumps. Add the milk and combine. Bring the mixture to a boil, then reduce to a simmer.

Simmer for about 10 minutes.

Meanwhile in a small saucepan, add 1½ cups water and ½ teaspoon salt. Bring to a boil over high heat. When it is at a rolling boil, add the reserved asparagus tips. Cover and cook for 2 minutes. Immediately drain in a colander and rinse with cold water to stop the cooking process. Set aside.

Remove the soup from the stove after it is done simmering & puree the soup until smooth** and then return it to the pot. Add the yogurt, lemon juice, and Parmesan and any additional salt and pepper to taste. If the soup has cooled too much, heat on high, stirring until the soup is as hot as you like. Serve with the reserved asparagus tips and shredded Parmesan.

Note: this was often made and preserved for future meals, so the batch isn't a large one. Easily doubled or tripled depending on the people needing to serve.

* Heavy cream was originally used; I like the yogurt for a lighter flavor.

** We prefer it not completely smooth so the soup as some texture to it.

Yield: Serves 2-4

Contestant, 2010

Ox Tail Soup
Linda D. Cifuentes, Mohamet, Illinois

It was a contest to see who could pile up the most bones next to their soup plate. The loser did the dishes.

My grandmother was not a very good cook, but my mom got married when she was 18 years old and learned to cook well. As a matter of fact, she was a great cook. My Grandma made this soup, but my mom turned it into a family favorite.

We come from a Czech background and lived in a Czech neighborhood in Berwyn Illinois. Back in the day this was a very inexpensive meal to make. Oxtails were 69 cents a pound and you could buy a "soup package" for 59 cents. The soup package contained parsnips, turnips, carrots and celery.

Unfortunately, today it is not so inexpensive a meal. Oxtails cost $4.29 a pound and the soup package doesn't exist, so you have to buy all the vegetables separately.

Photo by Catherine Lambrecht

When my Grandma made this recipe, she did not use the bouillon or the rice; that was my mom's addition.

This was an entire meal that was usually served for Sunday Supper for two reasons. Sunday supper was the special family meal of the week and it took all afternoon to make the soup. We always got to pick a meal for our birthdays and this was the meal my little sister picked. Her birthday is in December and my mom always made this the Sunday closest to her birthday.

This was also a very entertaining meal. My mom served the soup right out of the pot and we ladled it into very large bowls. She placed the oxtails, which come in various sizes, in a large colander set inside a bowl that was full of the ox tails. Once everyone finished their soup it was time to dig in. We ate with our fingers and everyone used ketchup to dip the ox tails in. It was a contest to see who could pile up the most bones next to their soup plate. The loser did the dishes. Now the bigger the ox-tail the more the meat, however I always grabbed the little ox tails because I could eat them fast and pile up a lot of bones. I hated to do dishes and by using this strategy I never lost.

> We always got to pick a meal for our birthdays and this was the meal my little sister picked.

Making this meal today I could not stop thinking about my Mom who has almost been gone for 5 years, she had Alzheimer's and unfortunately the last few years of her life could not cook. So please think of my mom Helen when you are eating her special soup today. And remember if you don't want to do the dishes grab the little ox tails. But if you want a lot of that meaty flavor go for the big ones!!!

Ox Tail Soup

Linda D. Cifuentes, Mohamet, Illinois

I wrote the recipe just as my mom had it. This is exactly what I put in:

Ingredients:

4 pounds ox tails
3 carrots
2 parsnips
3 stalks celery
2 turnips
1 onion
1 beef bouillon cube
½-cup instant rice

Directions:

Add ox tails to cold water. While oxtails are heating up clean and add whole to the pot: carrots, celery, parsnips, onions, and turnips. Let vegetables boil 35 to 40 minutes, take out of water and cool down. Cut vegetable into small pieces and put into another pot. After ox tails have boiled one and a half hours strain liquid into pot with vegetables. Add 1 beef bouillon cube. Optional-add rice and boil 10 minutes.

Photo by Catherine Lambrecht

Honorable Mention, 2009

Potato Soup with Rivels
Darlene Crider, Lincoln, Illinois

They were hardworking farm folk and this recipe was perfect for filling up hungry children on a cold winter's day.

The recipe for "Potato Soup with Rivels" was passed down to me by my grandmother, Wilma "Irene" Rouch (Grandma Rouch 1904-2001). She felt a strong desire to pass on her family history and made handwritten copies of her favorite recipes that she gave to her many grandchildren, particularly those recipes that had been in the family for a long time. This recipe was passed down to Grandma Rouch by her mother, Flora Hershberger Johnston. Grandma Rouch grew up in Grass Creek, Indiana, where she and her husband Lester Rouch, raised 5 children. She was always very proud of her husband's Pennsylvania Dutch heritage, but her ancestry, as we discovered after her death, was Black Irish on her father's side and Pennsylvania Dutch on her mother's side. They were hardworking farm folk and this recipe was perfect for filling up hungry children on a cold winter's day. It also adapts well today with the addition of ham, chicken broth or vegetables, like carrots and celery.

Photo by Peter Engler

Potato Soup with Rivels
Darlene Crider, Lincoln, Illinois

Ingredients:

Potatoes (one per person)
1 Onion
1-quart milk
1 cup flour
¼ tsp. salt
2 egg yolks (or one whole egg)

Directions:

Photo by Peter Engler

Peel and dice a potato for each person to be served. Peel and dice an onion and add to potatoes. Cover with water in a large pot with a heavy bottom, add salt to taste and cook until tender. Add 1-quart milk. Heat slowly.

To make rivels:

Stir together 1 cup flour, ¼ tsp. salt and 2 egg yolks (or one whole egg) with fork until it forms little balls.

Add to potato soup, stirring all the time. Cook slowly on low heat until rivels are tender.

Add 3-4 Tbsp. butter and pepper to taste.

Contestant, 2010

Saltibarsciai (salt-tib-bar-sky) (Cold Beet Soup)
Deborah Steele, Springfield, Illinois

A common dish, brought to America in the early 1900's by my great grandparents .... they left their village to brave "the new world" because of a famine .....

According to my grandmother, this was made often for lunch; as it would keep til the men could come in from the fields. She usually got the job of chopping the beets, the cucumbers, the dill. Sometimes they would make it with buttermilk, other times with sour cream. It depended on what was "on hand." I never got to meet my great grandparents ... Joseph died in the 1940's from tetanus contracted on the farm ... Catherine died shortly thereafter from "a broken heart." This was actually entered on her death certificate!

Photo by Peter Engler

My grandmother had a huge garden with dill surrounding it. That is my main memory of her. The smell of the dill in the summer heat and in this soup.

She taught her two boys, (my father and uncle) to make this soup .... and my father taught it to me. To me it is the perfect summer soup. Cold, refreshing, filling.

Now I am teaching my granddaughters to make the soup and they are helping me pick the dill in my garden so it spans five generations that I can account for. A common dish, a common thread ....

Saltibarsciai (salt-tib-bar-sky) (Cold Beet Soup)
Deborah Steele, Springfield, Illinois

Ingredients:

10 beets; greens removed
3 quarts water
¼ cup chopped dill (and 3 tablespoons chopped dill for garnish)
2 cucumbers, peeled and chopped coarsely
¼ cup white vinegar
½ teaspoon salt
½ teaspoon pepper
1-pint sour cream
2 potatoes, boiled and cooled
1 medium onion, finely chopped
3 tablespoons butter
3 tablespoons vegetable oil

Photo by Peter Engler

Directions:

Wash beets, place in 6-quart dutch oven pan. Bring to boil, and simmer til just tender. Should be approx. 20 minutes.

Drain the beets, reserve the beet water. Let the beets and water cool. Trim and peel the beets, chop coarsely. Add to water.

Peel cucumbers, chop coarsely, add to water. Add the vinegar, sour cream, salt and pepper. Wash the fresh dill. Chop up and add to water in pot. Combine very well.

Place in refrigerator at least three hours to chill. Overnight is best.

Boil potatoes ... and let cool, then peel and dice.

Add vegetable oil and butter to frying pan. Sauté the chopped onion in the pan til limp; add diced potato, combine well and heat through. Let cool.

Add the 3 tablespoons chopped dill to soup before serving. This was always served with black bread.

Serves 10 people.

Contestant, 2009

Tomato Soup
Carlene Carter, Lincoln, Illinois

... a good way to use up excess tomatoes in the garden.

This is a recipe from a cookbook that my grandmother (Irene Rouch, born 1904, died 2001) compiled for her many grandchildren to share recipes that were important to her. She was a farm wife in rural Grass Creek, Indiana and did a lot of canning and preserving to feed her husband and 5 children. Things were especially tight when Grandpa Rouch died in 1955, and left her a single mom, running the farm by herself. This recipe was a favorite of hers but would not be considered safe to can according to current USDA instructions. It does freeze well, though, and is a good way to use up excess tomatoes in the garden. Oleo was margarine from the forties. Mango was a reference to green peppers. This term may have originated in the Pennsylvania area, and as Irene's family was Pennsylvania Dutch, it may have come from that direction!

Photo by Peter Engler

52　Family Heirloom Recipes from the Illinois State Fair

Tomato Soup
Carlene Carter, Lincoln, Illinois

Ingredients:

8 qts. Tomato juice (made with onion and mango added to the tomatoes while cooking)
2 cups sugar
1 tsp. Chili powder
¼ tsp. Red pepper, optional
¼ cup salt
Mix well:
1 cup oleo
2 cups flour

Directions:

Slowly add juice to flour and oleo mixture until thin enough to add remainder of juice to prevent lumps. Simmer until a little thick.

Makes 18 to 20 pints

To serve you may add ½ amount of milk or as it comes from the can, heat at low temperature.

> Editor's Note:
>
> "One plausible explanation of the usage [calling a green pepper a mango] is this: Mangos (the real thing) that were imported into the American colonies were from the East Indies. Transport was slow. Refrigeration was not available, so the mangos were pickled for shipment. Because of that, people began referring to any pickled vegetable or fruit as a mango ... bell peppers stuffed with spiced cabbage and pickled ... became so popular that bell peppers, pickled or not, became known as mangos. In the early 18th century, mango became a verb meaning to pickle."
>
> Creed, Richard (5 September 2010). "Relative Obscurity: Variations of antigodlin grow". Winston-Salem Journal (Opinion).

Greater Midwest Foodways Alliance
FAMILY HEIRLOOM RECIPES

Illinois State Fair
2012

Salads

Beulah's Chicken Salad

Kidney Bean Salad

Grandma Mohr's Pasta Salad

Ruth's Pasta Salad

Dueling Potato Salads

Great-Grandma's German Potato Salad

Grandma Wierman's Mashed Potato Salad

Mother's Day Strawberry-Rhubarb Salad

Second Prize, 2010

Beulah's Chicken Salad
Jone Schumacher, Chapin, Illinois

We almost always were served the chicken salad for our evening meal after large holiday noon meals.

My mother-in-law, Beulah, was an excellent cook and she was well-known for her delicious food. One particular favorite of immediate and extended family was her chicken salad sandwiches. Everyone expected her to bring these savory sandwiches to reunions and church pot-lucks. They were especially delicious as a cool entree for a hot picnic day as she was always careful to keep the sandwiches well chilled. Everyone knew her sandwiches without looking for her name on her container (usually Tupperware), and I recall her dish being one of the first to be empty. We almost always were served the chicken salad for our evening meal after large holiday noon meals. This made a perfect menu as she was able to make the salad ahead and wasn't busy in the kitchen during afternoon family time.

Beulah was also very particular about presentation and always

Photo by Catherine Lambrecht

sliced off the crust of the sandwich-style bread. (She made bread crumbs out of the crust pieces so there was no waste.) One side of the bread was covered lightly with mayonnaise and the other with soft butter, which added to the flavor and was her unique style. She always cut the sandwiches diagonally and placed in sandwich bags with a fold on top to assure they would be very fresh. These sandwiches were prepared in advance of the event and chilled in the refrigerator to mellow.

Beulah's chicken salad has become a staple for our family gatherings as well. I feel blessed that it is easy to grind my chicken with my Kitchen Aid grinder attachment whereas Beulah used a hand meat grinder. We usually do not put the sandwiches together ahead as she did but usually make sandwiches on bread or home-made rolls. One of our grandsons, who is a little picky about eating, has adapted to his liking by eating the chicken salad as a dip on scoop chips. Many times, our daughter has to leave our get-togethers to go to her job as a nurse on the evening shift at the hospital, so she is very pleased to take one of her favorites for her meal at work and thus feels like she is taking a little of the party with her. These sandwiches also give me a feeling of nostalgia as I recall as a young child that my maternal grandmother served similar chicken salad for our evening Christmas meal. Although I have never searched German recipes for a chicken salad, since both Beulah and my grandmother both were from German descent, I wonder if this dish originated in Germany.

> These sandwiches were prepared in advance of the event and chilled in the refrigerator to mellow.

My husband thinks his mother learned to make chicken salad from her mother sometime in the 1930's. We frequently think of Grandmother when we enjoy Beulah's Chicken Salad and I hope the recipe will be preserved and used for generations to come. I hope my family will remember fondly my version of her chicken salad, now known in our family as Grandmommy's Chicken Salad.

Beulah's Chicken Salad
Jone Schumacher, Chapin, Illinois

Photo by Catherine Lambrecht

Ingredients:

2½ pounds chicken breasts
1½ teaspoon poultry seasoning
¼ teaspoons pepper
2 teaspoons chicken bouillon granules
⅔ cup sweet pickles
¾ cup finely chopped celery
1¼ cup mayonnaise
¼ cup reserved chicken broth

30 slices sandwich bread

Soft butter to spread, approximately 1 teaspoon per sandwich

Mayonnaise to spread, approximately 1 teaspoon per sandwich

Directions:

Grease large baking pan. Place chicken breasts in pan and season with the seasoning, pepper and chicken bouillon. Cover with foil and bake in pre-heated oven for 40 minutes or until cut breast broth is clear. Drain and cool. Place broth and chicken in refrigerator to cool. Remove bones and skin from chicken, cut in pieces and grind chicken with meat grinder. (I choose to use 2 lbs. boneless, skinless chicken breasts for healthier, easier choice.)

Grind pickles into the chicken and allow the pickle juice to fall into the chicken. Stir the celery into the chicken. Combine the mayonnaise with the reserved chicken broth and stir into chicken. Chill the chicken salad until ready to make sandwiches.

To prepare sandwiches, cut the edge of bread from the slices. Spread soft butter on one side of first piece of bread and mayonnaise on another slice. Spoon about ⅛ cup chicken salad on the mayonnaise bread, top with the buttered bread. Cut sandwich on diagonally and place in sandwich bag. Chill in refrigerator until serving. If taking to picnic, place on ice.

YIELD: Recipe makes approximately 5 cups chicken salad, making 15 sandwiches.

Photo by Catherine Lambrecht

Contestant, 2016

Kidney Bean Salad
Linda D. Cifuentes, Mahomet, Illinois

My mom's Kidney Bean Salad is famous.
No, I should say Infamous!! Why, you ask?
My mom loved her kidney bean salad,
unfortunately she was one of few people who did.

My mom made this recipe for every party and get together she was invited to and no one ate the salad but her! She also made the salad as a side dish and served it at dinnertime— no one in the family ate it but her! When I told my brothers and sister, I was making Mommy's Kidney Bean Salad for a contest they just giggled. I will get back to the biggest event that the salad was served at but not eaten, but for now let me tell you about my mom; Helen Holas.

Helen was born November 11, 1933 to Vince and Betty Brezinsky. She was first generation in the United States born to Czech parents and the youngest of three children. She was born and raised in Cicero, Illinois. She had a stay at home mom, a dad that

Photo by Peter Engler

drove a street car and a Babi (grandma in Czech) that lived with her.

At the age of 14 Helen met the love of her life-Tony Holas and she dated him all through high school. At the age of 18 she married him, and they were married for 53 years. They had four children; I am the oldest. My dad owned a flower shop and my mom helped him there once all of the kids were older, but before that she was a stay at home mom.

And boy could Helen cook!! She made great meals and baked wonderful things. I'm not sure what went wrong with the kidney bean salad-don't get me wrong it really doesn't taste bad; I just don't like it!! I don't like kidney beans and I am not fond of egg salad, so I think that is why I don't like this salad. I remember the first time I tried this salad; my mom served it with dinner. I took one bite and spit it out and said this is yucky. As my siblings came into existence the same thing happened with them. I talked to my sister this morning and she said you know there is nothing wrong with the salad our family just didn't like kidney beans.

> And boy could Helen cook!! She made great meals and baked wonderful things. I'm not sure what went wrong with the kidney bean salad …

The most infamous appearance of the salad was at our annual fish fry. I had three bachelor uncles who owned a house and cabin on a lake in Wisconsin. Going back at least 50 years our family took a vacation for one week at the end of June with one goal: get enough fish for the Fish Fry in August. We would all fish and catch crappie and bluegill.

Originally the Fish Fry was held in my parents back yard. And there were about 30 guests; family and a few friends. Thirty years later when we had the last fish fry it was spilling into three yards and there were over 125 people. It became the social event of the season at least in Berwyn. There was beer on tap, fried fish, and side dishes galore. Of course, mommy insisted on making kidney bean salad. My sister Cindy would say, "Mommy why are you making the kidney salad, nobody eats it?" She would say, "I don't care, I like it, I'm going to make it." As you probably guessed there were a few nibblers, but mom was the primary consumer; AGAIN.

Unfortunately, we lost mom at the age of 73. She had Alzheimer's and that is why the recipe she wrote is so special to me because the last few years of her life she could not remember any of her recipes. You may be asking why I asked for this particular recipe–I didn't. One day I gave my mom a blank cookbook and asked that she write all her typical recipes, so they would never be lost. I told her specifically her chili, and stew. When I got the book back the kidney bean salad recipe was in it! Not only does it make me smile when I see a recipe written in her hand, but I guess you noticed her recipe style-no measurements. On this particular recipe the bottom line cracks me up-may double recipe for parties. I really don't think she realized she was the only one that ate this. In the display I placed the salad in a plastic/Tupperware bowl because

that is the only way my mom would serve the salad. The picture in the frame is my mom when she was in her early 20's. And the other picture was taken the last summer of her life right before her and I got on the pontoon boat with Uncle Joe to go fishing in Wisconsin.

We were supplying for the last fish fry!

And No, I still won't eat the salad!!!!!!!!

Photos by Peter Engler

Kidney Bean Salad

Linda D. Cifuentes, Mahomet, Illinois

Ingredients:

1 can dark kidney beans; drained
chopped sweet pickles
cup chopped celery
Salt and pepper to taste
2 hard boiled eggs
cup mayonnaise

Directions:

Mix in order given. Chill

Note: Double recipe for parties/etc.

Photo by Peter Engler

Contestant, 2011

Grandma Mohr's Pasta Salad
Kitsy Amrheim, Springfield, Illinois

"... good, easy to make and makes enough to feed a regiment."

Grandma Mohr always shows up to any large gathering with her pasta salad. I'm not sure how long it has been in the family, but she learned how to make it from her mother, Great Grandma Brown. Grandma says she always brings it to the annual family reunion picnic because it is "good, easy to make and makes enough to feed a regiment."

She was a young bride during the Depression when money was scarce. They had little money to buy food for a growing family, so they grew most of their own vegetables in a large garden. Back in the day, Grandma made her own pasta. To it she would add lots of fresh vegetables from the garden. Thus, the pasta salad became a favorite summer dish on the dinner table. Grandma Mohr had 7 children. With that many mouths to feed, she needed something good, cheap and easy to make to feed that regiment of kids. The pasta salad was the answer. It got the kids to eat their vegetables too.

Photo by Peter Engler

She has grown her own garden up until about 5 years ago when she moved into a retirement center. Grandma loved to square dance and did so up until she fell and broke a hip at age 94. That was just two years ago. She would go every Friday night and often take her pasta salad to share with her friends. At every family reunion, funeral, picnic or potluck, she brought the pasta salad. People who don't normally like pasta salad say they like hers. She is often asked for the recipe and is most generous in providing it. Her 19 grandchildren, 43 great grandchildren four great great grandchildren have all enjoyed it over the years. We all take it to various potlucks and gatherings of our own. I took it to a potluck at work several years ago. Now whenever we have a potluck, co-workers ask me to bring it. Since it is so easy and makes so much, I am happy to oblige. Many siblings and cousins have reported they get the requests as well.

> At every family reunion, funeral, picnic or potluck, she brought the pasta salad.

Grandma brought it to my dad's funeral and a friend of mine had it. She naturally wanted the recipe. She took it to a family gathering of her own. Now whenever her family has a gathering, she is asked to make the pasta salad and bring it. The recipe is destined to be an heirloom in her family as well.

I grow my own garden like Grandma Mohr and try to use fresh veggies from my garden in the recipe when I can. But if you don't grow a garden or it is the middle of winter, you can still enjoy the pasta salad with a trip down the produce aisle at the local super market.

Grandma Mohr is now 96 and in a nursing home. When I told her I was entering her pasta salad in the state fair, she smiled and winked at me. No blue ribbon can top that.

She can't make the pasta salad anymore. Many other family members have volunteered to continue the tradition. The pasta salad will continue to be at all of our family gatherings for generations to come. Thanks grandma Mohr. We love you.

Grandma Mohr's Pasta Salad
Kitsy Amrheim, Springfield, Illinois

Ingredients:

1 16 oz. Pkg. Rotini Pasta
1 c. chopped onion
1 c. chopped cucumber
1 c. chopped tomatoes
1 c. chopped green and red peppers
2 t. parsley flakes
1½ c. sugar
1 c. white vinegar
1 t. prepared mustard
½ c. vegetable oil
1 t. salt
1 t. pepper
1 t. garlic powder

Photo by Peter Engler

Directions:

Cook pasta till soft. Drain. Add onions, parsley, cucumbers, peppers and tomatoes.

In another bowl, mix sugar, vinegar, oil, mustard, salt, pepper and garlic powder. Pour over pasta mixture. Let sit in refrigerator overnight for best flavor.

Keeps 2 weeks in refrigerator.

Contestant, 2014

Ruth's Pasta Salad
Jackie Bales, Springfield, Illinois

As her children and grandchildren have fanned out throughout the country many have made their own mark on the recipe.

When I saw the heirloom recipe competition for a recipe suitable for picnics or large gatherings, I knew what recipe I wanted to enter. My husband's grandmother Ruth's Pasta Salad recipe. But I knew nothing of the history of the recipe. Grandma Ruth passed away a few years ago. So, have my husband and mother in law. I can remember her making it and bringing to family reunions since the early 80's, but I had never asked her where she got the recipe. The recipe makes enough "to feed a regiment" as Grandma liked to say. She wrote it out on a recipe card for me which I still use whenever I make it.

In June, my daughter and I attended the wedding of my

Photo by Catherine Lambrecht

husband's uncle's daughter. Many of Grandma Ruth's children and grandchildren and even great grandchildren were in attendance. So, I asked around to find out what they all knew of the history of the recipe. It was a blast hearing all the stories about Grandma Ruth and her recipe collection. I learned that Grandma Ruth took the Chicago Tribune for years just for the recipe columns. I remember her cutting out those recipes and transferring them to recipe cards. She had boxes and boxes of card files. Aunt Nancy says that her mother's pasta salad recipe started out as a "Macaroni Salad" recipe that her mom got from the newspaper during the depression. It originally had a mayonnaise-based dressing and used elbow macaroni. The vegetables that are used in it depended on what was growing in the garden. The vegetable part really hasn't changed. In the 60's she found a "pasta salad" recipe that used a vinaigrette dressing. The 60's recipe did not include sugar, but the original mayonnaise-based dressing did. Grandma Ruth combined parts of the two recipes to create her pasta salad which is different than any other I have tasted because of the sugar ingredient. In the 80's the elbow macaroni was replaced with Rotini. I've used the tricolor Rotini for about 10 years. I also like to use yellow peppers in addition to the red and green for more color. I've probably been doing that since the mid 90's.

My quest for the history sparked a fun conversation at the wedding. Everyone talked about the different things they put in it. Someone always brings pasta salad to the family reunions. They all have Grandma Ruth's recipe, and all use the sugar. As her children and grandchildren have fanned out throughout the country many have made their own mark on the recipe. Mostly because of what grows in their regions or is popular in the regions they now live. A granddaughter in Wisconsin adds Swiss cheese curds to hers. A granddaughter in California always puts in olives. A daughter in Alabama adds okra. My own daughter who lives in Arizona prefers to use a couple of hot peppers and cilantro in hers. Squash, zucchini, peas, chickpeas and kidney beans were also mentioned as ingredients that have found their way into this family recipe. I think everyone agreed that they all started with the basic ingredient list listed on Grandma Ruth's recipe card which is the dish you're about to enjoy.

I often take this recipe to potlucks and am always asked for the recipe. While I can't call the sugar a "secret" ingredient (since I share the recipe); I can call it the "must have" ingredient that sets it apart from any plain ordinary pasta salad. Enjoy!

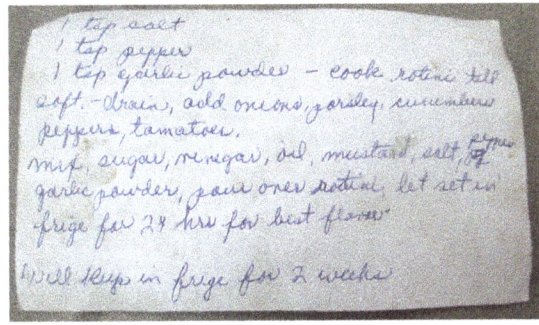

Photos by Catherine Lambrecht

Ruth's Pasta Salad
Jackie Bales, Springfield, Illinois

Ingredients:

1 pkg. 16 oz rotini
1 cup chopped onions
1 cup chopped cucumbers
1 cup chopped green peppers
1 cup chopped red peppers
1 cup chopped tomatoes
2 teaspoons parsley flakes
1½ cup sugar
1 cup white vinegar
2 teaspoons prepared mustard
½ cup vegetable oil
1 teaspoon salt
1 teaspoon pepper
1 teaspoon garlic powder

Photo by Catherine Lambrecht

Directions:

Cook rotini till soft. Drain. Add onions, cucumbers, peppers, tomatoes and parsley flakes. Mix sugar, vinegar, oil, mustard, salt, pepper and garlic powder. Pour over the rotini mix. For best flavor, chill in the refrigerator for 24 hours. Stir and serve.

The salad can be kept in the refrigerator for two weeks.

Contestant, 2014

Dueling Potato Salads
Pam Elliott, Waverly, Illinois

... each woman would bring their unique potato salad. And of course, the conversation always went to which one was "better."

In my husband's family there are 3 potato salad recipes. Each is a little different. One contains mustard, one contains black olives, and this one contains shrimp.

Two recipes belong to his grandmothers and this one to his great-grandmother, dating back to the 1930's.

Every holiday and birthday celebration the family would get together, and each woman would bring their unique potato salad. And of course, the conversation always went to which one was "better." Although each recipe is delicious, this one with the shrimp seemed to be the most favorite.

When my husband and I got married, he asked me to make this recipe to take to one of my family gatherings and it was an instant hit! It is now served at all holidays, birthdays, cookouts and sometimes just on a Sunday!

It has always been a favorite traditional recipe in the past, and with our daughters now making it, a family favorite for a whole new generation.

Photo by Catherine Lambrecht

Dueling Potato Salads
Pam Elliott, Waverly, Illinois

Ingredients:

5 lbs. of brown potatoes – boiled until soft, peeled and cubed
1 10 oz. jar of Manzanilla Olives – drained and chopped
2 cans of medium shrimp – drained
2 cups of real mayonnaise
8 hardboiled eggs – peeled and sliced
the juice of one lemon
2 tsp. salt
2 tsp. pepper

Directions:

Squeeze the lemon juice over the prepared potatoes (watch out for seeds).
Mix together

Add eggs and olives
Mix together

Add mayonnaise
Mix together

Add the shrimp, the salt and pepper
Mix together gently

Chill and enjoy!

Photo by Catherine Lambrecht

Contestant, 2013

Grandma's German Potato Salad as I Remember
(recreated by Jeanne Schultheis)
Jill Jackson, Grayslake, Illinois

How Great-Grandma's German Potato Salad Survived the Generations

lthough I was young, I remember my Great-Grandma well. My Mom, Sister and I, lived in the basement flat, my Grandparents on the first floor and Great-Grandma, Upstairs Grandma we called her, lived on the 2nd floor of the Chicago 2-Flat Home.

Great-Grandma was born Magdalena E. Hackemer on November 10, 1872 in Jersey City, Hudson, New Jersey. Her Father, Johann Hackemer, was born in Germany in 1847 and immigrated to the US in 1867. Her Mother, Magdalena Busch, was born in Bas-Rhin, France, where the native language was German. She immigrated to the US in 1869, met Johann and married in 1870 in New Jersey. This is the beginning of how the recipe became part of our family.

Photo by Catherine Lambrecht

They moved to Chicago where Great-Grandma met and married Eugene Gisselbrecht who was also born in Bas-Rhin, France, the same place as her Mother.

She brought the recipe with her and passed it on to her daughters, Selma Emma and Katherine Gisselbrecht. Selma married Otto Neubauer of Austria and had a child, my Mother, Jeanne in 1929. I never met my grandmother Selma, as she died in 1938. My Mother was then raised by her Aunt Katherine, who was married to Ervin Moninger. She was then always considered my Grandmother. And so, the recipe was then passed down another generation to my Mother and Aunt.

> What I never knew until recently, is that the recipe was never written down, just passed down over the generations by word of mouth and/or demonstrating.

I have always loved German Potato Salad. We must have had it at all special occasion dinners. I also remember my Mother making it when we were growing up. What I never knew until recently, is that the recipe was never written down, just passed down over the generations by word of mouth and/or demonstrating. It was never passed down to my generation. I remember every time I took my Mother to a deli, she would buy some German Potato Salad and rate it.

A few years ago, Mom in her 80's, had the foresight of writing down the recipe so it would not be lost. It looks as if she was writing it as she made it, as she remembered it, so she could get the ingredients accurate for us. Mom recently passed away from complications of a long 30 plus year fight with Myasthenia Gravis. It was after that when we discovered this recipe that we have grown up with. I hope that I can do the same justice with the recipe and then pass it on to my own Daughter.

Ancestors of Jill Sally Paschke

First Generation

Jill Sally Paschke was born on 15 Oct 1951 in Chicago, Cook, Illinois, United States.[1]

Second Generation

Jeanne Shirley Neubauer was born on 1 Jan 1929 in Chicago, Cook, Illinois, United States.[4] She was christened on 17 Feb 1929 in Chicago, Cook, Illinois, USA Pastor B. H. Leesman, St John's Evangelical Church, Chicago, IL.

Jeanne Shirley Neubauer and Gerald Gordon Paschke were married on 8 May 1948 in Chicago, Cook, Illinois, United States.[4]

She died on 12 Jun 2011 at the age of 82 in Barrington, Cook, Illinois, USA. Jeanne was buried on 16 Jun 2011 in Eden Memorial Park Cemetery, Schiller Park, Cook, Illinois.

Third Generation

Otto Ferdinand Neubauer was born on 18 Dec 1901 in Ottakring, Wien, Austria.[4,11] He immigrated in 1913 to Chicago, Cook, Illinois, United States.[12] He was naturalized on 18 Jun 1931 in US District Court, Chicago, Cook, Illinois, United States. Otto died on 20 Jun 1993 at the age of 91 in Evanston Hospital, Evanston, Cook, Illinois, United States.[13] He was buried on 24 Jun 1993 in Rosehill Cemetery, Chicago, Cook, Illinois, United States.[13] He was also known as Ottokar Ferdinand Neubauer. Immigrated to US 1913 with his aunt and male friend of his aunt; Naturalized after 1920

Occupation: 1920 Laborer, cemetery; 1930 Milk distributor

Selma Emma Gisselbrecht and Otto Ferdinand Neubauer were married on 27 Jun 1925 in Chicago, Cook, Illinois, United States.[14]

Selma Emma Gisselbrecht was born on 7 Dec 1901 in Chicago, Cook, Illinois, United States.[14] She died on 14 Feb 1938 at the age of 36 in Chicago, Cook, Illinois, United States.[14] She was buried on 17 Feb 1938 in Eden Memorial Park Cemetery, Schiller Park, Cook, Illinois, United States.[7,14] Funeral at St John's Evangelical Church, Moffat St and Campbell Ave.

Fourth Generation

Eugene Gisselbrecht[4] was born on 28 Apr 1874 in Baldenheim, Bas-Rhin, France.[14,24] He died on 28 Mar 1949 at the age of 74 in Chicago, Cook, Illinois, United States.[10] He was buried on 30 Mar 1949 in Eden Memorial Park Cemetery, Schiller Park, Cook, Illinois, United States.[7,14] Immigrated to US 1893; Naturalized 1903; 1920–born in Alsace-Loraine, native language French (also for parents)

Occupation: 1900 Woodworker; 1910 Manufacturer of window frames (employer); 1920, 1930 Mill worker in a Sash/door company (owner)

Magdalena E "Lena" Hackemer and Eugene Gisselbrecht were married on 31 Aug

1899 in Chicago, Cook, Illinois, United States.[5] Marriage License issued 31 Aug 1899; Vol 25, p.132, Lic# 296709

Magdalena E "Lena" Hackemer was born on 10 Nov 1872 in Jersey City, Hudson, New Jersey, United States.[14,25] She died on 19 Jul 1963 at the age of 90 in Chicago, Cook, Illinois, United States.[14] She was buried on 22 Jul 1963 in Eden Memorial Park Cemetery, Schiller Park, Cook, Illinois, United States.[7] Funeral Home: Matz Funeral Home, 3440 N Central, Chicago, Cook, IL

Fifth Generation

Laurent Gisselbrecht was born on 29 Nov 1843 in Baldenheim, Bas-Rhin, France.[24] He died on 27 Mar 1898 at the age of 54 in St. Elizabeth, Chicago, Cook, Illinois, United States.[10] He was buried on 29 Mar 1898 in Eden Memorial Park Cemetery, Schiller Park, Cook, Illinois, United States.[10,14] Laurent was also known as Lorenz Gisselbrecht. Came to US in 1893.

Salome Jehl and Laurent Gisselbrecht were married on 27 Dec 1871 in Baldenheim, Bas-Rhin, France.[24]

Salome Jehl was born on 25 Dec 1850 in Baldenheim, Bas-Rhin, France.[24] She died on 23 Aug 1908 at the age of 57 in Chicago, Cook, Illinois, United States.[10] She was buried on 25 Aug 1908 in Eden Memorial Park Cemetery, Schiller Park, Cook, Illinois, United States.[10] Came to US in 1893. Six children; 5 living in 1900. Cause of death: Tuberculosis

Johann Hackemer was born on 1 Apr 1847 in Hessen Lande, Germany.[5,25,33] He died on 2 Aug 1926 at the age of 79 in Chicago, Cook, Illinois, United States.[34] He was buried on 4 Aug 1926 in Eden Memorial Park Cemetery, Schiller Park, Cook, Illinois, United States.[13] Johann was also known as Johann Hackmeyer; John Hackemer. Came to US in 1867; naturalized 1884; 1870 census Hannover/Hanover; 1880 census Kier Hessen

Occupation: 1870 Carpenter; 1880 Millwright; 1881 Millwright, house es.; 1900 Grocer; 1910 Grocer (directory) Coffee roaster, wholesale house (census); 1917 Grocer; 1920 Proprietor grocery store.

Magdalena Busch and Johann Hackemer were married in 1869 or 1870 in Jersey City, Hudson, New Jersey.[14,35-36]

Magdalena Busch[4] was born on 16 Oct 1846 in Bas-Rhin, France.[10,25,35] She died on 27 Aug 1928 at the age of 81 in Chicago, Cook, Illinois, United States.[37] She was buried on 30 Aug 1928 in Eden Memorial Park Cemetery, Schiller Park, Cook, Illinois, United States.[13] Immigrated to US in 1869; 1920– born in Alsace, native language German (also for her parents) 1900: gave birth to 4 children, 2 living; 1910 gave birth to 2 children, 2 living. Possibly from Sundhausen or Mulhausen (Haut-Rhin)

Grandma's German Potato Salad as I Remember
(recreated by Jeanne Schultheis)
Jill Jackson, Grayslake, Illinois

Ingredients:

2 lbs. of Small Red Potatoes
8 Slices of Bacon
1 Medium Onion
1 T. Parsley Flakes
½ C. Sugar
3 T. All Purpose Flour
2 tsp. Salt
¾ tsp. Pepper
¼ C. Bacon Fat
1 C. White Vinegar
1 C. Water (from the potatoes boiling in)

Photo by Catherine Lambrecht

Directions:

Bring potatoes to a boil, then simmer for 20 minutes or until a fork can gently pierce them. In the meantime, fry the bacon until just crisp and cut into small pieces (not minced). Dice and fry the onion in the bacon grease, slowly, so they do not burn. Set aside 1 C. of the potato water and ¼ C. bacon fat.

Peel and slice the potatoes, place into a large bowl. Add the parsley flakes, bacon and onions. Keep warm.

In a separate bowl, blend together sugar, flour, salt and pepper. Set aside.

In a saucepan combine the bacon fat, vinegar and potato water. Bring to a boil. Slowly add the flour mixture, stirring well between additions. Boil 2-3 minutes, until mixture is thickened, stirring constantly to avoid and break up any lumps.

When thickened, remove from heat and pour over potato mixture, just enough to cover, and toss gently. Some sauce will be leftover.

Best to serve when warm, but cold leftovers are also great for a lunchtime addition!

Second Prize, 2014

Grandmother Wierman's Mashed Potato Salad
Christine Beckman, Sherman, Illinois

Mixing Up Memories

My Grandmother, Helen Marie Reisner Wierman, was born in 1913. Living through the Great Depression obviously created a need for creative cooking. She began making a version of this salad sometime in her 20's and it evolved into mashed potato salad in the early 1950's.

As far as the recipe goes, she never wrote it down. Each time she made it, it came from memory. So, it was never exactly the same. Funny though how it always tasted amazing no matter what tweaks she made. One time long before I came on the scene, my Mom remembers Grandmother attempting to sprinkle the celery seed into the salad. To her shock and surprise, the lid popped clean off and celery seed went everywhere! They attempted to

Photo by Catherine Lambrecht

scoop out as much of it as possible, but to no avail. Turns out that was the best batch of her potato salad ever and the excessive amount of celery seen became a permanent ingredient.

I remember as a child she would create a huge Thanksgiving feast with mashed potatoes to spare. The next day she would take the "extras" and create for me her most amazing dish. Mashed Potato Salad! She and I would mix it together taking turns with her old Sunbeam hand mixer, tasting ever so often to be sure it was just right. But during the spring and summer months, we could always count on Grandmother whipping up a large batch for the long weekends we spent at her place in Arcola, IL.

The best part is that it gets better with age. Somehow, each day kept in the fridge makes it smoother and tastier. The bowl in which Grandmother's potato salad is displayed today is the same bowl she used when I was a child. So many wonderful memories are tied to her via this recipe. These are priceless.

Surprisingly, no one else ever learned the recipe (not even my Mom), so I alone put it to memory. It was never really written down until now. I have always made it from memory, just like Grandmother, and I probably always will. Even though I've spent the past couple of summers trying to get the recipe exact, there is something to be said for cooking from your heart. It will be nice to have the recipe on paper to hand down to my children and grandchildren, but even nicer to teach them the way Grandmother taught me. By taste!

> I remember as a child she would create a huge Thanksgiving feast with mashed potatoes to spare. The next day she would take the "extras" and create for me her most amazing dish. Mashed Potato Salad!

Grandmother Wierman's Mashed Potato Salad
Christine Beckman, Sherman, Illinois

Ingredients:

5 lb. potatoes peeled, quartered, boiled, & mashed thoroughly
½ cup scalded milk
3 cups Miracle Whip dressing
1½ TBS. sugar
2 TBS. celery seed
1 cup sweet onion (coarsely chop all 6 vegetables)
1 cup celery
½ cup green bell pepper
½ cup red bell pepper
½ cup yellow bell pepper
½ cup orange bell pepper
12 hardboiled large eggs (chop 10 eggs, reserve 2 for slicing)
¼ tsp paprika

Directions:

• With an electric mixer, whisk scalded milk in to mashed potatoes. Cool and refrigerate overnight.

• Continue by mixing potatoes, Miracle Whip, sugar, and celery seed until well blended.

• Next, stir in by hand the onion, celery, and peppers.

• Gently fold in the chopped hardboiled eggs and transfer to a serving dish of your choice (glass is nice, so the colorful peppers can be seen). Refrigerate the extra for refills.

• Using an egg slicer (or sharp knife) slice the two remaining eggs into thin circular slices. Place egg slices on top of potato salad in a decorative pattern and sprinkle the entire dish with paprika. Serve well chilled.

Photo by Catherine Lambrecht

Third Prize, 2015

Mother's Day Rhubarb-Strawberry Salad
Jone Schumacher, Chapin, Illinois

...this salad was considered the traditional salad Beulah would serve our family for our Mother's Day lunch

I so fondly remember as a young child trips to our neighbor to help ourselves to their large rhubarb patch. I recall noting how large the leaves were and how pretty the red stems were. It is interesting to note that Ben Franklin is credited for bringing rhubarb seeds to this country in 1772; however, rhubarb was not widely popular until the early 1880's, at which time it was used mostly for making pies and wine. By the mid-1900s it gained popularity that continues to this day. It seems to me in the "Olden days" about every farm-stead had their own patch at the edge of their yard that was adorned with a large patch of rhubarb. I often wonder why my mother did not have a patch of her own, but our neighbors always seemed very happy to share some of their rhubarb. It seems there was always plenty to share. I was amazed

Photo by Peter Engler

when I asked my husband if they had rhubarb in their yard as they lived in town, and he replied they did have a rather large patch. It should then be of no surprise then that this beloved Mother's Day Strawberry-Rhubarb Salad should come from my mother-in-law, Beulah. Actually, this salad was considered the traditional salad Beulah would serve our family for our Mother's Day lunch when we would gather for the day after attending church together at our country church.

> Many times, Beulah would serve these individually and serve on a lettuce leaf on a salad plate ...

I hesitate to call any meal my mother-in-law, Beulah, served as "lunch" as actually our noon-day meal was always referred to as dinner and her meals were much to elaborate to be tagged as "lunch." I remember as a child watching my mother and grandmother prepare for their ladies' club meetings when it was held in their homes as everything was polished and sparkling and the best dishes and table clothes were used. My mother-in-law actually served her family dinners in the same immaculate manner. She would always have a white table cloth (sometimes lace), candle tapers burning, fresh garden flowers for centerpieces, cloth napkins, and glass coasters. I must admit, I'm rather glad the glass coasters have become out of style, because it would be embarrassing when the coaster would accidently stick to the glass bottom when one would take a drink and the coaster would go clanging down on the plate, and there was always concern for the "good china."

Last, but certainly not least was the salad. Many times, Beulah would serve these individually and serve on a lettuce leaf on a salad plate placed at each place. I recall Jell-O was very popular for salads and even deserts and I hear folks recalling and being amused with the idea that there never was a church pot-luck without there being at least one green Jell-O salad served. I always thought Jell-O was a rather "modern" food, but actually has quite a history. Charles Knox developed the first pre-granulated gelatin in 1894. In 1895, flavors were added, and

Pearl B. Watt renamed the desert "Jell-O." In 1902 an advertising company called it "America's most favorite Desert." In the early 1900's Ellis Island Immigrants were given a bowl of Jell-O as a "Welcome to America" gift.

Photo by Peter Engler

This salad is now my family's very favorite salad, one my adult children and their children all like. I anticipate in the future when my grandchildren recall the meals I have served, they will certainly recall this salad as this strawberry-rhubarb salad is served so frequently. We no longer call it the Mother's Day Salad since it is for basically all the family meals unless midsummer when fresh fruit readily available. I have streamlined the recipe for convenience, and now usually use Cool Whip lite and just stir the whole salad together instead of keeping some plain and the rest mixed with the whipping. Also, I usually double the recipe and put in one of my largest pink depression glass bowls to serve. One of our grandsons had a milk allergy, so I would always keep his separate and not add any whipped product and he would usually devour the amount saved for him while waiting for the rest of his meal! I am pleased that the children all like rhubarb as it is a healthy vegetable with many good nutrients. It amazes me how expensive this vegetable has become in some parts of our country when one considers it was once thought of as a very common farm border plant. I have searched for it in the south and some grocers don't even recognize what I am asking for and when I did locate it, it was priced at $4.95 a pound, which would really surprise some old-time farmers.

> I usually double the recipe and put in one of my largest pink depression glass bowls to serve.

I am pleased that we have a large rhubarb patch and I love pulling it in the spring and once again noting how beautiful and large the leaves are. It is such an easy food to prepare and freeze ahead for the winter. I really like searching for other "old-time" recipes to prepare yummy dishes, and I enjoy blending old family heirloom recipes into our family traditional meals.

Photo by Peter Engler

Mother's Day Rhubarb-Strawberry Salad
Jone Schumacher, Chapin, Illinois

Ingredients:

3 cups fresh or frozen rhubarb, cut into about 1-inch pieces
½ cup granulated sugar
½ cup water
6 oz. box strawberry Jell-O
1 container (9 or 10 oz.) frozen strawberries with sugar, thawed slightly
1 cup whipping cream, whipped with 2 tablespoons powdered sugar + ½ teaspoon vanilla
Optional trim: lettuce leaves, additional whipped cream and fresh strawberries

Directions:

Combine rhubarb, sugar and water in medium saucepan and cook over medium heat until rhubarb is soft, stirring frequently.

Remove from heat and stir in strawberry Jell-O until dissolved. Cut the strawberry mixture into about 4 large sections and add to the hot rhubarb mixture. Stir occasionally until strawberries are thawed and well mixed. Pour half of the mixture into an 8x8 square glass dish.

Set in refrigerator until almost set.

Gently fold the whipped cream into the remaining strawberry-rhubarb mixture and spoon over the salad in the dish. Return to refrigerator until completely set.

Cut into 9 servings.

Optional: Serve on lettuce leaf and top with a spoon-full of whipped cream and top with a fresh strawberry.

SERVINGS: 8-10

Greater Midwest Foodways Alliance
FAMILY HEIRLOOM RECIPES

Illinois State Fair
2013

Main Dishes

Grandma's Beef and Noodles

Updated Version Beef & Noodles

Old Version – Beef 'n Noodles

Grandma Guth's Stuffed Cabbage Rolls with Sauerkraut

Aunt Pearl's Chicken and Dumplings

Rouch Family Chicken and Noodles
Mashed Potatoes

Old Fashion Oven Fried Chicken

Svestkove Knedlicky (Fruit Dumplings)

Kluski (Potato Dumplings)
with Round Steak and Gravy

Grandma Delong's Meatloaf

Great Grandma's Meatloaf Cake

Original Oyster Dressing

Today's Oyster Dressing

Great Grandma's Pasties

Peixe a Lumbo (African Shrimp & Rice Stew)

Polenta with Meat Sauce

Ptacki (Rolled Round Steak)

Stuffed Peppers

Second Prize, 2015

Grandma's Beef and Noodles
Carmen Arnberger, Sherman, Illinois

For as long as I can remember, there have been two meals I could always expect to eat at my grandma's house: pigs in a blanket with cottage cheese and applesauce or beef and noodles.

Grandma, or Nan Nan as we called her, cooked her beef and homemade noodles during most visits, and it was just expected that beef and noodles would be served at every family reunion. The tender roast meat combined with the noodles and salty broth have always been a favorite of mine. Now that Nan Nan is gone, and the family reunions continue, enjoying her special dish keeps her a part of us.

Photo by Peter Engler

My ties with homemade beef and noodles are made more special when I understand the history of not only by biological family, but my church family as well. This story starts in Sheldon's Grove, Illinois. Sheldon's Grove is not too far from Browning, Illinois and is a grouping of houses you might miss if you blink while driving by. In Sheldon's Grove there is a tiny little church on top of a very large hill. The church was built in 1871 and was a community church that was attended by many denominations of people. Various preachers would take turns coming to preach each week at the church. In the early 1930's, my great grandmother, Helen Burgard along with a handful of other women, converted the church to a Methodist church and thus, Sheldon's Grove United Methodist Church (UMC) was born. This little country church has a history of the women of the church supporting it by any resources available to them. For example, one year they created a strawberry festival so that they could sell strawberries and strawberry products to support the church and missions of the church. They also sold chickens at one time. A more modern tradition has been for the women of the church to cook a turkey dinner in the fall. All the food is made by hand, including homemade mashed potatoes still peeled by hand with a knife. All this is done in the tiny little basement church kitchen with not many updates. It still looks like the 1950's when you enter the basement. Old Sunday School charts and pictures still hang on the walls. There is limited seating inside for those who wish to eat their dinner at the church, while many others opt for take-out orders. This annual tradition has been tremendously supported by members of the surrounding communities for many years, which includes my family. My family including my Nan Nan, mother, and other relatives have all come back to help at the tiny little church each fall for many years. Just down the road and down the hill from the church, is my great grandparents' home in Sheldon's Grove.

> My family including my Nan Nan, mother, and other relatives have all come back to help at the tiny little church each fall for many years.

My great grandma Helen and my grandmother, Arlene Burgard (Nan Nan) both lived during the time of the great depression and they were both members of the Sheldon's Grove Ladies Auxiliary at the church. They both grew up making the most of what little they had, not wasting resources, and working hard. Noodles were something that could be made at home without requiring a lot of ingredients. Noodles and broth could also stretch what little meat they might have at the time and could feed a lot of people economically. This is probably why Nan Nan always served beef and noodles. It was a recipe she learned while growing up from her mother and just kept making. In today's modern times, I know of few people who take the time to make noodles from scratch. It is much easier to just grab a bag of noodles at the store. However, store bought noodles don't taste the same and today people are much more willing to pay for a bag of homemade noodles than to make them. The Sheldon's Grove Ladies Auxiliary knew this and again used their skills and resources to begin another tradition of the Sheldon's Grove UMC. For the past 20 plus years, the women of the church have been making homemade noodles to raise funds for the church and mission projects. The very same noodles my Nan Nan has been using in her beef and noodle recipe my whole life.

> Noodles and broth could also stretch what little meat they might have at the time and could feed a lot of people economically.

I had never made Nan Nan's beef and noodles. I mean, why should I? Nan Nan was the maker of the noodles and it was her signature dish. One day a few years ago this all changed, when I was invited to join in on the fun and learn how to make noodles with Nan Nan and the church ladies. These ladies got up early in the morning and worked at it all day. The entire church basement was taken over for the project. At the end of the day the basement had been transformed by the tables full of noodles drying. The ladies typically use 13-14 dozen eggs at a time. Everything was still mixed by hand and cut by hand. There is definitely a trick to knowing just how thick the noodles need to be before they are cut. They can't be too thick or too thin. I had to redo mine a time or two! My day spent making noodles with my Nan Nan and the church ladies was full of stories of the "good ole days" and much laughter. The ladies joked that they were turning "dough" into dollars for the church. That "dough" was transformed into food baskets for needy, school shoes for impoverished children, and other local missions.

At the bottom the hill, from which Sheldon's Grove UMC is perched, my family gathers every year in May for the Burgard reunion. It is still held at my great grandparents' home. Although they are gone, the family has kept the house to use as a family gathering spot, which includes the reunion. Some years at the reunion, the family has walked up the hill to the church and worshipped inside its doors. There are even some family members that still worship there on a weekly basis. Other years we walk up the hill to the church and cross the road to the cemetery where my great grandma Helen and my Nan Nan are buried. We reminisce and hear stories, some old and some new. As I am reminded of them by these stories, I am proud of the legacy that my great grandma Helen and Nan Nan have left for me and my family. Their resourcefulness, faith, and love of family are what I taste as I eat grandma's beef and noodles.

Grandma's Beef and Noodles
Carmen Arnberger, Sherman, Illinois

NOODLES

Ingredients:

2 eggs
3 T. water
½ tsp. salt
1¼ c. flour

Directions:

Beat eggs, add water and salt. Add flour. Knead slightly. Roll into two balls. Roll each ball into paper thin circle. Place on tea towels and let dry until pliable. Fold circle in half, then half again, forming wedge. On short end slice ⅛" strips or to thickness of preference with a sharp knife. Shake out noodles and let dry completely on tea towel before using.

BEEF AND NOODLES

Ingredients:

3-4 lb. chuck roast
1 T. shortening
2 quarts water
1 T. salt
1 beef bouillon cube
homemade noodles as above

Photo by Peter Engler

Directions:

In Dutch oven, melt shortening and brown both sides of meat. Add water and salt. Bring to a gentle boil. Skim off fat as it bubbles. cover and let boil gently for 2 hours until tender. Remove roast. To remaining liquid, add 1-quart water and bouillon cube. Bring to boil. Add noodles a few at time to not reduce water temp. Boil 9-12 minutes. Cut up roast into small pieces and return to finished noodles.

Third Prize, 2018

Beef and Noodles
Amy Wertheim, Atlanta, Illinois

Family Heirloom Recipes....the things of legends, guarded with utmost secrecy and limitations.

The Family Heirloom Recipe Contest has been one of the longest continual contests at the IL State Fair for over 10 years now....long enough that I have begun to have a real dilemma on what to select for entry "this year." I don't want to repeat a recipe; and it's hard to come up with tried and true family heirloom recipes that I haven't used before. You see, most of our recipes that have been a part of our family for so long are quite honestly just family recipes that everyone has, not really "heirloom" in the true sense of the word.

Photo by Barbara Kuck

So, as I pondered what to try and make this year, I had to really reflect on what does everyone ask for when we get together... And what I discovered was that it truly depended on the event or season. For instance, for Christmas my sister and I have specific

MAIN DISHES

cookies that we bake for everyone to snack on during present opening; and at Mother's Day, we always have the 7-layer salad; and for birthdays, the birthday honoree gets to pick their favorite, so for Greg it's the German Potato Salad, Julie likes s'mores at a wiener roast; and for Nic/Dad/Amy, who unfortunately had to share their birthdays with each other along with two other grandparents and Thanksgiving, they were always stuck with chicken 'n noodles and beef 'n noodles.... Which when it finally came down to just Nic & Amy left, everyone bulked at possibly changing the routine meal even though they could finally choose their own meal. But honestly, in the end, they did want the chicken and/or beef 'n noodles....except they couldn't decide which one, chicken or beef.... Which lead me to this year's entry. Chicken 'n Noodles vs Beef 'n Noodles - which one is better, which one will reign supreme!

So, with the entry figured out for this year's Heirloom contest, the quest for the recipes began. You know how you keep treasured recipes in a specific location....and anytime you want them, you just go to your special stash and pull it out and whip it up....well, gosh, that would have been soooo easy, **IF** the recipes had been where **I KNOW** I put them. But no, they weren't there... hmmm....

Not to worry - for Christmas this last year, I had made four of my family groups homemade noodles & gave them handwritten copies of the recipes; just a simple phone call/text and I'd have the recipes and could pull the entry together. Best laid plans of mice and men.... I literally struck out with EV - E - RY -ONE!!! Yes, believe it or not, everyone went to their "special place" where they keep their treasured recipes and they **COULD NOT FIND THE RECIPES!!** No joke, all four family units cannot find their copies. So, here I was, literally dealing with a true heirloom situation, where no one, not even a single person, holds the key to the long-treasured recipes. So, without a copy, I now had to go on the great recipe treasure hunt through grandparent and great-grandparent cookbooks, handwritten notes, etc.

As you can see from the pictures, chickens and beef are long time agriculture commodities that both sides of my family have raised since the early 1900's. My mother's family, until the 1960's still

killed, boiled, plucked, and butchered chickens for their Sunday dinner. My mother can share countless stories of chickens chasing her and her sister as they collected eggs or her mother catching that unfortunate hen that was having trouble producing and snapping her neck with the flick of her wrist; it was so common place that the thought of buying a chicken at the supermarket was really never a passing thought. And my father's family were long time producers of beef, winning local and state awards; even having a rather large disbursement of breeding stock that was considered one of the largest auctions of the time... so given all of this, surely there was a note, a cookbook, **something** that I could find that had a recipe, even remotely similar to the family's version in it...

Two months later, yes, that is how long I had been working on the quest of the recipes; and after going through hundreds of cookbooks, handwritten notes, torn out newspaper and magazine articles, I was actually able to locate what I believe could have been the base recipes that belonged to my great-grandmothers on either side of my family. But.... were they the right versions....and so began the food trials! I mean, I needed to test the recipes out to make sure a) they were close to what we normally serve at the Thanksgiving/birthday dinner and b) they actually tasted good.

MAIN DISHES

After some tweaking, I was able to give a nod to the beef 'n noodle recipe found in the 1930 publication of *Mrs. Peterson's Simplified Cooking* from Chicago. By tweaking I mean removing carrots, tomatoes & peppers from the recipe. No real color is ever present in our chicken or beef 'n noodles - and I'm definitely NOT a fan of carrots, so out they went. As for the tomatoes, it's an oddity in my family, but several of us are allergic to tomatoes, so out with them also. Peppers, well, they didn't really add much flavor and let's be honest, we're eating this meal for the beef, not the veggies. We also stick pretty close to the "beef only" rule, but in our recipe, overtime, we've added some wine to give it some depth of flavor. Other than that, for the most part, this recipe is fairly close.

That only left the chicken 'n noodle recipe to track down. This one is rather ambiguous. My dad and I had discussed the chicken 'n noodle recipe when he became ill several years back and honestly, it was a "I cook up some chickens, throw some canned soup to thicken it up, add some seasonings and the noodles, there you have it..." no real leads there.... and I had made it for Thanksgiving a year ago based on that less than forthcoming conversation and everyone swore I had gotten it correct; but hey, Thanksgiving was a long time ago, and really, could no one not still find their recipes I wrote down for them?!?!?!? So back to the books I went....

I still wasn't having much luck when it dawned on me, I needed to check with Molly; Molly Goldberg that is, as in "the Molly Goldberg Jewish Cookbook." Whenever I needed a "go to" recipe, this is where I always found it; why I didn't just start with her, I do not know.... wait, yes, I did   I didn't start with her because like the handwritten recipes, this cookbook was MIA also. Oh, for pity sake, were the gods of conspiracy trying to keep me from the Heirloom Recipe contest?? Maybe so, I was not to be thwarted!

After tearing literally, the entire house apart, I finally stumbled upon Molly sitting in a stack of cookbooks that I had pulled to look for recipes to enter in the Blue Ribbon Competition back in April. No wonder she wasn't where she was supposed to be - I hadn't put her back yet just in case there was another competition/contest that I might need check it for reference - who knew how right I was!

I quickly turned to the index...no chicken 'n noodle recipe. Hmm. OK, I perused the meat section, nope. No chicken 'n noodle recipe. Really?? I checked in the bread section - I mean the noodles technically are kinda a quick bread.... SCORE!! A recipe for Mandlen....ok, not exactly the noodle recipe I was looking for, but the process sounded familiar and I vaguely remembered Dad making noodles this way a time or two; maybe I was on to something. But the footnote said to add them to consommés or beef soups at the last minute before serving. Yep, that sounded right; but where is the actual chicken recipe.... Off to the soup section I went!

Unbelievable ... here (minus those hideous carrots again) was the recipe I was seeking. And the ending comment mentioned the noodles. Finally, the long-lost chicken 'n noodle recipe had been found.

> Finally, the long-lost chicken 'n noodle recipe had been found.

So why give you two options?? Because at our family gatherings, whenever one is served the other is also. Some like the chicken, some like the beef, some take a little of both. But to serve one without the other is unheard of and would cause such a ruckus, the time/effort saved wouldn't be worth the effort. So, enjoy, and decide which side of the barnyard you fall into, Chicken or Beef or both. And never fear, the recipes are now typed, saved and preserved as a true heirloom recipe should be.

Beef and Noodles
Amy Wertheim, Atlanta, Illinois

Updated Version Beef & Noodles

Ingredients:

1 tablespoon oil - I prefer grape seed oil, but olive or vegetable oil is fine
1½ lbs. beef stew meat, cubed
¼ cup all-purpose flour
¾ cup chopped onion
¾ cup diced celery
3 garlic cloves, minced
4½ cups beef broth
1 cup red wine
1½ teaspoons dried marjoram
¼ teaspoon black pepper
16 oz. homemade noodles

Directions:

Add oil to a large Dutch oven over medium heat.

Place the meat in a medium mixing bowl and sprinkle the flour over the meat and toss to evenly coat cubes. Brown half of the coated meat in the hot oil. Remove from pan. Brown the remaining meat and remove. Cover & set aside.

In the same pan, brown the onion and garlic, adding more oil, if necessary. Drain off any excess fat and return all the meat to the pot. Stir in the broth, wine, marjoram, and pepper. Bring to a boil; reduce heat. Simmer, covered, for 1½ to 2 hours or until meat is tender. When meat is tender, remove with a slotted spoon and set aside to cool briefly. If the chucks are too big, shred them with a fork. Retain the broth for cooking the noodles in....

In the meantime, make your noodles ....

1⅓ to 1½ cups flour
¼ teaspoon salt
2 large eggs
2 teaspoons olive or other vegetable oil

Pour the flour and salt onto your working surface - make a mound and then a well in the middle. Break the eggs and place in the well area. Using a fork, slowly work the egg into the flour; when almost completely absorbed, add the oil and continue until completely combined. If the mixture seems overly moist, add a little more flour until you can easily handle the dough.

Let the dough rest a few minutes, then slowly knead it until the dough is silky and smooth. Add some more flour if still a little moist. It should take about 6-8 minutes of kneading to get the right consistency. Cover the dough with a damp cloth and let it rest for 10 minutes, or up to 30 minutes if you have time. This allows the flour to mellow the dough making it easier to roll out into your pasta shapes.

When you remove the damp cloth, the dough may seem moist - do not add more flour. Just lightly dust your work surface and hands and flatten out the dough ball. At this point, work quickly so the dough doesn't dry out.... Roll the dough til almost translucent about 24x30 inches - the thinner the better.

After rolling out the dough, let it sit for about 10 minutes, uncovered, or until the edges begin to dry, but not yet brittle. Then cut them into ¼-inch strips, hanging them to dry for at least 30 minutes before cooking in your beef mixture.

In a large stew pot place the beef broth and bring to a rapid boil. Add the pasta strands and give a quick stir. Pasta should be thoroughly cooked with 5 minutes; add meat and turn down to simmer. Let the beef and noodles cook down a bit as the noodles and meat absorb the broth. Serve immediately. Enjoy.

Old Version-Beef 'n Noodles
Mrs. Peterson's Simplified Cooking

2 lbs. beef
¼ lb. salt pork
2 cups tomatoes
1 onion
1 stalk of celery
1½ cups carrots
1 green pepper
2 tablespoons minced parsley
4 cloves
½ lb. of noodles

Wipe beef; cut into 1-inch pieces and roll in flour. Put diced salt pork in iron frying pan and cook until light brown. Add beef and continue cooking until meat is well browned, stirring constantly. Pour over enough water over to prevent burning and cook slowly for 2 hours. In another dish cook tomatoes with minced onion, chopped celery, carrots parsley, green pepper and cloves for 30 minutes. Add to meat, season with salt and pepper and serve with noodles, which have been cooked separately in boiling water for 30 minutes.

Contestant, 2014

Grandma Guth's Stuffed Cabbage Rolls with Sauerkraut
Denise Bollman, Springfield, Illinois

A recipe Grandma Guth had learned to cook during her childhood.

y great grandparents, Josephine and Frank Miller came to the United States in 1905. They had two children, my grandmother Carmellia, age 5 and her brother Carl, age 7.

When they arrived at Ellis Island and my great grandfather began looking for work, they moved to Pennsylvania where he first worked in the coke yards at the coal mine. The work was hard and dirty, with little pay. He eventually got a job with the Pennsylvania & Lake Erie Railroad. Although the pay was better and the work not so hard, the family had to continually move from town to town in the region to keep his position.

That is when my grandmother began to meet lots of other immigrants. A lot of the families had come from Poland. This is when she discovered the love for cabbage and sauerkraut. When she married my grandfather, Leo Guth, she would always make her favorite dish of Stuffed Cabbage Rolls with Sauerkraut she had learned to cook during her childhood. She would prepare the dish and take to all the families' gatherings, carried in a heavy crock or cast-iron pot with a lid and

Photo by Catherine Lambrecht

wrapped in a quilt to keep it warm.

She then handed down the recipe to my mother, Harriett Wolfe, when she married her son, Daniel. My parents moved to Indiana after World War II where my father found work in the steel mills. My mother, now 85 years old still makes a big pan of the tasty rolls for our family gatherings. And as tradition has it, I too make the dish for my family and friends here in Illinois.

My grandmother often used homemade sauerkraut and freshly made tomato sauce with brown rice. When Campbell's came out with their condensed tomato soup, the recipe quickly adapted this ingredient as well as the canned Silver Floss sauerkraut and Uncle Ben's quick cooking rice.

Grandma Guth's Stuffed Cabbage Rolls with Sauerkraut

Denise Bollman, Springfield, Illinois

Ingredients:

1 large head of cabbage
2 lbs. ground chuck
2 cups Uncle Ben's Original Enriched Parboiled Long Grain Rice
1 27-ounce can Silver Floss Shredded Sauerkraut
2 10.75-ounce can's Campbell's condensed tomato soup

Directions:

Preheat oven to 350 degrees

Fill a large stock pot with water and add cabbage leaves. Bring to a slight boil and continue cooking until cabbage is limp, drain water from cabbage with a colander.

Cook rice, according to directions on the box.

In a large bowl, mix together ground chuck, rice and half can of the tomato soup.

In a large heavy roasting pan, place the other half of soup into the bottom.

Lay cabbage leaves out and place one large scoop of meat mixture into the center. Fold leave over mixture and then tuck each end to center and roll up. Place rolls seams side down in roasting pan.

Cover cabbage rolls with sauerkraut and top with remaining can of tomato soup.

Cover with lid or aluminum foil and bake for one- and one-half hours at 350 degrees.

6-8 servings

This recipe is easily doubled for all your larger family gatherings.

Contestant, 2014

Aunt Pearl's Chicken and Dumplings
Carol Meadows, Springfield, Illinois

*One of the main dishes everyone
looked forward to …*

My husband was blessed because he came from a family of good cooks. I was blessed because they took me under their wings and showed me how a little bit of this and a little bit of that would change a bland recipe into something unforgettable.

Every year the "Meadows" held a family reunion in Dix, IL. A small town that was just a blink off the interstate.

The Meadows family loves to eat and so the women would show up with their signature dishes. Everyone knew you had to get everything you wanted on the first pass through because there was

Photo by Catherine Lambrecht

no going back for seconds because everything would be gone.

One of the main dishes everyone looked forward to, was Aunt Pearl's Chicken and Dumplings. Aunt Pearl was married to Uncle Lee. Uncle Lee always had a twinkle in his eye and a smile on his face. Aunt Pearl always had a smile on her face and a hug for everyone we loved them both.

One of the main dishes at the reunion was Aunt Pearl's Chicken and Dumplings. Uncle Lee would joke about being first in line, so he was guaranteed some of the chicken and dumplings. If you were unfortunate enough to be the last person in line it would be iffy that there would be any dumplings left. They were always the first to go. Aunt Pearl used the largest pot she had, and it was filled to the brim. When she was asked why she didn't make more she laughed and told everyone that was the largest pan she had in the house.

One of the main discussions was trying to figure out how Aunt Pearl made her dumplings because they were always so light and fluffy. For years the rest of the family would make chicken and dumplings, but they never tasted like Aunt Maude's.

One year I finely decided to ask her for her "Chicken-and-Dumpling" recipe. I remember she gave me a hug and laughed like it was a great joke. She described how she cooked the chicken and made the broth. She finally got to the dumpling part and laughed when she told me the dumplings were biscuits. She said Uncle Johnnie came home one evening and wanted chicken and dumplings for supper. She knew she did not have the time to make dumplings, so she used the biscuit dough she had mixed for supper. Uncle Johnnie liked them better than her homemade dumplings so after that she always used her biscuit dough recipe. She said she would mix up the biscuits and instead of rolling the dough out she dropped the dough into the chicken broth. She laughed and said if she was in a real hurry, she could use canned biscuits.

She said you just had to pop the roll open cut each biscuit into four pieces and drop them in the broth.

We now had the recipe!

Aunt Pearl's Chicken and Dumplings
Carol Meadows, Springfield, Illinois

Aunt Pearl and Uncle Lee are both gone now. But I have great memories every time I make Chicken and Dumplings (Biscuits).

BROTH:

Ingredients:

1 Chicken Cut Up or 3 Chicken Breasts
¼ Cups Carrots Grated
½ White Onion Finely Chopped
1 Rib of Celery Grated
1½ Teaspoon Poultry Seasoning
½ Teaspoon Sage
8 Bouillon Cubes
4 Cups Water Enough to Cover the Chicken
3 Cups Water (For extra liquid for dumplings)

Directions:

In a large pan place the chicken, carrots, celery, onion, poultry seasoning, sage, 6 bouillon cubes, and 4 Cups Water. Cook over high heat and bring to a boil. Reduce heat to simmer and cover and let cook for an additional 20 minutes. In a smaller pan add the 3 cups water and 2 bouillon cubes and bring up to a boil and reduce to simmer. Use the 3 cups water for additional liquid for the dumplings if needed.

Photo by Catherine Lambrecht

Dumplings: Biscuits

Ingredients:

¼ Cup Shortening
2 Cups Flour
3 Tablespoons Baking Powder
1 Teaspoon Salt
¾ Cup Milk + 1 Tablespoon
½ Teaspoon Rubbed Sage

Directions:

While the chicken is cooking you mix the biscuits. In a mixing bowl cut shortening into the flour, baking powder, salt, and sage. Once the shortening is cut into the flour add the milk and mix until you have sticky dough. The 1+ Tablespoon is used if the dough is dry. Remove chicken from the pan and shred into fine pieces. Set chicken aside. Turn the pan up to medium or medium high heat. Start adding the biscuit dough a tablespoon at a time into the boiling chicken broth. Make sure you stir the pot occasionally to keep the biscuits separated. Cook uncovered for 10 minutes cover and cook for 10 more minutes. Add the chicken back into the pot and gently stir to incorporate the chicken with the dumplings. Serve hot with biscuits.

Third Prize, 2011

Rouch Family Chicken and Noodles
Darlene Crider, Lincoln, Illinois

Rouch Family Reunion

Growing up in the Rouch family, headed by my widowed Grandma Rouch, (Wilma Irene Rouch of Grass Creek, IN,1904-2001) one of the best events was the annual reunion. It was always Grandma Rouch's determination to keep the family together that kept these reunions going strong. They were popular events in the ever-growing family and were always well attended, usually held at a large park with a playground for the children to run around in or at the Grass Creek fire station. There was always more food than we could ever eat, brought in as a potluck by the large family, but there were a few culinary constants at the Rouch Family Reunions. Uncle Bob would always bring ham (from one of his own pigs from his dairy farm), one of the aunts would bring "Rouch Salad" (lime Jell-O with shredded

Photo by Peter Engler

carrots) and carrot sticks, another might bring Cherry Delight or green beans with bacon and Grandma Rouch would bring Chicken and Noodles. The noodles were handmade, which she would make at home and give away to church sales as well as serve to her family. Feeding a family of 5 children in rural Indiana was never easy and the Chicken and Noodles were a reflection of her German and Irish background as well as being a frugal meal for feeding a hungry family in the 30's, 40's and 50's. Also, the ingredients were readily available on the family farm. The recipe is simple and easy to make, though it can easily be "dressed up" with the addition of veggies. But what made her Chicken and Noodles unusual was the way they were served. They were always served over a big dollop of homemade mashed potatoes! Early in my marriage, I served this dish to my city born and bred husband and he thought I had lost my mind! Chicken and Noodles over mashed potatoes? Is it a rural Indiana dish or just the Rouch's? I don't know. But my husband soon learned that it is a delicious and filling meal and honestly, I can't imagine it served any other way! We now serve it to our own family and they love it as well. I really appreciate my grandmother's culinary heritage, which she shared in a handwritten cookbook of all her best family recipes. She had so much to share with all of her children, grandchildren, great-grandchildren and great-great grandchildren and is greatly missed.

> ... what made her Chicken and Noodles unusual was the way they were served.

Rouch Family Chicken and Noodles
Darlene Crider, Lincoln, Illinois

NOODLES:

Ingredients:

4 egg yolks
1 whole egg
4 Tbs. cold water
½ tsp. salt
1½ c. all-purpose flour

Photo by Peter Engler

Directions:

Beat eggs and salt with a fork. Add 4 Tbs. cold water. Add 1 cup all-purpose flour and stir. Add ½ cup flour and stir. Dough should be stiff enough to turn out onto a floured board or counter top and knead slightly. If too sticky, add more flour. Divide dough into 3 parts. With rolling pin, roll out on well-floured counter. Roll out to desired thickness. Place on cloth to dry. Roll out other two parts. When nearly dry, cut into strips and then size as desired. Finish drying the noodles. Can also be put into freezer bags and frozen. One recipe of noodles will make a large batch of Chicken and Noodles, enough to serve about 12-15 people.

CHICKEN:

Ingredients:

1 whole chicken
1 tsp. salt

Directions:

Remove giblets and wash chicken. Boil whole chicken in a large pot with enough water to cover. Salt water. Cook chicken until it is falling off the bones, about 1 hour. Remove chicken from pot; cool until able to handle. Remove skin and bones, discard. Shred chicken meat and set aside. Return pot to stove, bring to a boil. Add noodles. Simmer until noodles are tender, about 20 minutes. Add shredded chicken. Salt and pepper to taste. Serve over hot mashed potatoes. It's also excellent with the addition of chopped celery, carrots and onions.

MASHED POTATOES:
(my recipe, not Grandma Rouch's)

Ingredients:

6-8 potatoes
½ tsp. salt
pepper
½ cup butter
¼ cup milk

Directions:

Boil peeled, diced potatoes (about 1 per person) in salted water until tender; drain. Add ½ cup butter and gently mash with beaters until butter has melted and potatoes are chopped into small pieces. Add milk; whip potatoes with mixer on high until light and fluffy.

First Prize, 2017

Old Fashion Oven Fried Chicken
Jone Schumacher, Chapin, Illinois

Chicken as an old-time favorite main dish serves up for many folks a vast variety of memories.

I have heard several senior members of our families recall one chicken dish in particular, Oven Fried Chicken. My mother explains this was a family favorite Sunday dinner dish. Her mother would fry fresh chicken pieces just until lightly browned and then place the chicken in a roasting pan, add some liquid, cover and bake in a slow oven. Her family would then travel to church and back in their horse-drawn carriage while the chicken baked. She further explained that her mother would fire up the oven with split wood in the summer and would use nut coal in the winter as the coal would get hotter than the wood. They also had a small old coal oil stove in the "wash room" and her mother sometimes cooked on this in the summer. Mother recalls the excitement of her mother when one day a large truck arrived and delivered a bottle gas stove that my grandfather had ordered to surprise my grandmother. This stove was much easier to use as they just had to light a match to ignite the stove and oven. It amazes me how Grandmother knew how much fuel to use to keep

Photo by Barbara Kuck

the oven glowing at the right temperature for the chicken to slowly roast all morning. I noticed quite a "glow" also on my mother's face as her memories take her back to savor that "fall-off-the-bone" tender chicken as her mother, daddy and sister gathered around the kitchen table at noon. Mother said Grandmother usually made chicken gravy also, and if they didn't have potatoes for the meal, they would eat the gravy on bread. Family meals seem to be some of the most special memories my mother has of her childhood as their life was a simple, hard-working farm family far away from the hustle and bustle of our modern lives.

When Mother speaks of "dinner," she means the noon meal, hence the "dinner bell" which was rung to call the men in from the fields mid-day. What "city folks" and I think modern folks call "dinner" now, was referred to by my mother's family as supper or the evening meal. I remember well the "everyday" dishes we used at my grandmother's when I was a child, and I am so pleased to have found several pieces of these dishes at various antique shops. I especially enjoy using these when serving Grandmother's oven fried chicken.

My grandparents still had chickens on their farm when I was a little girl and I loved taking Grandmother's basket and go into the chicken house to carefully collect eggs. I also recall being careful to watch where to step

Photo by Barbara Kuck

when walking outside around where the chickens strolled during the day. I also recall, with no such fondness, memories of my mother's "chicken dressing day," which we kids always wondered why it wasn't called chicken "undressing" day! Early on a week-day morning, my mother would go to a nearby neighbor and return with a wooden crate full of noisy "fryers." She would open the trap door and pull out one chicken, hold its neck over a stump and chop off the head with a sharp ax. We kids were so disgusted to see the headless chicken flopping around the yard splattering its blood everywhere. Then Mom would dunk the chicken in a bucket of very hot water and proceed to pluck off the feathers. To this day I can still smell the stench of wet feathers and have had absolutely no desire to sleep on a feather pillow. To remove the pin feathers, mother would hold the birds over a small fire in the yard to singe off the fine feathers. My great grandmother used to do this over an open burner of the kitchen stove and one time caught her apron on fire, so this could be a dangerous step! One by one, all the chickens were destined to the same fate. The chickens were next taken inside to the kitchen sink where the "innards" were taken out, the gizzard cleaned and kept along with the liver and heart. We kids thought dressing old hens were more interesting than the fryers because we were intrigued to watch Mom find eggs inside these chickens! Next, the birds were cut up, wrapped in plastic bags and frozen. I don't really recall if we had fresh fried chicken for our evening meal that night, but I don't think after all that commotion, chicken would not sound too appealing, and I think my mother would have been too tired to fry chicken. I must say it amuses me to hear young moms today complain about what a job it is to go to the grocery—to buy chicken nuggets to microwave, breaded chicken tenders ready to bake, or even to pick up a rotisserie chicken for dinner! Oh, what they don't know! Even though one could say I know how to dress chickens, I have to be honest to say this is not one family tradition of skills I have carried on.

> My great grandmother used to do this over an open burner of the kitchen stove and one time caught her apron on fire ...

However, I do want to carry on the tradition of Sunday oven-fried chicken with my family. After a couple recent trips to Kentucky Fried Chicken to pick up chicken after church for Mother's Day and again for Father's Day family meals, I have concluded this "old fashioned" oven chicken is much more economical! I have searched extensively for a recipe or directions for this dish. I have searched through many old family hand written recipe file boxes and many old cook books, including *Domestic Arts Edition of the American Woman* (copyright 1939) as well as questioned many seniors who admit they ate this chicken at their mother's or grandmother's home. I have come to the conclusion that this dish was something home cooks found so simple and common place that there was never the need to record as a recipe. It seems some of the best family foods were not kept secret but just prepared and the skill passed down through the generations along with the savory memories.

I have spent some delightful hours with my mother listening to her detail how her mother prepared this chicken and we now have the recipe documented! It is wonderful to have a fried chicken recipe that enables one to brown the chicken and have the mess cleaned up before mealtime. I am also so thankful I can set my oven to the exact temperature and not have to "fire it up!"

I recently prepared this chicken for my mother and she declared it delicious and very similar to what she remembers her mother prepared, and she seemed to sincerely enjoy this connection to her past. After the chicken dinner, we looked at her picture album and found some childhood chicken pictures to treasure. We also enjoyed looking back through the years with my picture album and I must say I'm not surprised or disappointed we didn't find any pictures of "chicken-dressing day," so instead I can just picture cherished memories of how my mother sometimes performed unpleasant tasks to provide the best quality food possible for her family. I am excited to be able to prepare this chicken for my children and 11 grandchildren as they now call this chicken "tender BONE chicken" to differentiate from their frequent meals of chicken tenders. I am also especially looking forward to preparing this dish again for my mother on her 90th birthday this coming October!

> After the chicken dinner, we looked at her picture album and found some childhood chicken pictures to treasure.

Old Fashion Oven Fried Chicken

Jone Schumacher, Chapin, Illinois

Ingredients:

CHICKEN:

1¼ cup all-purpose Flour
¾ teaspoon Teasoning (poultry seasoning)
¾ teaspoon Lawry's salt
1½ teaspoon fine chicken bouillon
2 teaspoon pepper
½ cup buttermilk or evaporated milk
4 pounds chicken pieces
4 cups solid shortening
12 oz. chicken broth

Photo by Barbara Kuck

OPTIONAL GRAVY:

3 tablespoons left-over seasoned flour
2-3 cups whole milk

Directions:

1. Pre-heat lard in a large skillet to 350 degrees.

2. Combine all seasonings and flour in a plastic or plastic bag.

3. Dip chicken pieces in the buttermilk and place in bag. Shake gently to coat with the seasoned flour. Carefully place chicken into the hot oil.

4. Let fry to light brown, turning after about 5 to 10 minutes to brown all sides.

5. Remove from skilled to blot off excess oil on paper towels.

6. Place chicken in roasting pan, pour on the chicken broth, cover and place in pre-heated 275-degree oven for 2½ to 3 hours until tender and reaches internal temperature of 180 degrees.

OPTIONAL GRAVY:

When shortening is cool enough to handle safely, drain skillet, being careful to leave the browned flour crumbs. Stir the seasoned flour into the fat that remains with the crumbs. Slowly pour in the milk, stirring constantly. Heat skillet to 350 degrees, continuing to stir until gravy is bubbling and thickened. (Additional milk can be added as necessary for desired thickness.) Keep warm until serving.

> PS: I realize some of the seasonings I have in my recipe may not have been available to my grandmother, but I have chosen to include them for the flavor boost. I believe that modern taste buds have been altered with all the strong international spices available, and I think the fresh dressed chickens of days past were so flavorful extra spices were not needed. I want to have a recipe that will last through the generations. Had I not been called away to babysit grandchildren in July and then combated bronchitis and an ear infection upon my return, my mother and I would have liked to have dressed a fresh fryer to bring to the fair!! I was unable to use lard in my recipe to fry the chicken in as some in my family cannot eat pork or pork products, and I choose legs and thighs as these are the favorites of my family.

Second Prize, 2017

Svestkove Knedlicky (Fruit Dumplings)
Linda D. Cifuentes, Mohamet, Illinois

For us kids, summer meant fruit dumplings.

Summer for most kids meant no school, vacations, and swimming. As that was true for us kids, summer also meant fruit dumpling. My mom only made these dumplings in the summer primarily because stone fruit is used, and summertime is when the fruit was fresh and less expensive. She only made them a couple of times throughout the summer and I think that is because they are a bit time consuming to make.

I remember my mom lining up all the apricots, plums, peaches, and cherries after she washed and dried them. Then came the big task; making the dough. She would mix up the dough in the pot and once the dough was made, she would flour up her board and her hands. She rolled out the dough and then cut it into pieces and wrapped around each of the fruit (3 cherries to one dumpling). After all the dumplings were made, they were placed in a huge pot of boiling water.

Photo by Barbara Kuck

118   Family Heirloom Recipes from the Illinois State Fair

Once my dad got home from work, we all sat down at the kitchen table and the feast and games began. My mom took all the dumplings out of the water with a slotted spoon and placed them in a colander. She left the dumplings in the colander and placed in a soup bowl to catch any extra dripping. Then she put a stick of melted butter in a bowl and also a bowl of sugar mixed with cinnamon on the table. You put the dumplings on your plate; broke them up; being careful to push the seeds aside; sprinkled with cinnamon sugar and doused with melted butter. I don't think I have ever eaten anything better than my mom's dumplings! Yum!!

Now here is where the fun began. There were actually two contests within this meal. The first was to see who ate the most dumplings—we counted the seeds. The other game was to find the cherry dumplings. These were most coveted for many reasons. First and foremost, they were by far the best tasting dumpling and EVERYBODY's favorite. They also had 3 cherries in each dumpling which gave you 3 seeds to add to your seed collection. Cherry dumplings were most coveted and were a little difficult to spot. We would all poke at a smaller dumpling and look for red juice, but we were often fooled for when we cut it open on our plate it would contain a plum. My dad's rule was if you took it you ate it. There were many a tearful meal, but my dad was steadfast to this rule. So, the game became ruthless looking for those cherry dumplings. There were several times I left the dinner table with fork marks on my hand from my brother Tony as we were both going after the same cherry dumpling. These are some of the fondest memories of my childhood.

> Now here is where the fun began.

Once I realized we should have my mom write down the recipe it was too late! She had Alzheimer's and could not remember how to make the dumplings. When my mom passed away in 2005, we thought the recipe was lost forever. My dad was bound and determined to figure it out. He called me one day in January 2007; just a little over a year after we lost my mom and said, "I think I figured it out," and he made a recipe using canned plums. I went to his house and heated the dumpling but never got to eat it or get the recipe. That same night I took my dad to the hospital; he was diagnosed with Leukemia; and died 5 days later. We thought the recipe was lost forever.

We were visiting my Uncle Joe last year (the only living relative in this generation) in Delaware. My cousin was also there, and we started talking about food we ate that was special when we were young. I was with my brother Tony and my sister Cindy and we mentioned how we would kill to eat my mom's fruit dumplings one more time but that the recipe was lost! My cousin Karen shocked us all when she pulled out this recipe and said this is your mom's recipe; my mom had it. You cannot imagine our joy!!

This recipe is from our Czech routes. Knedlicky is Czech for dumpling. Both my parents were born here in the United States, but three of my four grandparents were born in what is now the Czech Republic. All four of my grandparents spoke Czech as did both my parents. My Babi (grandma in Czech) spoke minimal English and my Dede (grandpa in Czech) spoke no English. I grew up in Berwyn 50 years ago and it was almost entirely a Czech area. The shopkeepers spoke Czech, the bakeries sold Czech products and even the high school I attended taught Czech. As a matter of fact, I took Czech my freshman and sophomore year.

When both my parents were young, they attended Czech school. It is not surprising that many of the foods my mom cooked were Czech based since her mom and mother-in-law passed down recipes. My mom Helen was a great cook and baker. I hope by presenting this little piece of our family history you will Get a feel for the Czech "experience."

These fruit dumplings are not the prettiest food to look at but are oh so tasty!! Besides how can you go wrong with something covered in sugar and butter!!

I have taken the liberty to set up a couple of dumplings on the plate like we would eat them, but I did not want to deprive you of the best part. So happy hunting for the cherry dumplings—beware of the plum dumplings (all though they are not bad).

Jist!! (Eat!!)

Svestkove Knedlicky (Fruit Dumplings)
Linda D. Cifuentes, Mohamet, Illinois

Ingredients:

2 eggs; beaten
2 tablespoons melted butter
1 cup milk
3½ cups flour
½ teaspoon salt

Directions:

In a large bowl combine eggs, milk, and butter. Mix flour and salt with wooden spoon until smooth and in a big ball. Cut dough in half.

Wash and dry stone-fruit (peaches, plums, apricots, and cherries).

Flour board and roll out dough. Wrap around washed fruit. Place in large pot boiling water with salt added and boil 20 minutes. Remove dumplings with a slotted spoon and place in colander to drain (this is how my mom served the dumplings).

Serve with melted butter and cinnamon sugar mixture.

Photo by Barbara Kuck

First Prize, 2009

Kluski (Potato Dumplings) with Round Steak and Gravy
Caroline M. Becker, Springfield, Illinois

As a child, I remember my mother making these dumplings from leftover boiled red potatoes.

The recipe for the kluski (potato dumplings) came from my maternal grandmother, Pauline Szymura, who was Polish and German. She and my grandfather Stanley owned and worked together in a butcher shop on Western Avenue in Chicago. My mother, who was born in 1913, was the second oldest of the girls. (Upright photo, c. 1921) My parents were married in August, 1945 and lived in Chicago where they rented an apartment in the same building as my grandparents. I was born in 1947, followed by my first brother in 1949, and a second brother in 1950. Because my Dad didn't want his children to have a concrete "yard", our family moved from Chicago to a home in Berwyn, about 10 miles away, when I was 5  years old in 1952. My youngest brother, born in 1953, completed our family. (Horizontal photo, May, 1954) Mom stayed home with us while my Dad worked as a maintenance man at a factory.

Photo by Peter Engler

Most of our family meals consisted of a meat, boiled potatoes and a vegetable. As a child, I remember my mother making these dumplings from leftover boiled red potatoes. I watched as she rolled the dough into a long, thin "snake" which she then cut into "pillows" that were boiled. She told me how her mother used to make these for her family when she and my aunts (c. 1920-30) were children living at home. Mom never measured anything for this recipe, but the kluski always seemed to turn out the same each time she made them. Prior to my marriage in 1968, I lived at home, didn't cook much and certainly never attempted the recipe. But having round steak, gravy and kluski (along with canned corn) was a strong and favorite childhood memory, so I tried making them on my own. Since my Mom never measured any ingredients when she made them, she couldn't provide much help. It took multiple efforts before I felt that I duplicated the product of my childhood memories! Eventually, I measured the ingredients and wrote the recipe in a cook book. Determining how to make the round steak was an easier task.

> Mom never measured anything for this recipe, but the kluski always seemed to turn out the same each time she made them.

Although I never felt deprived as a child, there were not many extras in our family and I somehow knew that finances were tight. In the early years of my own marriage, however, when our finances were meager because my husband was in graduate school, I realized that making kluski helped stretch our limited resources because it turned a smaller amount of leftover potatoes into a larger quantity of dumplings that could feed a family for more meals. My Mom was obsessive about fairness, and each of us only got 4 kluski at a meal. I have always loved the taste and texture of the dumplings, particularly when combined with the round steak and gravy. Now that I have grandchildren of my own, my only son, his wife and our granddaughters have enjoyed them with us at family dinners. Hopefully, since the recipe is written down now, the tradition of the Polish kluski will be carried on for another generation.

Kluski (Potato Dumplings) with Round Steak and Gravy
Caroline M. Becker, Springfield, Illinois

KLUSKI RECIPE

Ingredients:

5 cups cold boiled red potatoes (lightly packed)
3 eggs
2¼ tsp. salt
3½ cups flour

Directions:

Photo by Peter Engler

Peel and quarter 10-11 medium red potatoes and boil in salted water until they break easily when pierced with a fork. Drain and refrigerate overnight. Using a potato ricer or sausage grater, finely shred the potatoes. Measure 5 cups (lightly packed) potatoes, place in large bowl. Add eggs, salt and flour and mix by hand to form a soft but firm dough. Turn entire ball onto a large, generously floured surface, kneading for several minutes until the ball becomes smoother. Cut in half with a knife. Roll and shape each half, using your hands, to make a long, cylindrical "snake" about 1¼ " in diameter by 36" long. Using a knife, cut into 1 – 1¼ " in sections. Bring 6 quarts water to a boil in a large pasta pot with a colander insert. Gently place the sections from the first half of dough in boiling water, stirring lightly to keep them from sticking during addition. Kluski will rise to surface and float in 5 minutes. Continue boiling for another 10-11 minutes, stirring occasionally. Drain in colander. Repeat process with second half of dough. Makes approximately 66 dumplings.

ROUND STEAK AND GRAVY RECIPE

Ingredients:

2# tenderized round steak
8 slices bacon
1 tsp. tenderizer
1 tsp. salt
½ tsp. black pepper
⅛ tsp. sugar
¼ tsp. garlic powder
5 tbsp. beef soup base (can substitute 5 beef bouillon cubes)
2 tsp. liquid hickory smoke
6 tbsp. flour and 1 cup water for gravy

Directions:

Fry 8 slices bacon in a non-Teflon Dutch oven. While bacon is frying, season meat with tenderizer, salt, pepper, sugar and garlic powder. Remove bacon from pan and reserve for later use. Cut round steak into serving size portions (approx. 3"x4"), trimming excess fat. Brown round steak pieces in bacon fat, removing and reserving juices that accumulate during browning. Add enough water to reserved juices to equal 6 cups. Add beef soup base and hickory smoke to water. Continue browning round steak until very brown. Break bacon into smaller pieces and put on browned round steak. Add flavored water to pot (all meat should be covered) and simmer on very low heat for 3-4 hours until meat is very tender. Remove meat to serving platter.

Blend flour and 1 cup water in separate bowl. Pour into remaining juices in Dutch oven. Heat and stir until gravy thickens. Strain to remove any remaining pieces of shredded meat. Serve over kluski.

Contestant, 2016

Grandma Delong's Meatloaf
Janie Saner, Sherman, Illinois

My grandma was one special lady.

Mary Grace (Arvin) Delong was born on October 13, 1890. She and my grandpa lived at 322 South Park in Springfield. One of my favorite memories was riding the "city bus" with grandma. That was quite a big deal for this country girl. We would ride the bus downtown to shop at Kmart. We also walked to the nearby bakery on Saturday morning to buy butter cake. If you didn't get there early enough, it would be gone. I loved playing with her dog Trixie. Grandma and I played Chinese checkers and regular checkers, which she would sometimes let me win. We played give away checkers too, which was hard to play after playing regular checkers.

On Sundays, my family would often go to grandma's for dinner after church. One of our favorite meals was her special meat loaf. She would serve it on her pretty pink flowered china. I was later given this china and her china cabinet. Inside the door I found a note that says the name of the china is Nautilus and it was purchased at Bressmer's department store. The meat loaf is on Grandma's china platter.

I have been told by many friends and family that what makes Grandma's Meat loaf special is the piquant sauce which is spread on top of the meat loaf. The sauce contains the right amount of sweetness from the ketchup and brown sugar, but also has a bit of tanginess from the dry mustard. When I made our daughter a book of family recipes, I included this one. Her husband liked the piquant sauce so much that he asked her to double it when she makes the meat loaf.

I was named Mary Jane after my beloved grandma, Mary Grace. I share her love of cooking and gardening. She canned many vegetables over the years. Grandma saved money wherever possible. Her meat loaf was an economical dish to serve the family. This recipe has been in my family for well over 90 years. I am thankful that my mom put this recipe in my handwritten cookbook, and I hope the recipe continues to be passed on for many more years.

My grandma lived to be 100 years old. I still miss her, but I have great memories of her. One saying she had was "Take what you've got and make what you want out of it." I still say this today when I might not have exactly what I need for a project. My grandma was not wealthy, but she gave me a wealth of knowledge about life. I'm so glad that she also shared her love of God with us. My dad was her only child and she was 38 when he was born. I thank God for Grandma and I hope to pass on her love of cooking to our kids and grandkids.

Photo by Peter Engler

Grandma Delong's Meatloaf

Janie Saner, Sherman, Illinois

Ingredients:

⅔ cup dry bread crumbs
1 cup milk
1½ pounds hamburger
2 eggs, beaten
1 T dried onion flakes
1 tsp. salt
⅛ tsp. pepper
½ tsp. sage

Piquant Sauce:

3 T brown sugar
¼ cup ketchup
¼ tsp. nutmeg
1 tsp. dry mustard

Photo by Peter Engler

Directions:

1) Mix milk, bread crumbs, beaten eggs, onion flakes, salt, pepper, and sage in large mixer bowl at low speed. Add hamburger and blend together.

2) Place in greased loaf pan.

3) Mix piquant sauce ingredients in a small bowl.

4) Spread piquant sauce over top of meat loaf.

5) Bake at 350 F for 1 hour.

Contestant, 2017

Great-Grandma's Meatloaf Cake
Amy Wertheim, Atlanta, Illinois

Meatloaf - the food of nightmares

According to the history books, Meatloaf seems to have originated in Ancient Rome, where it appears in 5th Century cookbooks. However, Modern American references to meatloaf first appear in print in 1899, shortly after the invention of mechanical meat grinders.

Today's Meatloaf popularity seems to date back to the Great Depression and World War II due to economic hardship and wartime rationing. The various fillers that can be found in meatloaf, such as bread crumbs and eggs, helped to lower the cost of the meal by taking the place of some of the meat. But even beyond the United States, Meatloaf is a popular dish in Germany, Cuba, Greece, Mongolia and other countries. But I stand by my

Photo by Barbara Kuck

first statement ... Meatloaf IS the food of nightmares, at least my nightmares, as it was the method of murder my mother used to rid us of ... well, I'm getting ahead of myself.

Meatloaf has always been a staple, a standard, a special tradition in our family during certain eventful gatherings; specifically, my grandfather's birthday. Not a big fan of cake, my grandmother would fashion the meatloaf into sort of a "cake" for him, decorating with "ketchup icing", mashed potato "flowers" you get the idea. Every year it was a different theme, shape, decoration, etc. And then of course, other times when it wasn't his birthday, it was the typical half football oblong blob at Sunday family dinners. And since my dad "loved" meatloaf too, my mom made it like every other day for him; okay, maybe not every other day, but it sure seemed like it!

Now back in the day, you ate what was put before you. And God help me, the adults in my life were overly generous with the slice of meatloaf. There are only a few things I absolutely did not like to eat - spaghetti, chop suey, sauerkraut & brats, and meatloaf. And no matter how I tried, asked, begged, whined, cried, sat in pouty silence, I was always given a healthy slab of the yuck, er meatloaf.

At least I was until that fateful day in January, 1970 ....

It was a typical supper time - meatloaf with the cooked-on ketchup sitting on the table mocking me, knowing I was going to have to choke it down, or sit there until bedtime if I didn't. So, trying not to gag, and drinking a ridiculous about of water to try and wash the taste away, I finished every last bite, escaping to the back porch to play with Tutu, our spider monkey.

Tutu has come to us via my Aunt Libby, my dad's younger sister, who received it as an 18th birthday gift from their older sister Aunt Franny. But since Libby left for college that fall, and she couldn't take him, we got to keep him by default. That was back in the day, where every pet store sold monkeys, parrots, and other exotic animals.

Now Tutu could be so sweet, taking treats from you or he could be evil, screeching and throwing his feces at you. Luckily, Tutu and I were buds; Mom and Tutu, well, it was a day-by-day, "what kind of mood is Tutu in" kind of relationship. Mom has recently taken to feeding Tutu leftovers from dinner; although Spider Monkeys are primarily frugivorous preferring a diet of 90% fruit and seeds, Tutu loved his meat. I know, he was a strange one. Dad would even slip him a bite or two when he was grilling on the back porch (this was where Tutu's cage was located the majority of the year). So, it wasn't unusual that Mom brought Tutu some leftover meatloaf to enjoy. And off to bed I went ....

Only to awaken to a DEAD TUTU! Mom had poisoned my beloved monkey with HER meatloaf! And she'd fed me that same meatloaf - was I going to die?! Everyone tried to convince me that the meatloaf hadn't killed Tutu. They even took him over to the U of I medical clinic to find out what had happened ... the "official" findings were that Tutu was actually suffering from pneumonia, but in monkeys, they said we would have never known he was sick as they rarely show any signs of sickness until too late, but I KNOW, the REAL REASON Tutu died — it was the meatloaf and I have proof...

A few years later, my Aunt Franny adopted a pet chimpanzee, named Nicky. Nicky was adorable! But along about her second birthday, when chimps start to mature, it suddenly began attacking any males randomly; my dad or brother could just be sitting there, and she'd attack out of the blue, sometimes drawing blood! It was only after my dad threatened to feed her meatloaf if Aunt Franny couldn't figure out how to control her that Nicky was made to go to her cage when people were over so if it really was pneumonia, why mention the meatloaf???

And that is why, to this day, and since I was 4-years-old, I have never eaten another piece of meatloaf made by anyone, anywhere. And for all those family gatherings where meatloaf was the "featured" item, they always made a special meal just for me.

So please enjoy my family's long-standing killer, to die-for, one-of-kind meatloaf. And don't worry, you're not a monkey or a chimp, so what do you have to worry about?

Great-Grandma's Meatloaf Cake

Amy Wertheim, Atlanta, Illinois

Ingredients:

2 pounds ground beef
1 pound ground pork
½ medium onion, very finely chopped (½ to ¾ cup)
½ cup horseradish
2 teaspoons Worcestershire sauce
1 teaspoon dry mustard
2 eggs
¾ cup bread crumbs or cracker crumbs
1 teaspoon salt
½ teaspoon freshly ground pepper
4 cups of water for steaming in oven
2 tablespoons water
3¾ cup ketchup
½ cup of your favorite bbq sauce

Directions:

Preheat oven to 350°F.

Combine all ingredients except water and ketchup in a large mixing bowl. Use your hands to quickly and thoroughly combine. Refrigerate for at least 30 minutes to overnight.

Mix the ketchup and bbq sauce in a small mixing bowl; set aside. Place the meat into two (2) greased bread pans, dividing the ingredients evenly between the two pans and generously brush the tops with the ketchup and bbq mixture - saving approximately ½ cup for later. Place 4 cups of water in another cooking pan and place both the bread pans and pan of water in the oven, baking for 50 minutes or until meat tests done, approximately 155°F.

Remove and allow to cool for 10 minutes. Loosen the sides of the loaf from the pan and place on serving dish. Drizzle the extra ketchup/bbq sauce leftover from earlier on top much like the icing on a cake.

Garnish, parsley; serve and enjoy. Serves 8 to 12 servings

Third Prize, 2014

Oyster Dressing
Amy Wertheim, Atlanta, Illinois

Oyster Dressing ... the rest of the story

Like all families, we try to get everyone together at the holidays, especially Thanksgiving. This isn't always possible since some live so far away, but in order to always keep the same feeling in place, we, like many families, have traditions. Some traditions are good ones; and others, well wonder how they ever started or why we even continue them ....

Some of the better traditions at Thanksgiving is everyone at the table sharing one thing they are thankful for, either something that has happened in the last year, or just thankful in general. Another tradition is we always take a family portrait, err portraits ... from every angle, from each end of the table, from each side of the table, etc, etc, etc. And of course, the photos cannot take place until ALL the food is on the table. Which leads to the not so better traditions ....

Photo by Catherine Lambrecht

Taking pictures only after all the food is on the table; you know, the food that is supposed to be served warm, or even cold; because by the time the pictures are done, everything is all the same temperature. The other not to good tradition is you have to take at least a tablespoon of everything – even the foods you don't like. Even the oyster dressing – yuck! And while we are on the bad traditions, why would you ask do we even serve the oyster dressing anymore, well that is an interesting story ....

Along about five generations ago, the matriarch of the family was Aunt Teddy. Aunt Teddy had a love all things seafood; lobsters, clams, shrimp and oysters. Back then, around the 1900s, oysters could only be purchased around the holidays in 5-gallon wooden barrels. Folks would stop by the butcher, tell him how many they needed, and he would scoop them out, throw them in butcher's paper and on home they went for the holiday feasts. Well, Aunt Teddy was such a lover of oyster, her brother would buy her one of these barrels and she'd pop the lid off and scoop out these little pearls of "yumminess" and slurp them down. Now, one can only eat so many oysters, so they had to come up with something to do with the leftovers, hence the oyster dressing that was served at Thanksgiving, & Christmas, and every meal in between I imagine!

> Aunt Teddy had a love all things seafood ...

The really odd thing about this tradition is there is only one person in every generation that even likes the oyster dressing! Which begs the question, why do we serve a dish that only one person likes? Maybe it has something to do with "who" that oyster dressing lover is .... Aunt Teddy was the matriarch; and with the next generation, the oyster dressing fan was Aunt Lena. Although not necessarily the matriarch, she was the old spinster and you know how demanding they can be! And just like aunt Teddy she would pop the lid off the barrel, and scoop out those slimy, smelly little things and eat them raw & warm. And NO ONE was allowed to take his or her helping of oyster dressing until AFTER Aunt Lena has taken her portion (like we would!!!).

The next generation, my dad's generation, the oyster fanatic was his sister, my Aunt Frannie. She was another lid popper, oyster scooping, raw eating fan ... I remember asking my dad what in the world she was doing on the back porch bent over a dirty old barrel, I mean she was a well-respected doctor, but you wouldn't have known it seeing her trying to grab the slippery little devils. But that is what an oyster apparently does to a person – you are reduced to a cavewoman like being hovering over your barrel, ready to defend it from all others. Luckily, with this generation the oyster dressing took a dramatic turn for the better with the addition of oyster crackers on top and cream. Now, everyone had to opportunity to "take their tablespoon" from the cracker topping instead of having to eat any of the oysters. The only problem was if by the time it came around to you, if all the cracker topping was gone, well, you were stuck taking an oyster and trying to choke it down.

> ... the oyster dressing took a dramatic turn for the better with the addition of oyster crackers on top and cream.

For my generation, the oyster lover seems to be my cousin Anne; and the oyster no longer come in the oh-so-unsanitary barrels, but a nice plastic container from the deli. For those us who tend to sit at the end of the table, well, we've learned the art of pretending to take a helping of every item passed without really taking some. Believe me, I've earned a pass having to eat my share of oysters in the past ....

As far as the current generation, well no one has truly emerged as the oyster lover as of yet; but we do seem to have a large contingency of oyster cracker fans. So, as we use the traditional serving pan, we've started to reduce the number of oyster and to add more crackers. Sadly, the original pan that was inserted into the serving dish met its demise before my generation came along, hence the use of the aluminum pan .... Although I think they started using it to make it easier to throw out the uneaten dressing! So, we continue the tradition of the aluminum pan, and the oyster crackers, and the addition of the cream. I hope you enjoy my version ... and if you dig in deep, you'll find one of those slimy little suckers that only the end table has the "privilege" of enjoying.

Oyster Dressings
Amy Wertheim, Atlanta, Illinois

ORIGINAL OYSTER DRESSING

Ingredients:

16 oz. oysters
2 sleeves of crackers (we think it means saltines)
2 tubs butter (?)
a package of hot dog buns (8 or 12?) extremely stale & hard
1-quart heavy whipping cream
Oyster crackers

Directions:

Preheat oven to 350 F. Rub baking pan allover with butter; set aside.

Using a rolling pin or a bottle smash the crackers. (No mention on how much, small bits, medium bits, nothing). Then crush the hot dog buns, but not as small as the crackers.

Clean the oysters (again, no instructions) reserving the juice.

In the baking pan, place a layer of crackers, then pats of butter; throw in a handful of buns, half of the oysters and ⅓ of the cream and oyster juice. Add another layer and finish with oyster crackers and remaining cream/oyster juice poured over the top.

Cook until crust is golden; serve warm.

Photo by Catherine Lambrecht

TODAY'S OYSTER DRESSING

Ingredients:

1 tablespoon vegetable oil
1 cup chopped celery
1 cup chopped onion
8 cups dry breadcrumbs
2 tablespoons chopped fresh parsley
3 cups oysters, liquid reserved
3 eggs, beaten
1½ teaspoons salt
¼ teaspoon ground black pepper
1 teaspoon poultry seasoning
½ teaspoon dried thyme
Oyster crackers

Directions:

Preheat the oven to 325 degrees F (165 degrees C). Grease a 2-quart casserole dish.

Heat the oil in a large skillet over medium-high heat. Add celery and onion; cook and stir until tender, about 5 minutes. Mix in the breadcrumbs and parsley and remove from the heat. Add the oysters and eggs, and season with salt, pepper, poultry seasoning and thyme. Stir in enough liquid from the oysters to moisten and mix everything thoroughly. Transfer to the casserole dish.

Bake in the preheated oven until the top is toasted and a knife inserted into the center comes out clean, about 45 minutes.

Contestant, 2011

Great Grandma's Pasties
Dianna M. Wara, Washington, Illinois

A modem day marriage of turnover meets pot pie.

My husband's grandmother, the patriarch of the family, was well known for having her freezer stocked full of all kinds of baked goods to have on hand when visitors came to visit. She lived most of her adult life in Lead, South Dakota. So, as a young boy and teenager, my husband has very fond memories of visiting his grandmother who lived 2 driving days away from where he lived in Illinois. They were lucky if they got to visit 2 times a year. One of his favorite meals to eat when he arrived at his grandmothers has always been pasties. What do you ask are pasties? No, it's not some fancy pasta or a fancy pastry with fruit filling - instead, I would describe it as a modem day marriage of turnover meets pot pie. I got to experience pasties from his grandmother and she retold the story behind this wonderful food.

Her husband (my husband's grandfather) was from Finland. During hard times, he had to travel to where the jobs were. So, his family along with fellow friends from Finland came to the United States. The first jobs that they found were working the copper mines in Michigan. Grandpa wasn't there long before he and other Finlanders heard about better jobs opening up in Lead, South Dakota. The Homestake Gold Mine was looking for people to work

Photo by Peter Engler

their mines. So, my grandpa made the move to South Dakota. With him, also moved many of their Finish friends. Grandma said that Grandpa's family brought the recipe with them from Finland. However, the Cornish people that were already established working in the copper mines, had their own version. I don't think that we will ever know who actually created the recipe first but, both variations were created for the same purpose and that was to create a filling meal that the miners could easily take with them to eat. Grandmother was very particular on how her recipe was to be made. First, she said that the beef HAD to be in small cubes. The butchers years ago refused to cut it into small cubes for her and told her to buy ground beef instead. That was NOT the way a pasty was supposed to be made. So, she showed me how to chop it into cubes. Second, she said that when you seal the pasty, you want to create a thick edge/seal around it. The reason being, that part was typically not eaten. It was made thick enough so that the miners could eat the middle and throw way the crust. Because miners ate right where they worked - no running water to wash up before they ate. This thick edge gave them something to hold on to as they ate the middle part of the pasty. That way, even with the dirtiest of fingers, the miners were able to eat lunch. Then grandma wrapped the pasty in a newspaper and put it into grandpa's lunch. The pasty still had some warmth to it when he ate his lunch. My husband always thought it was odd that every day before the miners went home, they had to take a shower. The Homestake didn't want any gold dust to leave the sight. But yet the Homestake didn't have running water so the miners could wash their hands before eating.

Grandpa worked most of his adult life at the Homestake Gold Mine. Although he never "struck it rich with gold" he was a very wealthy man in that he had a family that loved him and grandchildren who thought the world of him! Grandma continued to make pasties for her family up until her passing a few years ago. But the tradition is still carried on. My mother-in-law still makes pasties. And I for the second time, will make pasties and carry on the tradition. Oh yes, I will honor grandma's wishes and cube my own meat!

Great Grandma's Pasties
Dianna M. Wara, Washington, Illinois

Ingredients:

Filling

3 cups cubed peeled potatoes
1 cup chopped carrots
1 medium onion, chopped
¾ teaspoon salt
¼ teaspoon pepper
2 pounds roast beef, small cubed
1 tablespoon butter, melted

Pastry Crust

4 cups all-purpose flour
1¼ teaspoons salt
1 cup solid shortening
¾ cup cold water

Photo by Peter Engler

Directions:

In a large bowl, combine the potatoes, carrots, onion, salt and pepper. Add the beef over potato mixture and mix well. Add butter and toss to coat; set aside.

For pastry, in a large bowl, combine flour and salt. Cut in shortening until mixture resembles coarse crumbs. Gradually add water, tossing with a fork until a ball forms. Divide dough into five portions; roll each into a 10-in. circle. Place 1 cup of filling in the center of each circle. Fold pastry over filling and seal edges tightly with a fork; cut slits in the top of each.

Place on a greased baking sheet. Bake at 375 degrees for 50-60 minutes or until golden brown.

Yield: 5 servings

Honorable Mention, 2015

Peixe a Lumbo (African Shrimp & Rice Stew)
Amy Wertheim, Atlanta, Illinois

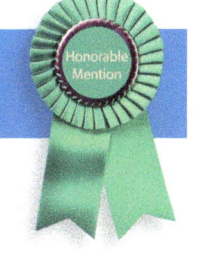

Nancy Frances Wertheim

The farm. It's where six generations of my family have learned about hard work, where their food comes from whether it be the animal or plant variety, and where they learned about the great outdoors. On the farm you can expect to get dirty whether from hard work and sweat or mud in the crick bottoms when you sneak off for a cool afternoon swim. On the farm is where love of the land and its creatures is learned. But on the farm several generations ago, it was also where girls learn that their place isn't necessarily out in the barns, or in the fields, and it's most definitely not in the calving pens or breeding house. No, young girls, and especially young ladies, would NEVER venture into THOSE kinds of places their place was in the home, with the mothers and grandmothers learning about sewing, and cooking, and cleaning, and other such boring, mundane, tedious, unfulfilling tasks … Just ask my Aunt Frannie ….

Nancy Frances Wertheim grew up on the family farm in the 1940's. And she did NOT like the inside chores, no question about it. She wanted to be in the barns where all the action happened. And she was going to be a big animal vet, the first WOMAN VET in the whole of central Illinois. She had a plan, she had a goal, her mind was focused …. and then her dad and brother intervened. No farmer, no rancher, would want a lady doctor tending to their animals – be a regular doctor, a people doctor they told her; and over time, they slowly wore her down until when the time came to apply to medical school it wasn't to the U of I Vet school, it was to Southern Il Medical School, but she didn't bend on one item, she would help bring life into this world, and so she became an obstetrician, a baby doctor.

Now, if you're wondering how this story could possibly lead to a family heirloom recipe, well as Paul Harvey used to say, here's the rest of the story ….

Although my dad and grandpa were able to talk Aunt Frannie out of being a veterinarian, they weren't able to ever quite squelch her need for adventure. And as a "people's" doctor, her skills were in great demand .... here in the US AND abroad .... way far away, abroad .... clear on the other side of the world in Mozambique & Zimbabwe; yup, my Aunt Frannie became a traveling doctor whenever her schedule would allow for it and off to Africa she'd go.

At first, the people who came to the clinics assumed she was a nurse, as there were many nurses there from the Red Cross (pic at right – Aunt Frannie top row, far rt). And of course, there were those that were quite skeptical of anyone who was practicing medicine without using the herbs and other potions like the Shona Witch Doctors (left); but most were just skeptical that a woman could be a doctor. But over time, the people of Mozambique & Zimbabwe forgot that she was a woman and were just thankful she was there willing to help them and their children.

Sadly though, these types of clinics are for people of humble and meager means, but they were so thankful for all the healing that they would try to give gift items to my Aunt Frannie .... goats, tribal shield, zebra drum, fertility statue (on the display) and meals.

> Aunt Frannie, as previously mentioned, was an adventurous soul.

Now, as everyone knows, most food is not safe for consumption in undeveloped countries for nonnative people to eat, but my Aunt Frannie, as previously mentioned, was an adventurous soul. Because of this, she was able to try many of the native dishes and bring them back home with her. And one such amazing dish was a shrimp & fish stew.

In Africa, the shrimp are different – they have yellow shrimp and red cherry shrimp – but for the most part, it is similar to our crawfish. And growing up on the farm did allow for the kids to learn how to catch crawfish; but Aunt Frannie was partial to shrimp, real shrimp, from the ocean not the muddy crick .... And thus, over time, the dish has slowing evolved with each generation has adding their twist or flare to the dish.

Photo by Peter Engler

Generation 1 – Aunt Frannie eliminated the fish altogether because it just became mush; and to add more shrimp, but because, well, is there really such a thing as too much shrimp??

Generation 0 – from what was once just a basic broth, my grandma suggested adding rice to make it a more heartier "stew' instead of a watery broth with shrimp floating in;

Generation 2 – my addition/change was to use coconut milk instead of regular milk for a sweeter flavor;

Generation 3 – my son's addition/change was to add jalapeno peppers for a little heat.

And of course, we only use the freshest ingredients from the farm – peppers, onions, tomatoes – and if we're really feeling up to it, we could still go down to the crick and catch some crawdads to add instead of store-bought shrimp.

Peixe a Lumbo (African Shrimp & Rice Stew)
Amy Wertheim, Atlanta, Illinois

Ingredients:

3 tablespoons olive oil
1 large white onion, sliced & diced
2 medium red bell peppers, sliced & diced
2 medium firm ripe tomatoes, skinned and diced
1 teaspoon ground coriander
1 small can green chilies
2 small or 1 large can coconut milk
2 pounds small-medium sized shrimp, uncooked
4 cups yellow rice

Photo by Peter Engler

Directions:

In a large skillet, heat the olive oil until shimmering. Add the onions and bell peppers and cook for about 5 minutes – do not let them burn – until soft. Next add all remaining ingredients except the shrimp and rice. Cover and simmer until liquid is reducing by ⅔'s and "stew" seems to thicken, about 35 minutes. Add shrimp and cook until shrimp are opaque, approximately 5 minutes. Set aside to cool slightly while preparing yellow rice.

In a medium size sauce pan, prepare your favorite yellow rice according to the directions on the box. Remove rice and place in serving bowl; pour shrimp "stew" over the rice and mix thoroughly; dish up and enjoy!

You can also cook both the rice and stew on a smoker grill for a hickory smoked flavor.

Serves 6-8

First Prize, 2018

Polenta with Meat Sauce
Michael Marchizza, Sherman, Illinois

*Growing up in an Italian family,
I heard many stories.*

Whether the stories I heard were about the "old country", or tales about oddly-acting relatives, or working in the coal mines, they were short tales and often repeated over and over to anyone with an open ear. One of my favorites was often told by my mom, about the family getting together and eating Polenta. Polenta is an Italian version of corn meal mush, but worlds apart in flavor and satisfaction. The dish actually had its origin here in the America's by Native American using maize. When Columbus came to the America's one of the things he brought back to Italy was maize and the Indian version of corn meal mush, which in Italy became Polenta. My family had traditionally been rather poor, and Polenta was considered a poor man's meal. It was very popular in the poorer northern regions of Italy around Lombardy near Milan and Venice. And it so happens

Photo by Barbara Kuck

that my maternal grandparents are both from northern Italy in the Gubbio region near Assisi. Coincidentally, they lived in villages just 20 miles apart, but did not meet until the early 1900's when they had both immigrated here around 1913-1914 and were both living in Riverton, Illinois. When my grandmother immigrated to America, the recipe for Polenta and her sauce came with her. She passed in 1945 and although my mom was only 13, she now took over the job of preparing meals because all of her other sisters were so much older, married and did not live there anymore. My mom remembered making and eating many meals with Polenta.

> ... the family would gather around the table, each with their fork or spoon, and dig in.

Once the corn meal and water were mixed and cooked, forming a creamy dish of Polenta, the polenta was spooned onto a wooden cutting board. The polenta was covered with a tomato sauce and sprinkled with Parmesan, and the family would gather around the table, each with their fork or spoon, and dig in. Yes, they all would eat from cutting board's mass of Polenta. Each starting in their corner or section and digging away at the delicious creamy mixture, often served along with Italian sausage. Interestingly, many times before they began eating, they would decide on a pattern to follow. Perhaps to dig with their forks and produce a map of Italy, or Illinois, or some cartoon character. It sounds like fun, except when you think everyone is digging in there with their own forks eating a communal dish. I don't know how sanitary that was, but that is what they did time and time again. My mom told me how she would upset their design by taking her fork and making a trail through the polenta to where the others were stationed.

One reason Polenta was considered a family meal was that it was usually only eaten on special occasions like Thanksgiving, Christmas, or Easter. I don't know how many ever sat down at

one time to consume a board of Polenta, but from stories I have heard I would say at least 6-10 people. I am sure it did not bother anyone as our family has always been very close. My mom's and my dad's parents, brothers and sisters and their families lived within 3-4 blocks of our house. I literally was neighbors to most of my aunts and uncles, maternal and paternal grandparents who were still alive, and my cousins. Since one of my aunts owned a tavern, that served as a hub for family get-togethers during Holidays and important family events. We ate a lot of Polenta in that tavern!

Their stories were mostly about eating Polenta during the depression and then World War II. It was a simple tradition brought over from Italy. By the time I arrived on the scene in the early 1950's, they had for the most part gone to eating Polenta on individual dishes. Also, for some reason (and it may have been my dad's idea), we started putting a slice of cheese in the layer of Polenta. The cheese would melt and just add to the flavor and appeal of eating the Polenta. Today, when I make Polenta, it brings back warm memories of my family, and I smile and always think of them carving out some map, some feature, enjoying the Polenta, forgetting for a moment that they were poor, and just loving each other. The Polenta I serve you today is covered with my meat sauce which has been derived from my mom's and my grandmother's recipes. There are slices of brick cheese inside, and it is being served with our traditional Italian meat sauce. Enjoy! Mangia!

Polenta with Meat Sauce
Michael Marchizza, Sherman, Illinois

POLENTA

Ingredients:

4 cups water
1 cup cornmeal
2 tbsp. butter
1 tsp. salt
2 slices brick cheese
2 cups spaghetti meat sauce

Photo by Barbara Kuck

Directions:

Mix together cornmeal, butter, and salt. Combine with water.

Microwave for 10-15 minutes. Stirring every 5 minutes.

Spread half of the hot, cooked polenta on a plate. Place brick cheese on polenta and cover cheese with remaining polenta.

Ladle meat sauce on top. Serve hot.

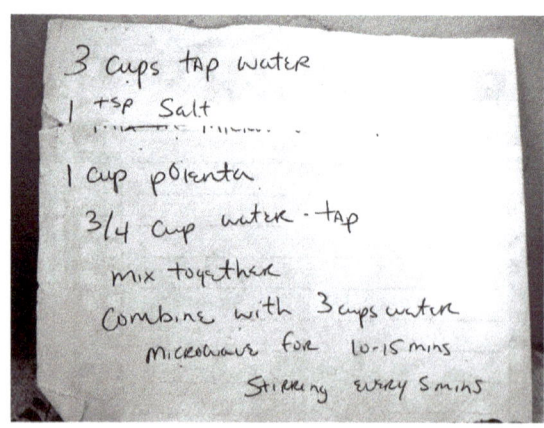

MEAT SAUCE

Ingredients:

1 lb. ground beef
½ lb. ground pork
1 tbsp. olive oil
5 cloves garlic, minced
2 med. onion, chopped
2 tbsp. basil
1 tbsp. Italian seasoning
1 tbsp. garlic powder
1 No. 303 can tomatoes (2 cup)
2-3 cans tomato sauce
2 6-ounce cans tomato paste
1 tbsp. salt
2 tsp. pepper
2 tbs. sugar
¼ cup parmesan
½ cup red wine

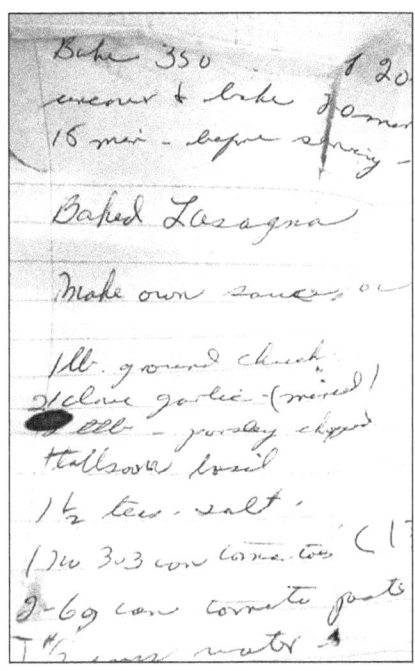

Directions:

I would first brown the ground beef (or chuck, depending on what was on sale), and along with that also brown some type of pork they might have used ground pork or pork ribs. While the meat is browning, I would add in some chopped onions and garlic. Then the basil and just a little Italian seasoning and actual garlic powder, and the salt and pepper. I would then add a can of crushed tomatoes, then 2-3 cans of tomato sauce, a can of tomato paste. I would stir all of that together and let it cook a few minutes together. The rest is all individual preference. I would add about ½ cup red wine, the parmesan cheese, and about 4-5 tbsp sugar. The sugar is needed to offset the acidity of the tomatoes. But again, I would taste it as I went along and adjust accordingly. I would then let the sauce simmer for 4-5 hours, sometimes even turn it off and leave it all night.

Contestant, 2009

Ptacki (Rolled Round Steak)
Linda D. Cifuentes, Mahomet, Illinois

Ptacki is a Czech word for birds and this dish is so named because they thought when the meat has the toothpicks in it, it resembled birds.

This recipe was passed down from my grandmother (she was born in the Czech Republic) to my mother and then to me. It uses an inexpensive cut of meat which becomes tender from the baking. This was an economical way to feed a family "steak" when times were tough which was often.

The original recipe did not have dill, but my father loved dill in the sauce; as a matter of fact, he would have a bottle of dried dill next to his plate to add more because he said you could never have enough dill! We ate this meal often when I was growing up. I grew up in Berwyn, Illinois which was a very Czech area.

As you can see the ingredients in this recipe are not very healthy but traditionally Czech cooking is not healthy as we used to say around our house, "Not really good for you, but really good."

I decided to let you choose for yourself-do you like Daddy's dill gravy or Grandma's sour cream gravy??? I made both.

Photo by Peter Engler

Ptacki (Rolled Round Steak)

Linda D. Cifuentes, Mahomet, Illinois

Ingredients:

1½ to 2 lbs. round steak
½ lb. Bacon
1 large onion sliced thinly
salt and pepper to taste
water as needed

<u>Sour cream mixture</u>
1 large sour cream (16 oz.)
½ cup fresh dill
1½ Tbs. Flour
2 tsp. milk

Directions:

Combine sour cream mixture ingredients and allow to sit at room temperature while meat is baking. Trim round steak and cut in long slices. Salt and pepper each piece. Place ½ strip of raw bacon on each slice of round steak. Top each with a slice of onion. Roll each piece of meat and secure with toothpicks. In small skillet, sauté remaining bacon that has been cut in bite size pieces. Remove with slotted spoon and reserve. Brown meat in bacon grease. Place in Dutch oven add ½ to 1-cup water, cover and bake in 350 F oven for 30 minutes. Add another ½ cup water and bake another 15 minutes. Remove meat from pan and keep warm.
Add small amount of hot liquid from the pan to the sour cream mixture--this will prevent the mixture from curdling. Add entire mixture to pan and mix well. Add reserved bacon. Return meat to mixture and heat another 5 minutes. Remove toothpicks.*

*Very important

Contestant, 2018

Stuffed Peppers
Linda D. Cifuentes, Mahomet, Illinois

My Dad, Tony Holas

I am from a Czech background and both my grandmothers made stuffed peppers. They were fairly cheap to make because hamburger was a fairly inexpensive cut of beef. They could grow the peppers and the recipe went a long way with a big family. My Mom, Helen had 2 siblings and my Dad Tony had 6 siblings.

Galumpky is the Polish name for stuffed cabbage rolls and this is a take-off on that recipe. As a matter of fact, when my mom made the peppers, she often times had left over meat/rice mixture and would serve that with the tomato sauce. She called it Galumpky without the Galump. Also stuffed cabbage was more difficult to make as well as tedious.

Photo by Barbara Kuck

As far back as I can remember in my childhood (I am in my 60's) I remember eating Stuffed Peppers. One day my dad Tony, decided that he was the supreme stuffed pepper maker and my mom never made them again. My story is going to focus on my Dad, Tony Holas.

Tony was born in Cicero, Illinois in 1928. As I said he came from a large family. When he was 12, he started working at Kolar Floral company in Cicero, sweeping floors. The story goes that when he was 16 everyone was gone, and he was the only one there. A man came in to get a corsage and my dad thought; what the heck!! I've seen them made a million times, I can do this. The customer came into the workroom and said. "I love watching an expert." My dad said he was sweating bullets but got the corsage made. I guess you can say the rest is history because they started letting him design and eventually, he bought the flower shop which he worked at for 40 years.

Photo submitted by Linda D. Cifuentes

Since my dad was a florist, I think this is what propelled his love of gardening. For the first ten years of my life we lived in Chicago. Every house on the block had a garage except ours. The entire space was taken up by a garden; tomatoes, peppers, onions, lettuce. You name it, Tony grew it. Tony did have help though, his devoted wife Helen and their 4 kids Linda, Tony, Joey, and Cindy. We eventually moved to Berwyn and that's where my parents stayed for the next 40 years. My dad still had his vegetable garden, but it was considerably smaller because now we had a garage. Since the garden was smaller and my dad had to downsize, he only planted peppers and tomatoes at which he was a master grower of both.

I think that is why he became the stuffed pepper "King." He had so many peppers that he mass produced the recipe and then froze them. We would eat them all summer and then in the winter take out dad's "prized" packages of stuffed peppers. It was like having a little bit of summer all year around.

Photo submitted by Linda D. Cifuentes

I fulfilled a dream and experienced one of the most precious moments of my life. I had been competing in the Blue Ribbon Culinary contest for a couple of years and in 2004 I got to cook against my dad in the Beef category. You guessed it; Stuffed Peppers!! Alas, I beat him, but it was an experience I will cherish for the rest of my life. We were able to cook next to each other.

I do want to mention that he always made the peppers in an electric skillet. He felt that they were cooked more evenly that way. Unfortunately, we don't have the electric skillet anymore, so I cooked them in the oven. My husband always says, "They don't taste like your dads"

I lost my mom 12½ years ago and my dad followed a year later. When we started to clean out their house, we went into the small stand up freezer and found dozens of small plastic containers holding 2 or 3 frozen stuffed peppers. What a gold mine!! We divided them up and could still enjoy a bit of Daddy's prize recipe. Finally, about 6 months after he died, I had the last ever Tony Holas stuffed Peppers and cried through the whole meal. They were the best ever!! I hope you enjoy the peppers as much as our family did.

Stuffed Peppers
Linda D. Cifuentes, Mahomet, Illinois

Ingredients:

1-pound hamburger
1 bag instant rice (cooked)
7 to 9 green peppers
1 large onion; chopped
Salt, pepper and garlic salt to taste
Small can tomato juice
1 can tomato soup
½ cup catsup

Directions:

Cook rice; set aside. Cut tops off peppers and chop for later use. Clean out seeds and extra pulp from peppers; wash and set aside on toweling upside down to drain. Mix meat, onion and seasoning. Add rice and mix. Stuff peppers with hamburger mixture and place in electric fry pan. Mix juice, soup, and catsup and pour over peppers. Place diced pepper tops in sauce. Cover and cook at medium Heat (325) for 35 to 45 minutes.***

*** we have no idea where dad's electric fry pan went so, I baked the peppers in the oven at 350 for 35 to 40 minutes.

Photo by Barbara Kuck

Greater Midwest Foodways Alliance
FAMILY HEIRLOOM RECIPES

Illinois State Fair
2014

2014 Winners

2014 Audience

Vegetables

Grandma Cook's Disappearing Baked Beans

Beans N'Such

Souffle de Zanahoria (Carrot Souffle)

Family Sweet Corn

Aunt Lynd's Infamous Corn Pudding

Lima Beans in Tomato Sauce

Spring Wild Greens

Tomato Cabbage

Contestant, 2009

Grandma Cook's Disappearing Baked Beans
c. 1921 by Florence M. Cook (my great-grandmother)
Crystal R. Smith, Farmer City, Illinois

Always the first dish to disappear.

As a young girl, my family would have huge cook outs and the family favorite was always the "Grandma Cook's Disappearing Baked Beans." My grandmother would make these for just about every family and social function we would attend, and they were always the first dish to disappear.

While the exact date of origin is unknown, we estimate these beans were "designed" around 1921 by my great-grandmother, Florence M. Cook of Elkland, Pa. Living during the depression, times were rough for many folks and with a huge family to feed, she had to figure out a way to feed at a reasonable price her ever expanding family. With this need, "Grandma Cook's Disappearing Baked Beans" was born! They have been passed down from generation to generation and have now came to me.

I was taught to make them by both my grandma and my mother as a young girl. Once I moved out on my own, I brought the recipe with me to make for my family and friends. Like years past, these are still a family favorite. A few shortcuts have been made over the years to save time and money but from time to time, I go back to the old way of making them, no matter how you cook them, they make everyone smile and drool and the smell of them.

Photo by Barbara Kuck

Grandma Cook's Disappearing Baked Beans
c. 1921 by Florence M. Cook (my great-grandmother)
Crystal R. Smith, Farmer City, Illinois

Ingredients:

1 lb. raw Navy Beans
1½ T. brown sugar
4-5 uncooked hotdogs (can use cooked bacon)
1 sm. can tomato soup
Season to taste (Mrs. Dash, Garlic Powder, Italian Season)

Directions:

Soak Navy Beans in water overnight in refrigerator for a minimum of 12 hrs. Transfer to stock pot and cook for 1-2 hours or until soft. Drain. Put in large mixing bowl, add brown sugar, tomato soup, hotdogs and seasonings. Transfer mixture to a well-greased 9"x9" baking dish. Bake at 350 degrees F for 30-45 mins or until bubble. Remove from oven and let sit for 15 minutes, serve immediately.

Note: you can also you Grandma Brown's Baked beans instead of the navy beans and cook in a Crock Pot

Contestant, 2017

Beans N'Such
Mary Gillespie, Springfield, Illinois

Baked Beans!... I'll drink to that ;-)
A crowd-pleasing, tasty recipe loved by
leprechauns and hungry guests, alike.

Circa August 1947, Springfield, IL ... Dick Gillespie, his "lil' brother" Roy, and best friend Joey Hildebrand headed out to enjoy a few hours at the state fair. After their fair visit, the trio was scheduled to paint the new apartment for Dick and his wife. As the three Northenders* departed for the fairgrounds, Dick and Roy's mother (aka Grandma Pat Gillespie), spoke up.

They were to bring her something from the fair - a crock, for her baked beans. She described it as 'shiny brown' (read: glazed).

Photo by Barbara Kuck

After a few hours of fun, the three figured they should get home and began walking towards the Exit. Uh oh, don't forget mom's bean pot, brown and shiny. Got it. The mile and a half walk home from the fairgrounds would wind them through Lincoln Park. Final destination, the 200-block of East Calhoun. Gosh, a mile and a half can get boring.

Family lore has it that one of the young men had a great idea. Like many of history's great ideas, it was a little fuzzy as to who actually (was to blame) is credited as having originated the idea. Dick remembered it was Joey or Roy. Joey thought it was Roy or

Dick. Lastly, Roy pled the Fifth (or drank one).

THE GREAT IDEA - football! Well, it would pass the time as they walked. Aw, can't play football. No football. Let's use the bean pot. Yeah. We're not gonna break - we're gonna catch it! The first two passes were without consequence; so, the tossing continued. One of them went out for the long pass. Thus, proving the third time IS NOT always a charm.

Grandma Pat never got her crock from the fair - that year. However, over the years, a glazed, brown stoneware bean crock made its way into her kitchen. To this day, family and friends still enjoy delicious baked beans - from Grandma Pat's recipe.

NOTE - betwixt the story and the recipe, the terms 'baked' and 'crock' has to make one smile!
*Northender - term of endearment for denizens of the northern area of Springfield.

> The Gillespie family's Irish-Scottish lineage makes it quite easy to add Jameson to an endless number and types of the family's recipes

The Gillespie family's Irish-Scottish lineage makes it quite easy to add Jameson to an endless number and types of the family's recipes (appetizers, entrees, side dishes, dessert, etc.).

Beans N'Such
Mary Gillespie, Springfield, Illinois

Ingredients:

1# dry navy beans
4 C. water
1 clove garlic – minced
4 C. beef stock
1 med. sweet onion - fine chop
5 sl. thick-cut bacon - chop into pieces

SAUCE

2 C. water
2 TBL. molasses
1.5 TBL. ground mustard
2 TBL. Worcestershire sauce
¾ C. barbecue sauce [chef's choice]
1 C. light brown sugar
¼ C. ketchup
1 C. Jameson Irish Whiskey
¼ C. apple cider vinegar

Directions:

> Night before - place beans in a larger pot and cover with water. Soak overnight...drain the next morning.

> Combine 4 cups of water plus 4 cups beef broth in a Dutch oven - add (drained) beans.

> Bring beans to a boil. Simmer for 30-40 minutes - drain.

> While beans are cooking - put bacon in a large skillet over MED heat.

> Cook bacon until crispy, and fat is rendered.

> Remove bacon from pan - drain on a brown paper grocery bag.

> Leave about 2 tablespoons of bacon grease in the skillet.

> Reduce heat to MED-LO

> Add onion, cook for 8-10 minutes, until translucent.

> Add in garlic, cook for 30 seconds, remove from heat. Set aside.

> In a 7 qt slow cooker, add water, barbecue sauce, brown sugar, ketchup, molasses, Jameson, ground mustard, vinegar, and Worcestershire sauce - whisk well to combine.

> Add in the beans, and the onion-garlic-bacon mixture (include bacon fat - optional).

> Cover and cook on LOW for 10-12 hours, stirring occasionally, (see Note)

> After 10-12 hours, turn slow cooker to the WARM setting or turn OFF completely.

> Let the beans sit anywhere from 30 minutes to 2 hours. This will help the sauce thicken.

Note: after 10-12 hours the liquid may still seem soupy. You have to allow the beans sit on the LOW or OFF setting - staying covered). This will result in a thick and syrupy sauce.

Second Prize, 2012

Souffle de Zanahoria (Carrot Souffle)
Linda D. Cifuentes, Mahomet, IL

The carrot soufflé was special because it was only prepared to celebrate her return ...

In the age of technology an innovation things of times past are often thought of as insignificant. There is however, for some of us, nothing more priceless and heartwarming than family heirlooms and traditions. To quote my husband, "If we don't know our past we don't know where we stand, and we have no clue where we are going."

I feel privileged to have received a family heirloom recipe from my 92-year-old mother-in-law. She passed the recipe on to her four daughters and to me her only daughter-in-law.

My mother-in-law was born in a small town nestled in the central mountain range of the Andes in 1920. The last time I was in Colombia I visited that town of Fusa with its beautiful central park and church where my mother-in-law married. Nowadays it is a bustling city with palm-tree lined line avenues, resorts, a university and flourishing businesses.

Photo by Victoria Moré

Back in the early 1920s my husband's grandmother (abuelita),

Dolores, was a very enterprising woman. She was mother of eight, and along with her husband Rafael she owned and managed a general store, a bakery, and the town's only Inn. She was in charge of purchasing which in those days was quite an undertaking. This was a weeklong affair, traveling on the old Colonial Camino Real Road on horseback along with a mule train and tagging along were 2 young helpers. This tortuous road often winds through the clouds up to the top of the mountain.

After this one-day ride, they arrived in a town where the railroad stopped on its way to the capital. She would take the train with one of the helpers while the other helper remained behind to care for the animals. When she arrived in the capital, Bogota, she spent the next several days buying the finest materials, toys, and merchandise imported from Europe to outfit the store. When the purchasing trip was complete, she would board the train with her treasures and return to where the pack mules were and load up for the journey back down the mountain.

So, you might be asking, where does carrot soufflé come into this story. Well, I was just getting to that.

> Dolores, was a very enterprising woman. She was mother of eight, and along with her husband Rafael she owned and managed a general store, a bakery, and the town's only Inn.

Before leaving the train station my husband's Abuelita would have telegraphed her approximate time of arrival. This was a joyous day in the family, his Grandpa would gather all the children and they would go with a couple of maids to the outskirts of town to the mahogany groves and set up a picnic feast under the shade of the magnificent trees. Specially prepared dishes to celebrate mom's return were brought to the grove and one of these dishes was carrot soufflé. The carrot soufflé was special because it was only prepared to celebrate her return which only took place four times a year. This was also a special time for my mother-in-law and her siblings because along with the supplies, a special toy was had for all.

My mother-in-law came to the United States in 1969 along with her family. She brought her many family traditions and one of those was the carrot soufflé which became a holiday staple in the Cifuentes' household.

> ... this beautiful and cherished recipe is still only made a few times a year ...

So, this beautiful and cherished recipe is still only made a few times a year but is always associated with happy and joyous occasions.

Her granddaughters are varying on the tradition putting carrot soufflé on their holiday table and I hope it will continue with their daughters.

Since I now have this coveted recipe my family also gets to enjoy this great recipe!!

Souffle de Zanahoria (Carrot Souffle)
Linda D. Cifuentes, Mahomet, IL

Ingredients:

5 medium carrots
bread slices to make up one cup of bread crumbs
1 cup of milk
2 tablespoons butter
3 eggs
4 tablespoons grated cheese (I used Parmesan)
1 teaspoon salt
5 tablespoons sugar

Directions:

Take a medium size pie mold, grease and set aside. Take the carrots and boil them until soft. Pour the milk over the bread crumbs. Beat the eggs. Next melt the butter and dump all ingredients together into a large bowl and mix by hand until well combined. Once this has been well mixed pour into pre-greased mold and bake at 350F checking often for doneness with tip of knife. Soufflé will be done when tip of knife comes out clean.

Taken from: "Recetas de la Abuelita" by Teresa I. de Cifuentes
Translated from Spanish by Bill Cifuentes

** Note Over the years for convenience sake my mother-in-law used a blender to mix the ingredients.

Second Prize, 2018

Family Sweet Corn
Jone Schumacher, Chapin, Illinois

Sweet Corn 'Puttin' Up

Photo by Barbara Kuck

The sweet sweet smell throughout the rural Illinois country side each hot July day brings fond childhood memories of enjoying fresh sweet corn on the cob and of the task of "putting up" corn for the long winter months. On second thought, maybe not all the memories are the most fond of my childhood, but probably helped to shape my good work ethics. My mother also tells of enjoying sweet corn as a child, and her mother would preserve some corn by canning as freezing was not an option for her family. For most of her childhood, her family only had an ice box, which they would stock with ice on occasion when the ice wagon came around. My father's mother, however, had one of the earliest freezers in the area and she was a "pioneer" in experimenting with preserving produce by freezing. My mother reports they always had a small patch of hybrid sweet corn, but she recalls talk of times when farm folks would watch the field corn and eat field corn before it dented and matured. This corn was not sweet and tender as the corn we are all accustomed to now.

As I indicated earlier, some of my memories involving corn were not my favorite. My father decided to add to our household income by having a fresh produce truck farm for several years. This provided my older sister and me with the opportunity to help hoe furrows, drop the seeds in the ground, cover the seeds and a few weeks later spend countless hours hoeing the long rows. At harvest time, I remember sitting under the big shade tree in the yard husking the corn. Mother then prepared the corn for freezing, blanching the ears, cooling in ice water in the large dish pan she received as a wedding present from her parents. Mother then froze our corn packed neatly in blue freezer boxes. Of course, we did have countless meals with fresh corn on the cob dripping with melted butter.

> At harvest time, I remember sitting under the big shade tree in the yard husking the corn.

When my children were growing up, they missed the garden experience I had as the sweet corn was planted with a 4-row planter on the edge of a corn field and was not hoed by hand. When it was time to freeze corn, my husband's parents hosted the "party" in their basement for our family and my husband's brother and family. The cousins loved getting together and it really didn't seem like work. The guys picked the corn and husked it outside, and we women worked in the cool basement where my in-laws had an electric stove and sink. For years, we blanched the corn while still on the cob in large pans, cooled with ice water in the sink, drained and cut the cooled kernels off the cobs with our sharpest long knife. The corn then was measured into pint and quart plastic bags and slipped into white freezer boxes. The tops and bottoms of the boxes were taped securely with freezer tape and the date inscribed on with a marker. There was a freezer in the basement where it was frozen to be divided up later. In the mid-90's, we learned of a more modern recipe that seemed easier as it allowed us to blanch larger volumes at one time. Clean-up remained about the same. My husband's mother would cover the basement floor with braided rugs and she was not at all disturbed with the mess of dropped sticky corn kernels. She always said it was not a problem to shake out and put the rugs in the washer after the corn preservation for the year was completed. Besides the fellowship of working together, the best part was the delicious meal we all enjoyed after our hard work. The traditional meal was grilled hamburgers, delicious potato salad, tomatoes from the garden, and of course buttered corn on the cob, which we enjoyed eating in the cool basement, all sitting around the ping pong table converted to our picnic table.

The wonderful tradition of "putting up corn" has continued for our family each summer. Three different plantings are planted, still with the old 4-row planter. Now the "party" is held at our farm home and the hardest thing is finding a time when our children and their busy schedules are available at the same time the corn is at its best. This year just two of our five children were able to join our work force, but they brought some helpful, hardworking grandchildren. We have different "work stations" around the farm. After picked, the corn is husked in  the shade behind the Morton building, washed, cleaned and silks removed in the yard in the shade of the magnolia tree, and finally brought into my kitchen to be cut off the cob with electric knives. Twelve heaping quarts of corn are measured into large pans, sugar, salt and water added, and the corn is brought to simmer for 4-5 minutes. Fortunately, I have a very long sturdy wooden spoon to use to keep it stirred and prevented from sticking. The hot corn is poured out into large 16x16 metal pans and taken to chill in a large cooler. Instead of using the freezer boxes, our corn is measured into quart zip-lock freezer bags. I do not put down the braided rugs, and although our little dog likes to help the cleanup process by eating some of the dropped kernels, my floor is quite a sticky mess at the end of the day. The amount of corn frozen and the type of freezing bags have changed somewhat, but the fellowship of working together and enjoying delicious "homemade" corn remains the same over the years. I know this was a cherished activity of my husband's mother, Beulah, as well, as she even painted covered corn serving bowls in ceramics for both families. Using this bowl brings back many fond memories of Beulah and the great memories of time spent together putting up corn. I am disappointed in "old days" we did not take picture of our "corn parties," but I guess it didn't seem like an event but routine then.

Growing all kinds of corn has a deep history with our families as my grandfather started a hybrid seed company and my husband's father was a charter employee of another local seed company. It is these seed corn companies that have been instrumental in developing some of the great varieties of sweet corn we still enjoy today. The variety we grow is called Coon's Choice and we can certainly testify the local coons love it. It is always a challenge to get the corn before the coons or deer have a feast. For that reason, my husband puts up double rows of electric wire around our patch, so we must be careful to unplug the power before checking the corn.

> ...my grandfather started a hybrid seed company ...

It is wonderful and easy to thaw quarts of our fresh frozen corn and warm in the microwave, drain and add a few pats of butter ready for meals. It is just expected to have corn at all our family meals and holidays throughout the year! We do not always eat all the frozen corn, and we find it keeps well for more than a year. It has gotten to be a family inside joke as to guess what year the corn is at a given meal. Tradition dictates it is always the newest year's batch served at Christmas! Our son-in-law, who grew up in Chicago, chuckles at the term "puttin'up corn" but pitches in and has learned to be an excellent "farm-hand" on our country corn days. Even though not everyone is available each year to work on the "corn crew," it is a family project and we generously share the treasured golden delicacy with all our children's families. I did wonder what we would need to charge for a quart for our corn if we had the business of preserving corn for sale, but I quickly calculated with the number of workers and the hours spent planting, watering, harvesting and processing, the price would seem unreasonable. Our family freezer corn is just "priceless!" I am proud to report that we "put up" 100 quarts this year and have one more planting yet to mature, so we will be ready for another year of memorable meals. I believe the ingredient of love is tasted by all, and I sincerely hope my family will keep my big pans and somehow continue to get together to "put up" country corn for years to come.

> Our family freezer corn is just "priceless!"

Family Sweet Corn
Jone Schumacher, Chapin, Illinois

PREPARING CORN FOR FREEZING, ORIGINAL METHOD

Pick corn when ears are full, and silks are brown and dry. Shuck corn and remove silks.

Bring a large pot of water to boil. Place corn ears into boiling water and return to boiling, time for 4-5 minutes. Remove ears from water with tongs and drop into sink or large pan filled with ice water to chill. Drain well when cooled. Cut corn off the cob with a long sharp knife. Measure into plastic bags and place into freezer boxes. Freeze as soon as possible.

FAMILY SWEET CORN, REVISED

Ingredients:

12 heaping quarts fresh cut corn
2⅔ cup sugar
2 tablespoons salt
3 cups water
2 tablespoons butter per quart when heating to serve

Directions:

Measure corn into a large pan. Add sugar and salt and pour water over and stir to mix. Heat to steaming and water simmering. Stir frequently, bringing the corn on the bottom of the pan to the top. Simmer for 5 minutes. Pour into large shallow pans to chill in cooler. When cold, measure into desired freezer bags marked with the date.

> Hint: This recipe is easy to divide and reduce to smaller "batches."

To serve: Place partly thawed or frozen corn covered Pyrex and heat on high in microwave for 3-4 minutes; stir and heat 3-4 minutes until steaming hot. Drain most of the water, add butter and heat additional 1-2 minutes until hot. The corn can so be heated to serve over the stove, although the microwave is easier.

Third Prize (tie), 2010

Aunt Lynd's Infamous Corn Pudding
Amy Wertheim, Bloomington, Illinois

> *... the corn pudding (if Aunt Lynd is cooking) will be runny and inedible.*

Every year, our family gathers for the big Thanksgiving dinner at my Great-Grandma's house. As the dinner time nears, we can hardly contain ourselves – OK, it might have something to do with the stated dinner time of 1 PM having passed at least two hours before ... but we know that when we finally sit down to eat, the turkey will be juicy, the cranberry sauce will get spilt adding yet another stain to the fancy tablecloth reserved only for these occasions, and the corn pudding (if Aunt Lynd is cooking) will be runny and inedible. Thankfully my mother has taken it upon herself in the last few years to see to it that no one gets "poisoned" anymore! She has been officially assigned the coveted title of "Official Corn Pudding Maker."

Photo by Catherine Lambrecht

No one knows how long the corn pudding recipe has been around. It's one of the staples of our Family Thanksgiving. In fact, our family prides itself on having the same foods that my grandma's mother used to make ... and although my mom has taken to tweaking the recipe to be make it something really special (and edible), the core recipe has stayed the same. She still uses cream from our neighbor's dairy farm, the corn is the sweet corn from her garden that she cans every summer and the eggs are from the hatchery in the next town over. It's truly a homegrown, Midwest treat that our family looks forward to every year at Thanksgiving! I hope you enjoy my family's Heirloom Recipe, just the way my mom cooks it

Aunt Lynd's Infamous Corn Pudding
Amy Wertheim, Bloomington, Illinois

Ingredients:

2 ears of sweet corn (or 1 can of corn)
2 tablespoons flour
2 tablespoons sugar
½ cup heavy whipping cream
1 cup shredded cheddar cheese
1 teaspoon salt
2 tablespoons butter
2 eggs

Directions:

Preheat oven to 350 degrees.

In a buttered 9×9-inch pan, mix ingredients in order listed. Bake until golden browned and thickened for approx. 30 minutes. Remove and allow to sit for 5 minutes before serving.

Serves 6–8*

For larger gatherings, just double or triple as needed; cook time also is doubled.

Contestant, 2012

Lima Beans in Tomato Sauce
Marilyn Okon, Springfield, Illinois

It was frequently served as a meal in itself.

This recipe for Lima Bean in Tomato Sauce has been in our family for at least 75 years. It was shared with my mother, Lillian Okon, by her mother as she was growing up. When she married in 1946, she brought along that recipe and it quickly became a favorite in the extended family. For big family picnics or get togethers, my mother could always be counted on to bring her lima beans. There was never anything left to take home.

The lima beans were also a staple in her immediate family as she raised her four children. It was frequently served as a meal in itself. After each of the kids left home, it was not unusual for us to request our mom to prepare her special lima bean recipe for us when we returned to visit.

Photo by Victoria Moré

Over the years this recipe has found its way into many church and community cookbooks. It was even submitted and accepted for entry into a published cookbook.

While I have not made the recipe as often as my mom did, I remember one time recently when I was visiting family in Michigan. I decided to make the lima beans and share them with both my brother and my sister. Both were surprised and delighted to see those lima beans in tomato sauce again. Right before returning home, I called my brother to say good bye. One of the things he made sure to tell me was that he had just finished eating the lima beans. They were his lunch that day. It brought back memories of when we ate those lima beans as a meal in itself. My brother returned the container I gave him the lima beans in before I left, hoping, I am sure, that it be filled again soon.

Lima Beans in Tomato Sauce

Marilyn Okon, Springfield, Illinois

Ingredients:

2 lbs. dry lima beans
2 qts. boiling water
1 tsp. salt
1 lb. bacon, cut into 1-inch pieces
1 medium onion, finely chopped
2 10-¾ oz. cans condensed tomato soup

Directions:

Wash beans in running water. Cover with boiling water; add salt. Bring to boil; boil 2 minutes. Set aside to soak 1 hour. Bring to boiling point. Reduce heat; simmer 1 hour. Drain, reserving water. Fry bacon until soft. Drain off excess fat. Add onions and fry until soft. Add tomato soup and reserved cooking liquid. Add more water if needed. Pour mixture over beans. Season to taste with salt and pepper. Serves 8.

First Prize, 2013

Spring Wild Greens
Kimberli Yount Goodner, Edwardsville, Illinois

*"Spring Wild Greens,
Good for the Body and Soul."*

One day, I invited my aunts over for lunch. I am in the military and finally got an assignment back home. I love my aunts and cherish my time spent with them. As we sat around eating, we talked about old recipes and the subject of the "greens" came up. Aunt Alma is the oldest. She explained, "Mom walked with me through the woods and taught me what weeds I could pick for greens to cook." Yes, weeds. I was shocked. She explained that she picked dandelion greens, poke, lamb's quarter, dock, blackberry and elder leaves, and plantain. "Young tender weeds are the best, more poke and dandelions, add the others as you want, maybe even a little more lamb's quarter. It is best to pick in early spring as these are the tenderest." Yes, my aunt can be seen going through the neighborhood picking weeds. Did I mention my uncle has a nice pension & she can afford store bought food, but she still goes out and collects her Spring Wild

Photo by Catherine Lambrecht

Greens for herself and of course brings some to the reunions?

Dandelion

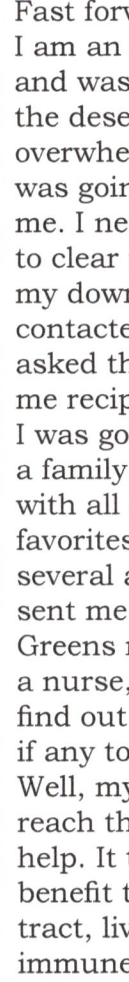
Dock

Lambsquarter

Blackberry Leaves

Elderberry Leaves

Plantain

Queen Anne's Lace

Fast forward to 2011, I am an Air Force Nurse and was deployed to the desert. I was overwhelmed by what was going on around me. I needed something to clear my head during my down time. I contacted my family and asked them to send me recipes and stories. I was going to make a family recipe book with all our beloved favorites. I received several and Aunt Alma sent me the Spring Wild Greens recipe. Being a nurse, I wanted to find out the benefits if any to these weeds. Well, my aunts didn't reach their 80's without help. It turns out they benefit the digestive tract, liver, skin, boosts immune system, reduce inflammation, help purge harmful toxins in the body, lower cholesterol, are high in Iron, calcium and vitamin C, stimulate circulation and much, much more.

When I returned home,

Pokeweed

Aunt Alma took me out and showed me what weeds to pick. Every spring since, she and I have shared the "Spring Wild Greens.' This past June at our family reunion, I gave each head of family a notebook with all our family recipes and stories. I shared the weeds story as my cousins looked on in amazement. But you know what dish was the first to be eaten? Yep, the weeds.

I credit these greens with not only benefiting my health but also with my emotions. You see, the weeds story was passed around during my deployment. It was something we all could laugh about during a hard time and I proudly shared the recipe. Now when I eat my greens, I fondly think of my Aunt Alma and of those nurses and medics I served with.

Spring Wild Greens
Kimberli Yount Goodner, Edwardsville, Illinois

WARNING: ONLY gather from a yard or garden that has NOT been sprayed with chemicals

Ingredients:

2 cups Young Tender Poke weed
2 cups Dandelion Leaves
   (the smaller are better and more tender)
1 cup Lamb's Quarter
1 cup Plantain
1 cup Dock
1 cup Tender Blackberry Leaves (1st to 4th from the end)
1 cup Elder Leaves (1st to 4th from the end)
3 slices of bacon or fat back (I used bacon)
¼ cup cider vinegar
1 tsp. Salt (I use sea salt)
1 tsp. Pepper

Directions:

Wash leaves in 3 waters (wash in water 3 times – wash, rinse, etc.). Fill large pot ¾ full of water, tear leaves and place in pot. Boil, then drain, Boil again. Fry bacon up until brown and a little crispy and crumble. Dip leaves out of water, place in skillet with bacon. Add vinegar. Add salt and pepper. Simmer for 15 min. When it has cooked down, it's ready to eat.

Cut a stem of Queen Anne's Lace and place in a vase. This is a weed that will add a touch of class to your table. It was also my Grandma's favorite Flower (the root is like a carrot and also edible). Bon appetite!

> Editor's Note:
> Please use a reliable field guide to identify these wild greens. If in doubt about any wild green identification, DON'T USE.

Contestant, 2011

Tomato Cabbage
Cindy Petriw, Schaumburg, Illinois

A Thanksgiving Tradition

Most people when they think of Thanksgiving they think of Turkey and Stuffing. When I was growing up, we would go to my Babi's (Bohemian for Grandma) for Thanksgiving dinner. One day I asked my Babi why she was making that (Tomato Cabbage.) She explained to me that it was a recipe that was passed down to her from her mother. Babi then passed it on to my mother. When I got married and started to host Thanksgiving at my house, I started to make the Tomato Cabbage. Having a boy, he was not as curious. Now I have a Granddaughter (now sixth generation) and I hope when she gets old enough to understand that she will ask me the same, "Grandma, why do you make that?" and I can share the same story my Babi (Grandma) shared with me.

Photo by Peter Engler

Tomato Cabbage
Cindy Petriw, Schaumburg, Illinois

Ingredients:

1 cabbage (small to medium)
2 small cans tomato juice
1 - onion chopped
salt
vinegar (to taste)
sugar (to taste)
caraway seed

Directions:

Sauté onion in a little margarine in a large saucepan. Add shredded cabbage, tomato juice, salt, caraway seeds, vinegar and sugar. Cook until cabbage is tender. Add thickening made from about 2 tbsp. margarine (melted in small frypan). Add about 2-3 tbs. flour mixing constantly until smooth and a little brown. Add to cabbage mixture stirring constantly and cook for about 10 mins. on low heat.

Almost like Babi's recipe.

BABI'S ORIGINAL RECIPE:

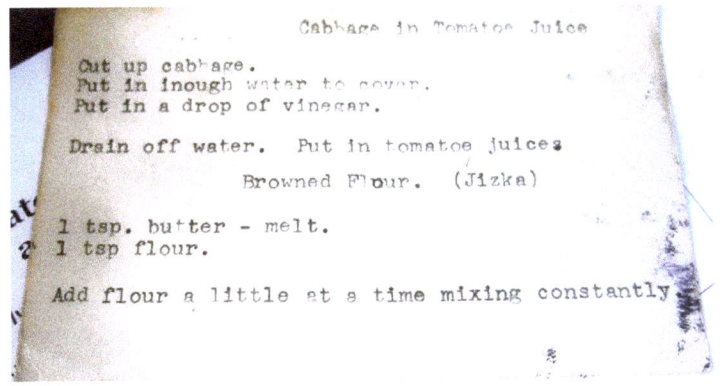

Greater Midwest Foodways Alliance
FAMILY HEIRLOOM RECIPES

Illinois State Fair
2015 - 2016

Desserts

Cakes

1-2-3-4 Cake

Cherry Cake, Grandma's Birthday Cake

Chocolate Sour Cream Pound Cake

Sarah Leonard's Family Fruit Cake

Grandmother's Gingerbread Cake

Prune Cake

Upside Down Cake

Contestant, 2009

1-2-3-4 Cake
Marilyn Okon, Springfield, IL

Cherries and walnuts make this cake special.

The 1-2-3-4 Cake and Best Frosting recipes were handed down to me by my mother, Lillian Sitko Okon as we were growing up in Inkster, Michigan near Detroit. I am not sure where they came from, but it was the cake and frosting that my mother always made for birthdays. I remember using those recipes myself when I learned to bake in the middle 1950's. (So, it had to have been around before then.) It was not only the gimmicky name of the cake but the special addition of cherries and walnuts (always black walnuts hand-picked from my grandfather's farm near Ann Arbor, Michigan. The family especially liked the frosting because it was smooth and not too sweet. My mother usually decorated the cake with two colors of frosting and alternated the colors in a pie shape which I have tried to replicate here.

Photo by Peter Engler

1-2-3-4 Cake
Marilyn Okon, Springfield, IL

Ingredients:

1 cup shortening
2 cups sugar
3 cups sifted flour
4 large eggs
3 tsp. baking powder
½ tsp. salt
1 cup milk
1 tsp. almond extract
¾ cup maraschino cherries, chopped
¾ cup black walnuts

Directions:

Cream shortening and sugar slightly. Add eggs and mix thoroughly. Sift and add dry ingredients alternately with milk and flavoring. Fold in the cherries and the nuts.

Bake in 2 greased 9-inch layer cake pans 375 degrees for 30 to 35 minutes.

BEST FROSTING

Ingredients:

5 Tbsp. Flour
1 cup milk
½ cup shortening
½ cup butter, unsalted
1 cup granulated sugar
½ tsp. salt
1 tsp. vanilla

Directions:

Blend flour and milk thoroughly. Cook to a very thick paste, stirring constantly. Set aside to cool.

Mix shortening, butter, sugar and salt until light and fluffy; add to lukewarm paste and add vanilla.

Beat until of spreading consistency.

(If mixture begins to curdle just keep mixing. It will eventually form a nice smooth frosting.)

Add food coloring and decorate as desired.

Contestant, 2011

Cherry Cake (Grandma's Birthday Cake)
Linda D. Cifuentes, Mahomet, Illinois

Happy Birthday Grandma & George Washington!

You might be thinking this is a strange looking birthday cake and that is exactly what I asked my mom. She explained that my grandma; Elizabeth Sekera Brezinsky was born on February 22, 1903. Since my grandma shared the same birthday as George Washington her mother decided it was fitting, she should have a cherry cake for her birthday. Grandma was born in Prague, Czechoslovakia and I think her mother wanted to make a good old American cake for her; so this became grandma's birthday cake.

The recipe was handed down from my great-grandma to my grandma to my mom then to me. This was the first cake I ever helped my mom make.

I was about 7 years old and I remember watching my mom make this cake. She beat the egg whites with a hand crank beater and I remember asking her when she was done if I could turn them upside down because I had seen this done on tv, she told me not to do it--But guess what? I did it anyway and the egg whites stayed in the bowl.

This was the beginning of many baking adventures with my mom, but it was so special because it was a Sekera family recipe. I don't have any children, but I have a God daughter and a God son and when they were married this recipe was passed down to them in a family cookbook to carry on the tradition.

Whenever I make this simple cherry cake, I immediately think of my grandma and her birthday!

Cherry Cake (Grandma's Birthday Cake)
Linda D. Cifuentes, Mahomet, Illinois

Photo by Peter Engler

Ingredients:

½ cup shortening
1¼ cup sugar
2 cups + 6 tablespoons cake flour
½ cup broken nut meats (I used pecans)
20 maraschino cherries; cut in quarters
3 teaspoons baking powder
¼ teaspoon salt
¾ cup liquid-¼ cup cherry juice and ½ cup milk mixed
4 egg whites

Directions:

Cream shortening, add sugar gradually and cream together thoroughly. Mix nuts and cherries and dredge with 2 tablespoons of flour. Combine remaining flour with baking powder and salt. Add flour mixture alternately with liquid. Stir in fruit and nuts. Fold in egg whites which have been beaten until stiff but not dry.

Pour batter into a greased and floured 10-inch tube pan. Bake 50 minutes in moderate oven (350).

Cool 10 minutes in pan and then turn onto rack to continue cooling. When ready to serve may sprinkle with powdered sugar.

Contestant, 2014

Chocolate Sour Cream Pound Cake
Pamela Lynn Sage, Monmouth, Illinois

No melted cakes.

My Mother, Julia Fields, was a natural born baker. Her parents immigrated from Hungary and she was one of 7 children, born in America. Every special occasion and holiday called for a special dessert: cakes, pies, yeast nut or poppy seed sweet rolls, cobbler and of course apple strudel. At Christmas we had at the least 8 or 9 different cookies. She was always trying new recipes.

For summer get togethers or picnics she would always bake a pound cake. When I got older, I asked her why she always took a pound cake and she explained that it was rich cake that did not need frosting and people could usually carry it in their hands to eat. So, no melted cakes. This chocolate sour cream pound cake was a family favorite!

Photo by Catherine Lambrecht

Chocolate Sour Cream Pound Cake

Pamela Lynn Sage, Monmouth, Illinois

Ingredients:

1½ cups butter, softened
3 cups sugar
5 eggs
3 cups Flour
½ cup cocoa
1 teaspoon baking soda
¼ teaspoon salt
1 cup sour cream, 8 ounces
1 cup boiling water
2 teaspoons vanilla extract

Directions:

Cream butter; gradually add sugar, beating well. Add eggs one at a time, beating well after each addition. Combine flour, cocoa, soda and salt; add to creamed mixture alternately with sour cream, beginning and ending with flour mixture. Mix well after each addition. Add boiling water and mix well. Stir in vanilla. Pour batter into a greased and floured 10-inch tube pan. Bake at 325 degrees for 1 hour and 20 minutes or until cake tests done. Cool cake in pan 10 to 15 minutes; remove from pan, and cool completely on a rack. Yield one 10-inch cake. Dust with powdered sugar.

Third Prize, 2016

Sarah Leonard's Family Fruit Cake
Brazilla A. Leonard, Harvel, Illinois

"Great Irish Cake"

Fruitcake is sometimes known as the "Great Irish Cake," the traditional holiday dessert into which every Irish cook sinks her reputation. Spiced, sweet desserts like this cake have been a part of Irish holiday celebrations for centuries and were highly prized because they included spices and dried fruits that were once difficult and expensive to obtain.

Along with thousands of other Americans, my husband's family has always been proud of their Irish heritage. My husband's great-great grandmother, Rosa Knowles Hoysted was a widow during the Great Famine in Ireland. She traveled with her daughter and son to the United States in search of a better life for her family. Her young son died on the voyage and she arrived in New Orleans in February 1851 with her daughter Anna. It is difficult to imagine two women alone in a new country. They did have some friends

Photo by Peter Engler

and neighbors who also were aboard the ship, namely Martin Brown and his brother Daniel. Martin traveled north to Illinois and became a farmer in the Farmersville/Harvel area. He later returned to Ireland and brought back the rest of his family. Their family became farmers in the Farmersville-Harvel, Illinois area where we still live today. Martin and his brothers were among the first in the area to tile the farm fields, using knowledge of the Irish bogs and utilizing teams of oxen and battling snakes. They also helped to establish the St. Isidore Catholic Church and St. Martin's Cemetery.

Martin never forgot the little girl on the ship and found her and Rosa living in St. Louis working in their own dress shop. Martin married Anna and brought them both back to Illinois. Our home and farm have been in the family for five generations and we appreciate the hard work and sacrifice of Rosa Hoysted, Anna and Martin Brown and all the others who made it possible for us to live in the United States and enjoy this country lifestyle.

This recipe has been passed down from each generation to the next with love and fond memories. While not everyone can say they love fruitcake, once they taste "Grandma's", their opinion changes. Not only is it delicious, it evokes memories of family gatherings past. It has always been on the Christmas menu and proudly displayed among all the other "special" holiday foods. If there is a family reunion, someone is sure to bring "the fruitcake" as it is fondly known. My husband's father, Lyle Leonard, served his country during World War II and was gone for four long years. This fruitcake was his favorite dessert and I can imagine that "Grandma Sade" was only too happy to make this for his homecoming.

I hope you will enjoy it and think of the immigrants to this nation and the frontier housewives who used what they had available; farm fresh eggs, hand-churned butter, sour cream from the family cow and the treasured spices, candied fruits and nuts.

I can only assume that sweet fruitcakes were reserved for the most special of occasions and I can think of nothing more special than representing our family in the 2016 Illinois State Fair!

Sarah Leonard's Family Fruit Cake
Brazilla A. Leonard, Harvel, Illinois

Ingredients:

Part I:
¼ Cup White Sugar
¼ Cup Brown Sugar
3 TB. Cocoa
1 Cup Boiling Water
1 tsp. Baking Soda

Part II:
1 Cup White Sugar
½ Cup Butter
2 Eggs
1 Cup Sour Cream
3 Cups Flour
1 Tsp. Baking Powder
1 Tsp. Nutmeg
¼ Tsp. Cloves
1 Tsp. Cinnamon
½ Cup Chopped Cooked Prunes & Juice
1 Cup Raisins
1 Cup Dates
1 Cup Walnuts
½ Cup Fruit Peel
½ Cup Candied Cherries

CARAMEL ICING:

¼ Cup Brown Sugar
¼ Cup White Sugar
2 TB. Butter
⅓ Cup Cream
1 tsp. Vanilla

Combine first 4 ingredients in saucepan and cook until mixture reaches soft boil stage.

Add vanilla and beat.

Pour over cake.

Directions:

Combine all ingredients in Part I. Set aside to cool. Cream sugar and butter, add eggs and incorporate thoroughly. Alternately add cooled mixture, flour and sour cream. Beat well. Add baking powder, cinnamon, nutmeg, cloves, prunes and juice. Roll raisins, dates, nuts, fruit peel and cherries in flour. Fold into the batter. Pour into tube pan and bake at 325 degrees for 1½ hours. Cool completely.

Contestant, 2016

Grandmother's Gingerbread Cake
Gail Long, O'Fallon, Illinois

As a child, I didn't like birthday cake.

When I was young, our family didn't have much, so we never received much in the way of birthday presents. My mother would always bake us a birthday cake, though. As a child, however, I was a problem for my mother. I didn't like cake. Every year she would make me a beautiful cake and I would refuse to eat any. This went on for several years, much to her chagrin. One fall, though, she caught me grabbing crumbs out of the pan that she had used to make a gingerbread cake for the family. When my birthday rolled around, she put a gingerbread cake on the table and I gladly ate a piece. She always referred to it as "Grandmother's Gingerbread Cake." I never thought to ask her if she meant my grandmother or her grandmother, so I will never know, but it solved the situation I had presented her with. Later she added the frosting, knowing how much I loved cream cheese, and I have changed it from a 9×13 single layer cake to a cake made in two 9-inch round pans.

Photo by Peter Engler

Grandmother's Gingerbread Cake
Gail Long, O'Fallon, Illinois

Ingredients:

½ c. sugar
2½ c. flour
1 c. hot water
½ c. butter
1½ tsp. baking soda
½ tsp. salt
1 egg
¾ tsp. cloves
1½ tsp. cinnamon
1 c. molasses
1½ tsp. ginger

Icing:
16 oz. cream cheese
8 c. powdered sugar
1-3 Tbsp. milk
½ c. butter, softened
2 tsp. vanilla

Directions:

Cream butter and sugar. Sift together flour, baking soda, salt, cloves, cinnamon, and ginger. Add beaten egg, molasses, and flour mixture together. Add hot water and beat until smooth. Grease 2 9-inch round baking pans. Pour in batter and bake 35 minutes at 350 or until cake tester comes out clean. Cool slightly in pans, then turn out and completely cool.

Beat cream cheese and butter until blended. Add vanilla. Add powdered sugar. Start with 1 Tbsp. milk and add more if necessary. Place one layer of cake on cake plate and frost. Top with second layer and completely frost.

Contestant, 2018

Prune Cake
Barbara (Luchtfeld) Hopgood, Sherman, Illinois

Mom knew what Dad liked.

My parents were married in 1939 and every birthday from Feb. 6, 1940 on my Mom made Dad a prune cake for his birthday until his passing in 1999 at 93. I'm sure she got the recipe from his mother. The recipe card I found which Mom had written later on only gives the ingredients, but I remember helping her make it as a child. On my Dad's 100 year birthday all 4 of us siblings living in different areas made the prune cake not knowing what each did until we talked later that evening. The plate I have it on was the original cake plate Mom used every year only for that cake.

Photo by Barbara Kuck

Prune Cake
Barbara (Luchtfeld) Hopgood, Sherman, Illinois

cream together:
1½ cup sugar
½ cup butter
2 eggs

add after sifting:
2½ cup flour
1 tea. baking powder
1 tea. Cloves
1 tea. Cinnamon
1 tea. Allspice
1 tea. Soda
1 cup sour milk

after combined add:
1 cup prunes (cooked)
1 tea. vanilla

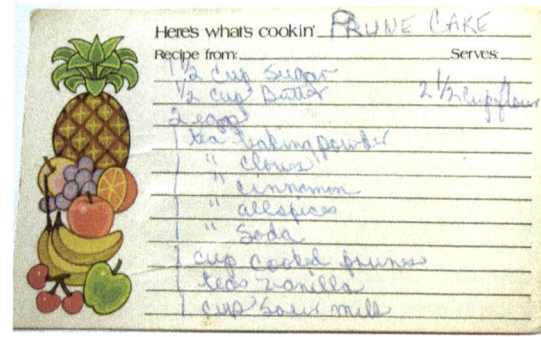

pour in 9-inch cake pans and bake at 350 degrees for 35 min till tooth pick comes out clean, cool 20 min in pan then on cake rack

ice with chocolate icing:
1 lb. confectioners sugar
¼ cup + 1 tbsp milk
1 tsp. vanilla
1 stick softened butter
1 tbsp cocoa

mix all together

Photo by Barbara Kuck

Contestant, 2017

Upside Down Cake
Mary Joan Miller, Pleasant Plains, Illinois

Cooking was an art to my mother.

Amelia Mildred Caflisch was born in 1888, the first of nine children born to Swiss and German immigrants. Hard work was part of her upbringing, including quitting school after the fourth grade to help her mother with the farm and the other children. Mildred met Roy Glasford from Peoria and married later in life, when Mildred was 39 years old. Mildred and Roy never had their own children, but raised several foster children, including myself. The love and joy I received from my parents, Mildred and Roy was abundant, and I am blessed beyond words to have had these two-wonderful people in my life and for giving me the solid foundations that I cherish to this day.

My youngest memories were of my mother cooking wonderful

Photo by Barbara Kuck

meals and tending her garden full of berries, luscious tomatoes, melt-in-your mouth sweetcorn and bushels full of a colorful assortment of vegetables. Her flower garden was the envy of the neighbors. Cooking was an art to my mother. Her thanksgiving dinner was extraordinary. And Roy was a hunter and fisherman, so often pheasant or catfish were the centerpiece dish at family gatherings. Food was a mainstay in our family and her love of cooking has been passed down through me to my five children as well.

> What a treat to taste the sweet pineapple with the moist cake that melted in your mouth.

My mom kept her most treasured recipes in a spiral notebook that has yellowed with age and the edges are frayed from use. Of all her many recipes, one of my most-cherished memories was of her Upside-down cake. What a treat to taste the sweet pineapple with the moist cake that melted in your mouth. It always made a beautiful presentation at large family events and church dinners.

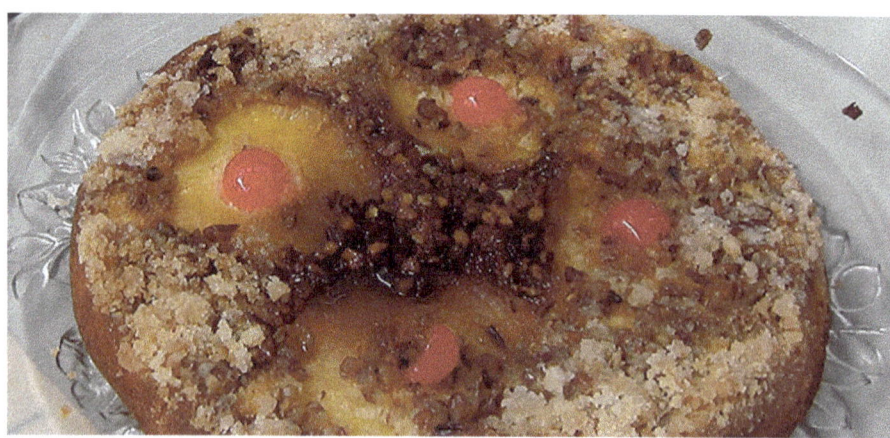

Photo by Barbara Kuck

Upside Down Cake
Mary Joan Miller, Pleasant Plains, Illinois

Ingredients:

¼ cup Butter
2 cups sugar
1 can sliced pineapple (8 oz.)
2 eggs - beaten
1 cup flour
1 teaspoon baking powder
⅓ cup hot water (or use pineapple juice instead - it is better)
½ cup nuts

Directions:

Melt butter in iron skillet and sprinkle with 1 cup sugar. Add nuts to butter/sugar mixture. Arrange 4 pineapple rounds in bottom of cast iron skillet.

Sift flour and baking powder together in large bowl. Add beaten eggs, hot water (or pineapple juice) and additional 1 cup sugar. Stir well. Pour mixture into cast iron skillet over pineapple.

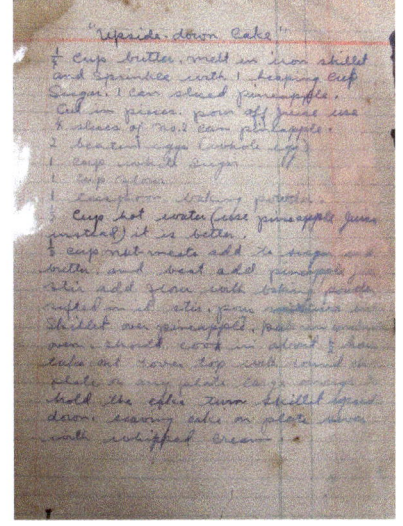

Put in moderate oven (350 degrees). Should cook in about ½ -hour. Take out, cover top with round china or any plate large enough to hold the cake. Turn skillet upside down leaving cake on plate. Serve with whipped cream.

*My mother didn't add Maraschino cherries to her recipe, but she always put the red cherries in the middle of each pineapple slice in the skillet.

Greater Midwest Foodways Alliance
FAMILY HEIRLOOM RECIPES

Illinois State Fair
2017

Desserts

Candies

Grandma's Black Walnut Fudge

Peanut Brittle

Cookies

Great-Great Grandma Rouch's Brown Sugar Cookies

Molasses Cut Out Cookies

Pfeffernusse Cookies

Grandma Rouch's Sweet Legacy Sugar Cookies

Contestant, 2013

Grandma's Black Walnut Fudge
Nancy Bathurst, Girard, Illinois

*A fudge which, in today's lingo,
people would say was "to die for."*

My Grandma (Lena Zimmerman) Johnson was born in 1886 in Jebshein, Alsace-Lorraine, France. The family immigrated to the United States in 1893 when she was seven years old.

My grandmother and grandfather (George Johnson) were married in 1910. Six years later, they moved to Illinois and began farming. It was a small family farm, very primitive by today's standards. Even when I was a child during the 1940's and 1950's, they had none of the modern conveniences such as indoor plumbing! Grandma had a stove that burned corncobs to generate the necessary heat for cooking and baking. I cannot imagine how she accomplished all the fantastic meals, but she most certainly did.

She tended chickens and sold her eggs in town. Grandpa had a few milk cows and he took the time to show me how to milk the cows (always by hand – no fancy milking machines!). Grandma would then run the milk through a separator and this wonderful very thick cream would be at the top. She would also make her own butter.

Photo by Catherine Lambrecht

As an only child, it was the highlight of my year when we would travel to Sheridan from Ottawa to visit Grandma and Grandpa. It was a time of family and play as we were always joined by my cousins who lived in Sheridan. I was looked at as the "city girl" even though Ottawa was only a town of 19,000.

One summer I wanted to bring my best girlhood friend, Marcia, with me for my week's stay at Grandma's. Mom said it was fine and neither one of us thought to ask Grandma if it was all right. After the week was over, my mom told me Grandma was very upset that I had brought a "city girl" because she was embarrassed that their home was so primitive. Primitive? I thought it was the most fun, wonderful place I had ever been! And so, did Marcia!

> There were never any fancy desserts at our family dinners, but we had something better …

There were never any fancy desserts at our family dinners, but we had something better … the very best sugar cookies you will ever eat and a fudge which, in today's lingo, people would say was "to die for." It was a very simple recipe and I have enclosed a copy written in my mom's handwriting over 50 years ago. It is titled "Mom's Fudge" and the "Mom" referred to is my Grandma Johnson. Over the years my mom and I tried to duplicate this fudge but never had any luck – it just was not Grandma's fudge. Of course, she used her own cream and black walnuts from their very own tree. I now know how difficult it is to just get the black walnuts out of those shells. I remember my husband's father telling me the only way to crack black walnuts was to run over them with a car!

Even though I have been competing at the Illinois State Fair for several years, I had never entered this particular contest. However, when I was reading about it this year, all could think about was Grandma's fudge. Could I duplicate it if I tried again? A light bulb went off – what if I used the double Devon cream that is used in England for scones? It is very, very thick and looks just as I remember the cream Grandma made.

> A light bulb went off – what if I used the double Devon cream that is used in England for scones?

Luckily, I found it at a local grocery store in Springfield. Therefore, I gave it a try. Did it come out like Grandma's? Close – not perfect – but close. I thought about displaying the fudge on a beautiful pedestal plate I have but that would not be right. Grandma never had such a plate; her fudge would be served on a plate that may be cracked or a chip out of it. Although my display may not be pretty, it is fine for Grandma and it pays tribute to a simple but beautiful lady.

Whether or not I receive a ribbon today, I thank the culinary department of the Illinois State Fair and Greater Midwest Foodways Alliance for giving me this opportunity to relive some beautiful memories of this beautiful lady – Grandma Johnson!

Grandma's Black Walnut Fudge

Nancy Bathurst, Girard, Illinois

Ingredients:

2 cups sugar
⅓-cup white corn syrup
½-cup water
3 – 1-ounce squares of semisweet chocolate
1 – 6-ounce bottle Double Devon Cream
2 ounces heavy whipping cream
1-teaspoon vanilla
1-cup black walnuts

Directions:

Mom's Fudge -
2 C. sugar
½ C. syrup
½ C. Water
3 sq. Chocolate
Cook until it spins a thread. Add 1 C. heavy sweet Cream. Cook to soft ball stage. Add 1 C. nuts (black walnuts) 1 tsp. Vanilla. Stir until creamy and thickened

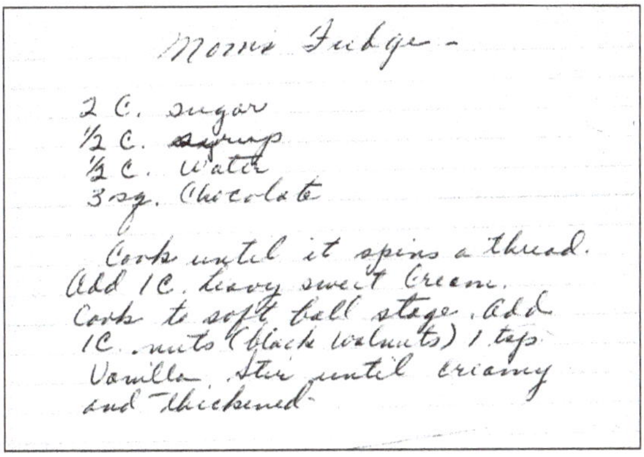

Combine sugar, white corn syrup, water, and chocolate in a heavy saucepan. Cook until it spins a thread. Add Double Devon Cream and heavy whipping cream. Cook until soft ball stage. Remove from heat. Add vanilla and black walnuts. Beat until creamy and thickened. Pour into a butter plate. When cool, cut into squares.

Second Prize, 2011

Peanut Brittle
Amy Wertheim, Bloomington, Illinois

What once was lost ...

On November 15, 2004, time stopped. Our family business, R.G.W. Candy Company, was burned to the ground due to faulty wiring in a light fixture. Not only did we lose all of our equipment & over 500 pounds of prepared confections, we lost all of the family recipes that our candies were made from. Every recipe had been hand-written by my grandparents & great-parents, and now ... they were gone. Of everything we lost, that was the most devastating.

Although we were able to rebuild, & Dad was able to recreate the recipes, every once in a while, a passing comment or reference to the lost recipes would arise. As silly as it sounds, the lost parchments of paper, most barely readable, left a very big hole in the heart of the candy shop.

Fast forward to the summer of 2010 ~ a local antiques dealer was dispersing his collection & of course, I had to go. There were 14 boxes of around 500 cookbooks & I had every intention of getting each one of them (yes, I have a cookbook issue!). As the bidding began, the price stalled at $14, my bid. Sold! "How many do you

Photo by Peter Engler

want?" "I'll take them all!" .... but wait, I, like everyone else, thought we were bidding on the box - - nope, it was by the book. Well, that quickly changed things & I picked up only one book that I had glanced at earlier & had dismissed. Why I picked it out, who knows! As the bidding resumed (now by the box), I quickly won the bid & was soon carrying out my treasures, forgetting about the one cookbook I'd left sitting on a chair.

As the auction came to a close, one of the auction assistants brought the 'lost' book over. Without a glance I tossed it into one of the boxes. Once home, I started reading thru the cookbooks looking for different or unusual recipes. It seemed like every time I reached over to pull out another cookbook that one book kept getting in the way. Finally, I gave in & glanced at it. What I thought was a cookbook ... wasn't a 'cookbook' at all, but more of an autograph book for recipes; people wrote recipes on the pages for a soon-to-be bride, etc. It was dated 1913 ... maybe there would be some interesting recipes after all. As I turned the pages, I started seeing names I recognized ... long-time family friends. How strange ... I stopped looking at the recipes & just turning pages to see who had written in the book ... and then I saw the name, Mother Hoblit. What?? Unbelievable, my Great-Grandmother had written in this book, by why did she sign it Mother Hoblit? Only the family ever called her that ... & then I found it. On the next to last page of the book, stuck in the folds, was a folded-up piece of parchment. My hands were shaking as I unfolded the crackling

> My hands were shaking as I unfolded the crackling paper ...

paper ... there, in my Great-Grandmothers handwriting was our lost peanut brittle recipe.

The book you see displayed is the book from the auction, & the brittle recipe is the handwritten copy I found. I have submitted peanut brittle as my entry because at every family gathering & at every community (church) meal, my Great-Grandparents, Grandparents, & now my parents, take peanut brittle as their dish to share. There is no better way to end a meal than with a dessert or sweet.

I can only speculate why out of all the cookbooks I picked up that one ... We still cannot believe that after all this time, the book and the recipe found its way home. But I do know it has helped heal the missing gap in the candy shop. Enjoy!

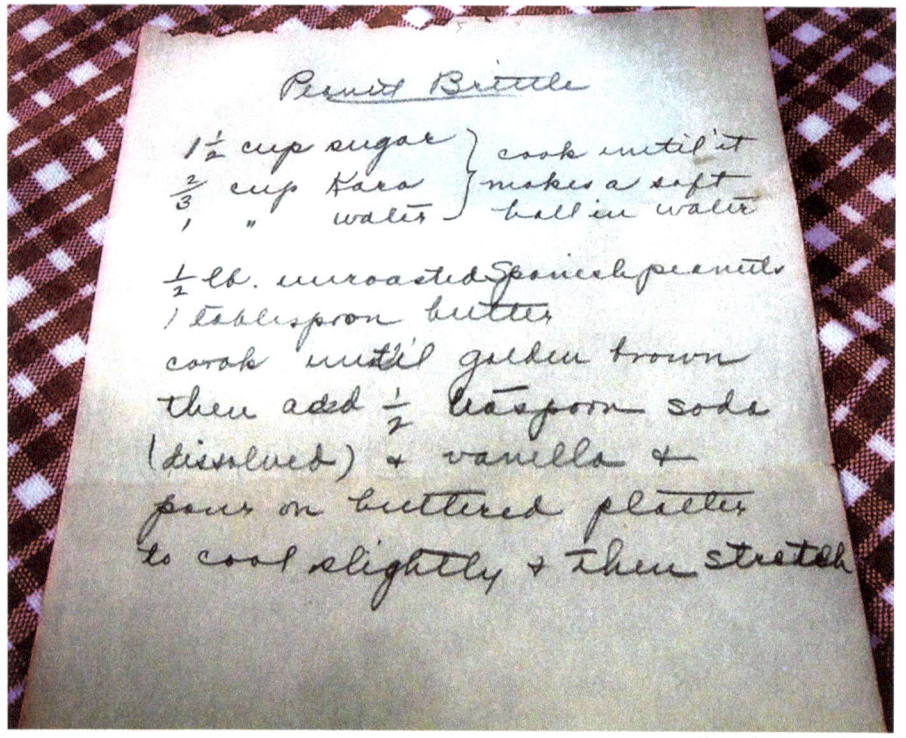

Photo by Peter Engler

Peanut Brittle

Amy Wertheim, Bloomington, Illinois

Ingredients:

1½ cup sugar
⅔ cup glucose (Karo for the home cook)
1 cup water
½ pound unroasted Spanish peanuts
1 teaspoon butter
½ teaspoon baking soda
½ teaspoon vanilla

Directions:

Cook sugar, glucose and water until it makes a soft ball in a water bath (drop a few bits of syrup in water and if it balls, then it's at a soft ball stage).

Add peanuts and butter to the syrup and cook until golden brown. Add the soda and vanilla, stirring quickly and pour onto a marble slab or buttered platter. Allow to cool slightly, and then stretch until thin and brittle.

Break into pieces and enjoy.

Makes enough for 4 people. Can be doubled, tripled as desired.

Honorable Mention, 2009

Great-Great Grandma Rouch's Brown Sugar Cookies
Elizabeth Carter, Lincoln, Illinois

Closer to a biscuit than a traditional cookie and uses common farmhouse ingredients.

This recipe originated with my Great-Great-Grandmother, Ida Rouch and so it has been in the family for approximately 100 years. It was written down by my Great-Grandmother Irene Rouch (b. 1904 d. 2001) as a part of a cookbook that she made for her Grandchildren to share her favorite recipes, a copy of which was in turn passed down to me by my Mother. The Rouch's were a farming family in Rural Indiana for generations.

Photo by Peter Engler

Great-Great Grandma Rouch's Brown Sugar Cookies
Elizabeth Carter, Lincoln, Illinois

Ingredients:

2 cups brown sugar
1 cup shortening
2 eggs
1 cup buttermilk
2 tsp. Baking powder
1 tsp. Baking soda
Pinch of Salt (⅛ tsp. Salt)
Flavoring (2 tsp. Vanilla)
Flour to make a soft dough (4 cups all-purpose flour)

Directions:

Cream brown sugar and shortening, add beaten eggs and stir well. Add buttermilk and flavoring. Beat. Add baking powder and soda 2 cups of flour and stir into the mixture. Add more flour to make a soft dough (add remaining flour). Chill dough. Cut off portions of dough, roll out, cut into desired shapes. Place on cooky sheet. Bake in moderate oven (350 degrees F.) for perhaps 8 or 10 minutes.

First Prize, 2011

Molasses Cut-Out Cookies
Jone Schumacher, Chapin, Illinois

Baked in a wood-burning kitchen stove.

One of my sweetest memories of Christmas as a child was the molasses cut-out cookies baked by my father's cousins and served at my grandparents Christmas dinner. What made these cookies so extra special was that they were baked in a wood-burning kitchen stove that is considered quite the antique today. Dad's cousins, Martha, Julia and Ethel Robinson were three sisters who never married and lived their entire lives in their parents' home-place about three miles north of Concord, Illinois. Their home never had electricity or indoor plumbing. The house was never painted and sat on the top of a hill, hidden from view from the road by the growth of pine trees and brush similar to a pasture. The yard was not mowed and instead of a sidewalk, a narrow "cow-path" curved up to the side-porch. I still recall my mother taking my siblings and me up that path to visit. Oh, how I wish I would have taken pictures inside that home to have a record of the unique family antiques in their natural surroundings. The sisters loved our

Photo by Peter Engler

visits and enjoyed having children in their home. They very seldom left their home to go anywhere except for church, as none of the sisters ever learned to drive. They wanted to live this way, as they refused family offers to help them modernize their home.

My grandmother and her sister would drive to the Robinson home on Christmas Eve afternoon to take them Christmas presents and to invite them to Christmas dinner. They would accept the invitation and would quickly reply that they would need to get busy and bake their Christmas Molasses cut-out cookies. Hence, they were very fresh and melt-in-your- mouth delicious. I wonder how long into the night they worked to bake these treasured cookies. They used lard that they had rendered themselves, which gave the cookies a unique flavor. They were evenly browned which must have been a challenge with the wood burning oven. Even as a child, I marveled at how pretty the Robinson cookies always looked with very simple decorations. They used cookie cutters that left marks on the cookie to show the detailed design of the cut-out object. My cousin recently reminded me that they frosted the bottom side of the cookies, so you could turn the cookie over and still see the intricate design. We children used to think they frosted the cookies up-side-down compared to the way our mothers frosted sugar cookies. We recall that Martha would mix the cookie dough and Julia and Ethel would cut out and bake the cookies. Julia was in charge of the frosting and decorating. Now I have learned that every year at Christmas time Martha and Ethel would try to find a new and different cookie cutter for Julia, so the cookie baking must have been more of her project.

> Even as a child, I marveled at how pretty the Robinson cookies always looked with very simple decorations.

My mother, my sister, several of my cousins and I still make these cookies for our family Christmas gatherings. I always make the full recipe, but some just make a one-half of the original recipe, as one full recipe yields about 12 dozen cookies, depending on the size of the cookie cutters. I use Butter Crisco, so my cookies do not taste quite the same as the Robinson cookies. I have been making these cookies in my home for my family for over 40 years, and it just wouldn't seem like Christmas if I didn't spend the time making and frosting these favorites. My children are all grown, and now grandchildren join the generations who enjoy these cookies. Some years I have only had time to bake and freeze the cookies unfrosted in large Tupperware containers. These years then, frosting and decorating these cookies has become a fun family pre-Christmas project after my family arrives home for the holidays. We have a great time decorating the cookies and the project gets done so quickly, although it makes quite a mess!

> We have a great time decorating the cookies and the project gets done so quickly, although it makes quite a mess!

I do not have any of Julia's cookie cutters, but I have some that I think were the same design. I do hope whoever inherited the cookie cutters realize how precious they were. My sister has the oak kitchen table that the Robinson ladies used to roll out the cookies on. I tried to frost my cookies for the fair as closely as I picture the way Julia did. For my display, I also included a few of my grandchildren's favorites: the large tree, candy cane and the mitten, and I used the edible glitter that gives a festive sparkle that they enjoy. I think Martha, Julia and Ethel would really marvel at the variety of unique decorations available today, such as the snowflakes I used, and they would not be able to believe the hundreds of cookie cutter shapes available on the internet. I usually do not make Santa cookies, as I strive to make my cookies with more of a religious theme to keep the true meaning of Christmas foremost. This is the first Christmas that I am retired from my nursing job, so I am hoping to have time to bake the nativity scene from the cookie cutter set my sister gave me.

This recipe was originally known as "Scotch Cookies", but our family has always referred to them as Molasses Cookies. These cookies have been an important part of our family Christmas celebrations for over 100 years. I am so pleased that I am able to create fond memories of cut out decorated cookies for my children and grandchildren, as I have cherished memories that I savor from my childhood.

I know this recipe will continue to be enjoyed in years to come as everyone enjoys the cookies so much, and several family members enjoy baking about as much as I love to bake special cookies like the Molasses Cut-Out Cookies.

Molasses Cut-Out Cookies
Jone Schumacher, Chapin, Illinois

COOKIE DOUGH:

Ingredients:

3 cups granulated sugar
2 cups lard
4 eggs, large or extra-large
1 cup molasses, bold flavor
½ cup boiling coffee
2 tablespoons baking soda
2 teaspoons vanilla
2 teaspoons salt
8-10 cups all-purpose flour

Directions:

In large mixing bowl of mixer, blend the sugar and fat until fluffy; blend in the eggs until well mixed. Blend in the molasses. Measure the baking soda into the boiling hot coffee, stir and blend into the fat-sugar mixture. Blend in the vanilla. Measure the salt into the first cup of flour and blend into the dough. Continue to add flour until is somewhat stiff and not sticky. (I have added to directions to chill in refrigerator until cold, as chilling helps to roll out using less flour.) Lightly flour a pastry board. Place approximately ¼ of the dough onto the prepared board and lightly flour the dough surface. Roll out to approximately ¼-inch thickness. Lightly flour the surface of the rolled dough. Lightly flour the inside of the cookie cutter and cut out shapes. Place on ungreased cookie sheet and bake in pre-heated 350-degree oven for 8-10 minutes until lightly browned. Remove cookies from cookie tray and cool on wire rack.

FROSTING:

Ingredients:

4 pounds powdered sugar
2 sticks of butter
4 teaspoons vanilla
¾ to 1 cup milk
food coloring
variety of colored sprinkles,
candy decorations as desired

Directions:

Blend softened butter with half of the milk and the vanilla. Add the powdered sugar and blend. Add additional milk until consistency to spread. Divide into separate bowls and stir in the desired colors. Spread frosting on the cookies and sprinkle with decorative sugars and add candies to trim. Let rest for 2-3 hours until frosting is completely set. (I prefer to make in advance of Christmas. To freeze, place cookies in appropriate containers with tight lids. Allow the cookies to defrost in sealed containers before placing on serving tray or place frozen cookies on tray and immediately cover tightly with plastic wrap.)

Yield: approximately 12 dozen

Honorable Mention, 2014

Pfeffernusse Cookies
Betty Moser, Decatur, Illinois

Pfeffernusse means 'pepper nuts' and the cookies are actually made with black pepper along with other exotic spices and honey.

Augusta Kraemer was born in Hanover, Germany in 1863 and immigrated to the United States in 1885. Augusta was a very diminutive woman - less than 5 feet in height. She met Henry John Thomsen, who had also immigrated from Germany, and they were married in March of 1892. He ran a cigar store, The Ridgewood Smoke Shop, in Brooklyn. As many as 18 people made cigars in the workroom of the street level shop. Henry and Augusta lived in the upstairs apartment where they raised a family - twin girls (Anna and Meta), a son (Henry) and another daughter, Frieda, who was my husband Ken's Mother. Ken remembers visiting his grandparents in this Brooklyn apartment many times. Like all women who immigrated, Augusta brought family recipes with her. At Christmas time Ken remembers singing carols in German while enjoying her special pfeffernusse cookies.

These deliciously fragrant cookies provided a delightful rush of warm spices and holiday cheer as they were being prepared. The word pfeffernusse means 'pepper nuts' and the cookies are actually made with black pepper along with other exotic spices and honey. At Christmas time Augusta would make dozens of these cookies, store them in a barrel and offer them as treats to friends and family. She would prepare enough cookies to last from Christmas season until Easter time. Our family has continued the tradition of making pfeffernusse at Christmas time.

Photo by Catherine Lambrecht

Pfeffernusse Cookies

Betty Moser, Decatur, Illinois

The original recipe needed to be cut down - the one I have makes about 40 cookies.

Ingredients:

¾ cup honey
2 tablespoons butter
1 beaten egg
2 cups flour
½ teaspoon salt
½ teaspoon soda
½ teaspoon baking powder
1 teaspoon nutmeg
1 teaspoon allspice
¾ teaspoon cardamom
½ teaspoon black pepper
¼ teaspoon anise seed powder

Directions:

In a large bowl, heat the honey and butter together and stir in the egg. Sift the dry ingredients together and add to the honey mixture. Let stand to stiffen. Shape into ¾ -inch balls and bake for 10 minutes in a 350-degree oven.

Prepare a glaze:

One beaten egg white
1 Tablespoon honey
½ teaspoon anise seed powder
¼ teaspoon cardamom
1 cup of confectioner's sugar

Drop several cookies into the glaze and stir them about to coat thoroughly.

Third Prize (tie), 2010

Grandma Rouch's Sweet Legacy Sugar Cookies
Diane Crider, Lincoln, Illinois

Visits to Grandma Rouch's farmhouse in Grass Creek Indiana were always a pleasure.

Whether it was exploring Grandma Rouch's attic full of treasures or visiting the animals in the farmyard we always had fun. She always had a full jar of cookies waiting for us hungry grand kids. My favorites were always her sugar cookies. Most people would make small, thin, crispy sugar cookies but hers were always large and soft and rolled in sugar. In a child's hands they seemed huge! She would serve them to us with frozen strawberries (that she had picked herself) and preserved in the "deep freeze" that we would then suck on to cool off on the hot summer days, as she never did approve of air-conditioners. Wilma "Irene" Rouch was born in 1904 and was always a very hardworking farm wife. She was widowed young and had to finish raising her family and maintaining the farm on her own. At the time of Grandpa Rouch's death, he had just purchased a new parcel of farm land and she scrimped and saved for years to be able to make the payments so that the land would stay in the family. So frugal recipes like her sugar cookies, which could fill up hungry children with very little expense, were a necessity. This recipe has been in continuous use for over 60 years and possibly longer. I am not sure of its origin, but it has made several generations of children very happy! The cookies are displayed in Grandma Rouch's pink depression glass cookie jar (pink was her favorite color) that was kept full of cookies in her kitchen. When she passed away at home at the age of 96, the jar still had crumbs in it!

> **This recipe has been in continuous use for over 60 years and possibly longer.**

Grandma Rouch's Sweet Legacy Sugar Cookies
Diane Creder, Lincoln, Illinois

Ingredients:

½ cup oleo (or margarine or butter)
½ cup lard (or shortening)
1½ cups sugar
2 eggs
3 tablespoons milk – it can be sour milk
1 teaspoon baking soda
4¼ cups sifted all-purpose flour

Directions:

Cream the oleo and lard and sugar. Add the beaten eggs. Stir. Add the milk and vanilla. Sift the flour, soda and salt together and add to the above mixture. Chill the dough. You may roll it out with the rolling pin on a bread board using powdered sugar, so it won't stick to the board and use cooky cutters or make balls, dip in sugar, place on cooky sheet and flatten with bottom of glass or Foley cup (metal measuring cup). Bake 8-10 minutes. 350-degree oven.

Photo by Peter Engler

Greater Midwest Foodways Alliance
FAMILY HEIRLOOM RECIPES

Illinois State Fair
2017

2017 2nd Prize Winner

2017 3rd Prize Winner

Desserts

Pies

Butterscotch Pie

Grandma Daniel's Spicy Peach Pie

Religiouse (French Pastry)

Best Strawberry Pie Ever

Sugar Pie

Zwieback Pie

Contestant, 2009

Butterscotch Pie
Amy Wertheim, Bloomington, Illinois

2:54 ... 2:55 ... 2:56 ...
"Oh, please, why is the clock moving so slow?"
2:57 ... 2:58 ... "Come on!" 2:59 ...

Ding! Finally, the bell rings and Tommy jumps up from his seat and runs out the classroom door. 1- 2- 3 - 4 - 5 - 6 - 7 steps ..... out the main door, just two blocks to go! Almost there ... ding dong rings the chime on the front door. Slowly the door opens and there stands a pleasantly plump old woman, with a twinkle in her eye as she asks, "Why Tommy, what are you doing here?" "It's Tuesday Great Aunt Cora. I've come for my pie!"

Yes, indeed. It was Tuesday and that meant that Great Aunt Cora had made Tommy's favorite pie, Butterscotch. One whole pie just for him, and one for everyone else. No one remembers how Butterscotch Pie day started, it just was. And every Tuesday, Tommy would leap from his chair as soon as the bell sounded and would run to get the special pie made just for him. No one else had a special pie, just Tommy.

Photo by Peter Engler

Even as the years passed and Tommy became Tom, Great Aunt Cora would still bake two pies on Tuesday. But soon came the day, when Great Aunt Cora passed on, and the pie was only made on special occasions, i.e. birthdays, anniversaries, Father's Day. Except today - today there were two pies made. One for you to enjoy, and one for the man once called Tommy, now known as Tom, or as I call him ... Dad. Just like Great-Great Aunt Cora used to make - one just for him and one for everyone else.

Original Recipe was published in the Atlanta Women's Club Cookbook in 1927; Great-Great Aunt Cora received the recipe from her mother so best guess is that the recipe is over 100 years old. The story above is true - and yes, I did make Dad his own pie, so he would not have to share. My grandmother is the person who taught me how to make it - she told me if I ever wanted anything, "just make your Father this pie."

> No one else had a special pie, just Tommy.

Butterscotch Pie
Amy Wertheim, Bloomington, Illinois

Ingredients:
Crust
1 coffee cup flour
2 tablespoons lard
½ coffee cup water
½ teaspoon salt

Filling
1 coffee cup brown sugar
1 coffee cup milk
2 eggs
1 pat of butter
3 tablespoons flour or corn starch
1 teaspoon vanilla

Directions:
Keep whites of eggs for top of pies. Brown in oven.

"MODERN" RECIPE

Ingredients:
Crust
1¾ cups flour
½ teaspoon salt
½ cup plus 2 tablespoon shortening
¼ cup water, cold

Filling
1 cup brown sugar
3 tablespoons corn starch
1 cup heavy whipping cream
2 egg yolks, reserve whites
1 tablespoon butter
1 teaspoon vanilla extract
½ cup sugar

Directions:

Pre-heat oven to 325°.

Prepare Crust - Combine flour, sugar, and salt in a medium bowl. Cut in shortening. Add water and toss mixture until evenly moistened. Gather gently into a ball, transfer to a lightly floured board and roll into a circle slightly larger than a 9-inch pie plate; flute and bake for 10 - 12 minutes or until lightly browned; set aside to cool.

Prepare Filling - In a medium saucepan, combine brown sugar and cornstarch; mix well. Gradually stir in cream, mixing until smooth. Over medium heat, bring to boil, stirring occasionally; boil 1 minute. Remove from heat. Stir half of hot mixture into beaten egg yolks, mixing well; pour back into saucepan. Bring back to slow boil, stirring occasionally; boil 1 or 2 minutes longer, until thick. Remove from heat. Stir in butter and vanilla; pour immediately into pie shell.

Topping - Place egg whites in a cold glass mixing bowl and whip until soft peaks form; add sugar one tablespoon at a time and beating well until mixed; whip until stiff peaks form. Spread meringue over pie, sealing the edges at the crust. Bake in the oven for 10 - 12 minutes or until meringue is light brown and dry to the touch.

Serves 8 (or 1 Tommy)

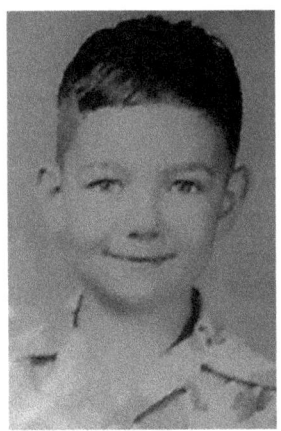

Contestant, 2012

Grandma Daniels Spicy Peach Pie
Carol Meadows, Springfield, Illinois

Grandma would let me have the first taste to make sure the "pickled peaches" were ok.

When I was young my grandmother lived with us until I was twelve. Due to an illness I was confined to bed for two years. A hospital bed was set up in the dining room, so I could be part of family activities. Some of my best memories was of my grandma setting by my bed teaching me how to sew, crochet, and embroidery. She also gave me my first adventure into cooking. I can remember in the summer she made spiced peach pies. In the summer she would can peaches and also make her "pickled peaches." She would save the "pickled peaches" for holidays and special occasions. I would wait with anticipation for her to open the jar because she would let me have the first taste to make sure they were ok. I remember she would take the peaches and cut an "x" on the bottom put them in hot water for a while and put them in cold water. When the cold-water pan got full of peaches, she would bring the pan in by my bed so I could take the skin off the peaches and she would cut them in half and take the pit out. Looking back, I know that having me help her added to the time she would spend canning the peaches. It was a special time. She took extra time to make me feel useful. I will never forget the special hours I spent with her. I have her recipe for "pickled peaches," and try to can several jars to use for our holiday dinners.

Photo by Victoria Moré

The peaches are very similar to spiced peaches in the ball canning book. She always had a few pickled peaches left over so she would make a pickled peach pie. She only made two a year one when she first made the pickled peaches and the second at the beginning of peach season when she need extra jars. I have tried to pass on her legacy to my nieces and great nieces. Many of my newer memories is of time I spend with my nieces, great nieces, and nephews in the kitchen. The kitchen is truly the heart of the house.

Grandma Daniels Spicy Peach Pie
Carol Meadows, Springfield, Illinois

Ingredients:

Crust:
3 Cups Flour
½ Teaspoon Salt
2 Teaspoons Sugar
2 Teaspoons Baking Powder
8 Ounces or 1 Cup Shortening or Lard
7 Tablespoons Cold Water
1 Egg Beaten

Filling:
8 Peaches (Skinned and Sliced)
2 Cups Sugar
½ Teaspoon Cinnamon
⅛ Teaspoon Ground Cloves
½ Teaspoon Ginger
6 Tablespoons Cornstarch
¾ Cup Peach Juice

Directions:

In a large bowl mix together salt, baking powder, flour, and sugar. Cut in lard or shortening until flour mixture resembles peas. Start adding water one tablespoon at a time. You want the dough to look like rags. Divide dough into two equal pieces and cover with plastic wrap. Refrigerate until time to roll out. Using the ½ cup of flour lightly dust the surface and roll out bottom crust into a 11-inch round circle. Place the bottom crust in a deep-dish pie pan. Add cooled filling. Roll out top crust and place over filling. Crimp together the edges and bake in a 350-degree oven.

In a large bowl combine peaches, sugar, cinnamon, cloves, and ginger. Mil well. In a mixing bowl combine peach juice and cornstarch. Mix well and add to peaches. Place filling in pie crust. Bake in a 350-degree oven until filling bubbles in the middle.

Contestant, 2017

Religieuses (French Pastry)
Michael Marchizza, Chatham, Illinois

Religieuses is a French word for cream pie. It was usually made for religious holidays.

Although my family is mostly Italian, I did have one grandparent who was French. Not only that, but in the small town I grew up in, the locals that lived on my side of the tracks were also mostly Italian or French. So, I not only grew up with Italian cuisine, but was also familiar with many French dishes and recipes also.

As far back as I can remember (and I am 66 now, so that's pretty far back), one of our unique and special dishes was only served during major holidays, especially at Easter and on New Year's, and sometimes at weddings. It was called Religieuses. It was a French word meaning religion. On New Year's Day our family would get together at my aunts tavern/bowling alley. We would have our traditional Italian meal of spaghetti and roast pork or

Photo by Barbara Kuck

some other meat, but after dinner we would have Religieuses. Religieuse is a French pastry that has a "blanc mange" or white pudding-like filling. In the early days, my mother would also put eggs in the filling and it was more yellow, but in later years she quit adding the eggs. (I'm not sure why). After eating the pastry, all of us children would go around the neighborhood and wish everyone a Bonne Annee, Bonne Sante. This simply meant Happy New Year and here's to your good health. The recipients of the greeting would give us nickels, dimes, or quarters in return.

My mother (Norma Draoulec) was quoted in a newspaper article from 1994 in which she says she had been making this pastry since the 1950's. Her mother-in-law had been making it many years before that.

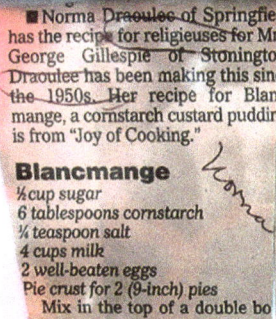

THE STATE JOURNAL-REGISTER

■ Norma Draoulec of Springfiel has the recipe for religieuses for Mr. George Gillespie of Stoningto Draoulec has been making this sinc the 1950s. Her recipe for Blanc mange, a cornstarch custard puddin is from "Joy of Cooking."

Blancmange

½ cup sugar
6 tablespoons cornstarch
¼ teaspoon salt
4 cups milk
2 well-beaten eggs
Pie crust for 2 (9-inch) pies
   Mix in the top of a double bo the sugar, cornstarch and salt. Gradually add the 4 cups milk while stirring well. Place the mixture over boiling water and stir constantly 8 to 12 minutes. Mixture should begin to thicken. Cover and continue to cook for about 10 minutes more. Stir 1 cup of this thickened mixture slowly into the two eggs. Return to the milk mixture and continue to cook for 2 minutes, stirring constantly. Do not overcook. The pudding will thicken more as it cools. Remove from heat, stirring to release the steam, then add to the pie crust.
   You can make your own pie crust or use the type of purchased pie crusts that can be unfolded. Roll out the 2 crusts together for the size of your pan. Place on the bottom of a pan, trim the dough so no dough is overlapping, just even around the pan. Bake the crusts according to directions and let cool.
   Make the blancmange and pour into the bottom crusts. For top crusts, slide crusts onto the blancmange. Ice while hot with 1 cup powdered sugar, ¼ teaspoon vanilla and 1½ tablespoons milk for a glaze consistency.
   Draoulec doubles the recipe for the blancmange and makes two double pie crusts to fit two 15½ by 10½ inch pan with sides.
   Serves 16.
   Nutritional analysis per serving: Calories 179.1, protein 3.8 g, carbohydrate 21.8 g, fat 8.5 g, cholesterol 17.5 mg, dietary fiber .6 g, sodium 206.1 mg.

Photo by Barbara Kuck

Religieuses (French Pastry)
Michael Marchizza, Chatham, Illinois

There are three steps in making the Religieuses: the **crust**, the **filling** and the **glaze**.

For the crust, combine 1¼ cup flour, ¼ tsp. salt and ½ cup chilled (been in the freezer a few hours) butter diced into smaller pieces. This should be processed in a food processor. Once you start getting small crumbs, add ice cold water one tbs. at a time until a dough forms. Do not add more than 4 tbsp. water. You will need to roll out two crusts, each the size of the cookie sheet pan you are using. Fix and press one crust into the bottom of the pan and up the sides. Use a fork to prick the prick the pie crust along the bottom and sides of the pan. For the second crust, flip a cookie sheet upside down and roll or press the pie dough to cover it. (This will be used for the top of the pastry later). Bake the pie crusts at 350 for 10-15 minutes or until brown.

> Blanc Mange is French for white pudding.

To make the filling, or blanc mange, you will use a double boiler. In the top of the double boiler stir in ⅓ cup sugar, ¼ tsp. salt, 3 tbsp. cornstarch, and finally, very slowly, add 2½ cups of milk. Cook over medium heat, stirring constantly until the mixture starts to boil. Allow the mixture to boil for 1 minute. Remove from heat and add 1½ tsp. vanilla. Pour this hot pudding filling into the pie crust. Then slide the second pie crust over onto the top of the pudding mixture. (For larger pans you may need to make a double batch of the filling).

To make the vanilla glaze, you will heat ⅓ cup butter until it is melted. Then stir in 2 cups powdered sugar and 1½ tsp. vanilla. Finally stir in 1-4 tbsp. hot water until smooth and of desired consistency to pour over the top crust.

1st I **bake the crusts**. You can do it the night before. You can make your own pie crust or use the type of piecrust that can be unfolded (I use Pillsbury piecrust in the red box).

Roll out two crusts together for the size of the pan. Place crust on the bottom of pan and up the sides, then do the same again using the bottom of another pan (this crust will be used for the top crust). Do not overlap your dough on bottom pan. I spray bottom of pans. Bake crust using instructions on box. Let crust cool.

To **make your Blanc Mange** (cornstarch pudding) or (white pudding)

Mix in top of double boiler
⅓ cup sugar
¼ tsp. salt
3 tbsp. com starch

Stir in gradually 2-¼ cups milk.

Cook over medium heat, stirring constantly until mixture boils. Boil 1 minute. Remove from heat.

Blend in 1½-tsp. vanilla

Pour hot pudding into bottom crust, then slide top crust from pan onto the pudding mix while hot.

Vanilla Glaze

⅓ cup margarine or butter
2 cups powdered sugar
1½ tsp. vanilla

2 to 4 tbsp. hot water. Heat margarine until melted. Stir in powdered sugar and vanilla. Stir in desired consistency. Stir in water:
1 tablespoon at a time until smooth and of desired consistency. Glaze top crust.

ENJOY. Norma

HINTS:
I make a double batch of pudding and I use 15½" by 10½" pan with sides Also have glaze made before making the pudding. You may have to patch the piecrust to fit the pan.

Contestant, 2014

Best Strawberry Pie Ever
Kitsy Amrhein, Springfield, Illinois

The best strawberry pie ever.

My great-grandmother made a good strawberry pie. She made her crust with lard, flour and sugar. She taught my grandmother to cook. My grandmother made a better strawberry pie than my great-grandmother. She made her crust with butter, flour and sugar. They both used the same ingredients in the filling. My grandmother gave the recipe to her daughter in law who was my mother. That was when she married my father in 1952. My mother made a great strawberry pie!

My mother used the same recipe but did something different when cleaning the strawberries. My mother was raised by her grandmother who taught her to cook. Her grandmother had taught her to remove the center core from strawberries when

Photo by Catherine Lambrecht

you clean them. So that is the way my mother cleaned the strawberries. My grandmother and great-grandmother just cut off the tops when cleaning the strawberries. By removing the core of the strawberries, it gives the pie a smoother texture. It might be my imagination, but the flavor seems better too. I guess the strawberry cores take away from the natural sweetness of the berries.

My mother experimented with margarine instead of butter and Cool Whip instead of the whipped cream. She also used a ready-made frozen crust from time to time. All those different variations made a good pie but not a great pie.

I learned to cook from both my grandmother and mother. I make the strawberry pie with the real crust and real whipped cream. I always clean the strawberries the way my mother taught me. Just like her grandmother taught her. No cores. I have taken my strawberry pie to many pot lucks and picnics. I've been told on several occasions that it is the best strawberry pie ever.

I love strawberry pie. It is my favorite pie. I have ordered strawberry pie in restaurants supposedly known for their wonderful strawberry pie. I have been served strawberry pie at picnics and dinner parties. None has ever been as good as the strawberry pie my mother made with that little variation from the recipe my grandmother gave her when she was first married. I'm proud to say it really is the best strawberry pie ever.

Try a sample and see if you agree.

Best Strawberry Pie Ever
Kitsy Amrhein, Springfield, Illinois

Crust:
1 cup flour
½ cup melted butter
3 tablespoons sugar
Pinch of salt

Preheat oven to 400 degrees.

Mix flour, sugar and salt. Add melted butter. Stir. Press into a 9-inch pie plate. Bake 8-10 minutes until golden brown. Remove from oven and let cool.

Filling:
1-quart strawberries
1 cup sugar
1 cup water
2 tablespoons cornstarch

Mix sugar and cornstarch. Add water and stir till smooth. Add 1 cup cleaned strawberries. Cook over medium heat, stirring occasionally until thick and clear. Mixture will be a bright red. Cool for 15 minutes. Add ¾ cup strawberries. Pour into prepared pie crust. Chill for 3 hours.

Topping:
1-pint heavy cream
½ cup powdered sugar
1 teaspoon vanilla

Whip cream till it forms peaks. Fold in powdered sugar and vanilla. Spread over pie.

Garnish with sliced strawberries.

Enjoy!

Second Prize, 2013

Sugar Pie
Dianna M. Wara, Washington, Illinois

I just inherited my grandmother's rolling pin!

I know, it doesn't mean much to you. Anyone can go and buy a rolling pin. But this one has been used by my great grandma, my grandmother and my mom. This rolling pin, my rolling pin, means the world to me! Oh, if my rolling pin could talk. I wonder what stories it would tell. Let me tell you my story … My great grandma came to America from France and brought her daughter (my grandmother) with her. They came to America shortly before World War I. Mom told me that my grandmother was 8 years old when she came to America. Mom use to tell me that the one thing grandmother remembered about that time was looking up and seeing the Statue of Liberty. They settled eventually in a small town in Iowa called Mystic. That's where my story begins.

Imagine this, two French speaking ladies in the middle of small-town USA. Ok, that makes me laugh just thinking about it. But

Photo by Catherine Lambrecht

the reason they moved there was because it was a town that was heavily populated with other French speaking immigrants. Great grandma never did learn to speak English but after a while, my grandmother did. I still remember going to grandmother's home. I was about 5/6 years old and I remember walking up the steps and into her house and these people carrying on conversations that made no sense to me. I was scared, uncomfortable and didn't want to be there. Looking back on it, that would have been so cool to listen to the conversations going on in that house.

I was born and raised in Illinois. So, when we would visit great grandma & grandmother, it was a 4-hour drive to get there and 4 hours to get back. So, when we would visit, we would stay for a few days. I remember many times visiting grandmother's house and all the activity going on in the kitchen. Sure, grandmother had a living room but, the family lived in the kitchen! I remember sitting at her kitchen table, many times and watching the women of my family cooking together. My grandmother always made pies, my great grandma made the bread, and my mom would do the rest. I was too young to help but they still gave me things to do. Like, picking the green beans for dinner, or picking fruit from her trees for pie, or going to the cellar to get something. When you're little, you don't want to sit still, help out or visit with the family (especially because I couldn't actually understand what they were talking about because they spoke in French) – not me! I would do whatever was asked of me then I'd rush back to her kitchen table and watch the women of my family work together creating a meal. I loved my grandmothers' yard! It was HUGE! She had a big garden, lots of trees, fruit bushes, and a chicken coop. How cool is that! Living in a big city, all that stuff was not things that a small child would see on a daily basis. My grandmother is what I would call self-sustainable. She cooked/baked with the ingredients that she grew. I remember going outside to pick berries for one of her pies. I think it was just the times and economy she grew up in. Living in rural Iowa, there

> I remember sitting at her kitchen table, many times and watching the women of my family cooking together.

wasn't a Walmart on every block for her to buy what she needed. She had to grow it herself! AND she never wasted a thing!

My grandfather owned a store. In fact, it was the only store in Centerville, Iowa for a while. My mom used to tell me stories of his store. I kind of imagine it to look like Oleson's Mercantile in Little House on The Prairie. I always thought the Oleson's were rich and people who owned stores were rich. That was not the case! My grandmother worked every day in the store with her husband. When my mom would get home from school, she was the one in charge of making dinner for her family. My mom has two siblings. She has an older sister (EllaMae) and a younger brother (John). There is a 17-year age difference between my aunt and my mom. So, my aunt wasn't around a lot to help. My mom's job was to make the meals for the family. One of my mom's favorite things to make for dinner was chicken & noodles. She would make the dough and roll it out before school then come home after school, cut them and use them for dinner. My mom made that dish many times while I was growing up.

My mom is a GREAT pie baker too! I'm sure she picked that up from her mother. My mom made pies for school functions, funerals, and as dessert for her family. Just as I did for my grandmother, one of my jobs growing up was picking the fruit for her pies. I LOVED watching mom make pies. So, one day, when I was about 8 years old, she invited me to make a pie with her. She had just made a full pie for a neighbor and she had leftover pie dough. She showed me how to make this wonderful pie called Sugar Pie. She had made it for us many times but, now I get to make it. Great grandma created it when there was extra pie crust dough. Remember, nothing was wasted in her family! This was her solution when there was extra dough leftover. This pie doesn't look pretty, it doesn't fit in a pan perfectly, and let's just admit it, at a bake sale, on looks alone – this pie would not get sold. However, just one bite into this pie and you will see why it's part of my heritage for 4 generations. The crispy crust and the buttery thin goodness on your lips – Y U M! Mom said that grandmother would bake this all the time for me when I was little. My mom has a cool

> I LOVED watching mom make pies.

rolling pin and I remember some time ago asking her if it was her mom's pin. Grandmothers' rolling pin produced some of the best pies that I have ever eaten. I'd love to have her rolling pin and as my own daughter grows, I would like to use it and pass it down to her. I would love to show her how to make sugar pie using grandmothers' pin. Mom told me that she did not have the rolling pin. When my grandmother passed away her sister took almost everything including pictures. There was no division of property. I can only imagine what my mom must have felt like. I guess it caused major friction between mom and her sister for years. If I had a fairy godmother and she granted me one wish, my wish would be ... being able to cook with the women of my family at grandmothers' house. I would have so loved to cook with all these women. Great grandma and grandmother were taken away before I could really cook with them!

> Grandmothers' rolling pin produced some of the best pies that I have ever eaten.

For the last few years, for whatever reason, my aunt has let loose of some of grandmother's treasures and let mom have them. These treasures aren't valued much in money but, most have sentimental value that is priceless. In February of this year, my mom called and asked me if I would like one of grandmother treasures. Not even asking what it was, I said yes without hesitation. I have only one other thing that belonged to my grandmother. Well, not really, it belonged to my grandfather. It's an ash tray from his store. So, mom didn't tell me what treasure it was only that she would give it to me the next time she saw me. In April, shortly before my birthday, mom gave me my grandmother's rolling pin! I have very few memories left of my great grandma and grandmother but sitting at her kitchen table watching her make pie is still very vivid in my head. Going out in her yard collecting fruits for her pie is another one. The same rolling pin that my mom made noodles for her family. I feel like my grandmother is here with me and as silly as it sounds, I feel closest to her when I put my hands on the very same spots as she did while I roll the crust for the Sugar Pie. If my rolling pin could tell me a story, would it be in English or French?

It is with great pride and joy that my entry for you was created by my great grandma, who taught her daughter (my grandmother), who taught her daughter (my mom), who taught me when I was 8 years old how to make. It's called "Sugar Pie." My mom is a pinch of this, a handful of that, a smidge of this kind of cook. There is nothing wrong with that except, her handful is not the same as my handful. It's not an exact recipe because you never know how much pie crust will be left over! So, in order to create a "standard recipe" I will be using a full 9-inch pie plate. The 3 staples of this pie are always the same, brown sugar, milk, and butter. According to mom one other ingredient was sometimes added depending on the season. That ingredient was nuts.

> If my rolling pin could tell me a story, would it be in English or French?

Grandmother had pecan and black walnut trees. I'm not sure if this type of pie actually came from France with Great Grandma or maybe perhaps a recipe created because of the times, accessible ingredients or just the fact that NOTHING was thrown away. But my great grandma and grandmother baked something that is out of this world in flavor. I do know that this pie was ALWAYS made with the left-over pie crust. A pie crust was never made specifically for this recipe. I've even tried to look this pie up on the internet and have found nothing remotely close. So, from my rolling pin to you, enjoy our family's Sugar Pie!

I have included a picture of my grandmother working in the kitchen and a picture of grandpa in their beautiful garden. The same garden that I would pick from so grandmother could make her pies and then make me my Sugar Pie out of the leftover dough!

Sugar Pie
Dianna M. Wara, Washington, Illinois

Pie Crust

Ingredients:

1½ cups all-purpose flour
¾ teaspoon salt
½ cup lard
2½ tablespoons water

Directions:

Preheat oven to 375°F. Sift together flour and salt. Blend lard into sifted flour with a pastry blender until the size of small peas. Add water all at once. Shape into a ball. Roll into a 9 – 10-inch pie pan; set aside.

Sugar Pie Filling

Ingredients:

½ cup brown sugar
3 tablespoons whole milk
1½ tablespoons butter, small cubes
2 tablespoons chopped pecan or black walnuts (if in season)

Directions:

Sprinkle the brown sugar in the bottom of the pie crust. If using nuts, the nuts would go on now.

Evenly spread the milk. (The brown sugar will absorb the milk – that's what you want.) "Dot" on the butter cubes. Bake in preheated 375 oven for 35-45 minutes. Crust will be golden brown, and filling will be bubbly. Take the pie out of the oven and let it cool.

NOTE: I did add black walnuts. My dad went to his farm in Iowa and picked them for me. His farm is about 1 mile away from my grandmother house!

Contestant, 2010

Zwieback Pie
Kitsy Amrhein, Springfield, Illinois

Zwieback is a German word meaning double baked.

Zwieback Pie has been in my family since at least 1894, when my great grandfather, Christoph Amrhein immigrated to the United States from Germany. He settled in Springfield, IL and started Amrhein's Bakery. One of the things he baked in the early days of the bakery was Zwieback toast. Zwie means 2 in German and back means bake. Double baked bread is Zwieback. My great grandmother would use the toast to let my grandfather teeth on. It was marketed as teething toast for babies. Both Nabisco and Gerber sold Zwieback toast for years but discontinued it about 10 years ago. Four generations of Amrheins have literally cut their teeth on Zwieback toast. My great grandmother would also grind it up to make a pie crust. This recipe was passed down to my grandparents. During World War II, my grandmother made Zwieback pie more than any other because of rationing. She couldn't get much sugar or flour for personal use, but Zwieback was plentiful for a family that owned a bakery. She is the one that taught me how to make Zwieback pie. I taught the next generation to make it and they will no doubt continue to teach future generations. It has long been my absolute favorite pie and still is today.

Photo by Catherine Lambrecht

Piecrust is made from Zwieback toast. Zwieback is a German word meaning double baked. I make my Zwieback from scratch, but you can use store bought (if you can find it) and put the toast through a grinder or food processor.

Desserts - Pies

Zwieback Pie

Kitsy Amrhein, Springfield, Illinois

Ingredients:

1 package active dried yeast
4 fl. oz. milk
2 oz. sugar
2 oz. butter
pinch salt
¼ teaspoon cinnamon
¼ teaspoon nutmeg
3 eggs (unbeaten)
12 oz. flour

Directions:

Gently warm the milk until tepid and add the yeast. Set aside for 5 minutes, to allow the yeast to activate.

Melt the butter and add to the mixture, along with the sugar, cinnamon, nutmeg and eggs. Stir until thoroughly combined.

Add enough of the flour to form a dough, then knead well until the dough is smooth – you may need to add extra flour as you knead.

Set the dough aside and leave it to rise.

Once it has doubled in size (around one hour later), divide it into 3 equal pieces and form into loaves Place on an ungreased baking/cookie sheet and allow to rise again (around 30 minutes).

Bake for 20 minutes at 400 degrees F, and then cool.

Lower the oven temperature to 200 degrees F and slice the loaves into ½" slices.

Return to the oven and bake for a further 15 mins, until the zwieback toast is dry and hard.

Pie Crust:

1¾ cup ground up Zwieback toast
2 teaspoons cinnamon
¼ -pound melted butter

Combine above ingredients and press into a glass pie dish.

Filling:

½ cup sugar
3 egg yolks
2 cups milk
1 tablespoon cornstarch
1 teaspoon vanilla
Pinch of salt

Combine ingredients and cook over medium heat while stirring constantly till thick. Pour into piecrust.

Meringue Topping:

3 egg whites
2 tablespoons sugar

Beat eggs with a mixer and gradually add the sugar. Beat until stiff. Spread over pie.

Bake in a preheated 400-degree oven till meringue topping is lightly brown.

Chill for at least 3 hours before serving.

Greater Midwest Foodways Alliance
FAMILY HEIRLOOM RECIPES

Illinois State Fair
2018

2018 2nd Prize Winner

2018 3rd Prize Winner

Desserts

Varied Desserts

Apple Dumplings

Grandmas Old Fashion Blackberry Bubble

Grandma's Cobbler

Date Nut Pudding

Grandmother's Raspberry Sauce
Grandmother's Meringue Shells
Grandmommy's (My) Fudge Tarts

Grandma's Rhubarb Dessert

Rhubarb Roll Up

Old Fashioned Baked Rice Pudding

Contestant, 2012

Apple Dumplings
Darlene Crider, Lincoln, Illinois

*Not fussy or pretentious.
It's just good, solid farm food.*

Grandma Rouch (Wilma Irene Johnston Rouch) was a remarkable woman. She was an incredible example of the strength and endurance it took to be a farm wife during the depression. Her passion was for her family and her home, which was always run with energy and dedication as a farm homemaker. She was married to a farmer, Lester Rouch in 1924 and had four children. His sudden loss in 1955 was devastating. She was left with a farm to run, children still at home (the youngest, my father, only 9 years old) and a mortgage on newly purchased farm land. But with grit and determination she was decided to see that her husband's last act, the purchase of that land, would not be in vain, despite the challenges and hardship. She worked even harder, adding extra odd jobs to her already heavy load to make the payments on that loan. She did without and lived below her means to do so. Amazingly, she accomplished her

Photo by Victoria Moré

goal! She paid the mortgage off, leaving a large amount of land to her children when she passed away, still living in her beloved home, at the age of 96. In fact, all of the original land that her husband had purchased still belongs to the family. All this while caring for her farm and her 5 children, being involved as a 4-H leader, a member of Grass Creek United Methodist Church, in the Ladies Aid, a member of several Extension Homemakers Clubs, and the Historical Society. She loved to teach other women new skills as homemakers so that they could learn to use their resources well as farm women. And she was fascinated by her Pennsylvania Dutch ancestry. This recipe may have been a result of that ancestry, but its origins are lost in time. And of course, she was a fantastic cook and left a wealth of wonderful recipes behind for her family. Rouch family get togethers were always a gastronomical treat with lots of hearty homemade dishes.

> ... she was fascinated by her Pennsylvania Dutch ancestry.

She was truly a remarkable woman. Her recipe for Apple Dumplings is like her, not fussy or pretentious. It's just good, solid farm food. It's rich, quick to prepare and nourishing, delicious and filling, using what was available on hand. The dumplings are great for family get-togethers or to fill up hungry bellies at the dinner table. My mother borrowed this recipe from Grandma Rouch and made it for me and my sisters, so it nourished our generation. Now I make it for my family and my children love it too, especially hot out of the oven and served with ice cream! So, the recipe has been used by at least 3 generations, possibly more and I hope it will continue to be passed down, illustrating the values that were so important to Grandma Rouch.

The dumplings are displayed on a table runner that Grandma Rouch embroidered. Honestly, I don't know how she found the time!

Apple Dumplings
Darlene Crider, Lincoln, Illinois

Ingredients:

Syrup:
1½ cups sugar
1½ cups water
¼ tsp. cloves
½ tsp. cinnamon
½ cup butter

Dough:
2 cups flour
2 tsp. baking powder
1 tsp. salt
¾ cup butter
½ cup milk
3 large or 5 small apples, chopped or grated

Directions:

Preheat oven to 350 degrees. In a large saucepan, mix together sugar, water, cloves and cinnamon and bring to a boil. Boil exactly 5 minutes. Remove from heat, add butter and let sit while mixing dough. Mix flour, salt and baking powder, rub in butter. Add milk; mix gently until combined and can form a ball of dough. Roll out into a rectangle, ¼-inch thick, on a floured counter-top. Cover dough with the chopped apples and sprinkle with sugar and cinnamon. Make into a roll and cut into 1-inch slices. Place in a 13x9x2 baking dish. Pour syrup over dumplings. Bake until brown and bubbly, about 30-45 minutes. Serve hot or cold.

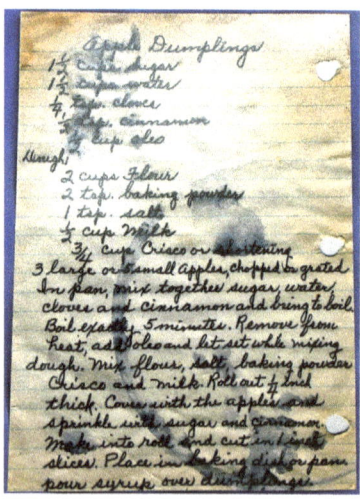

Contestant, 2011

Grandmas Old Fashioned Blackberry Bubble
Earl Meadows, Springfield, Illinois

Summary Memories

This recipe has been handed down in the family. It was from my Grandma Meadows. My brother and I couldn't wait when we were young until summer came and we could go to Centralia and spend the summer with my grandparents. Wakening to the smell of fresh baked bread and fresh honey from her bees. I can remember her handing us a pail and telling us if we found enough blackberries, she would make a bubble for supper. Back then blackberries grew wild along the railroad tracks. We would walk the tracks checking for ripe blackberries all the time the thoughts of grandma's bubble in our head. She had a white granite-porcelain pan with a red stripe around the top that she used for the bubble. I was fortunate enough to find a pan like grandmas in a local antique shop. If it was a special occasion, we would have homemade ice cream to go with the

Photo by Peter Engler

bubble. So, while the bubble was in the oven baking, we would be outside cranking the old-fashioned ice cream maker. Nothing in the world tasted better than grandma's blackberry bubble warm from the oven with a scoop of homemade ice cream. Some of the best memories of my childhood was the summers spent with my grandparents.

Grandmas Old Fashioned Blackberry Bubble
Earl Meadows, Springfield, Illinois

BOTTOM CRUST:

Ingredients:

1½ Cups Flour
½ Cup Crisco or Lard
¼ tsp. Salt
1 tsp. Baking Powder
4 T. Ice Water

Directions:

In a large mixing bowl combine flour, salt, sugar, and baking powder. Mix well. Cut in the Crisco or lard. Add water a tablespoon at a time until dough forms. Wrap dough in plastic wrap and set aside.

FILLING:

Ingredients:

2 T. Butter
6 Cups Blackberries
5 T. Cornstarch or Flour
1 tsp. Cinnamon
1 Cup Sugar
1 Cup Brown Sugar
½ tsp. Salt

Directions:

In a large bowl combine blackberries, sugar, cinnamon, and cornstarch. Mix well. In the bottom of a 9x13-inch pan roll out crust and fit into the bottom of the pan half way up the sides. Add filling and bake in a 350-degree oven until filling starts to bubble and the juice turns clear.

TOPPING:

Ingredients:

2 Cups Flour
1 T. Sugar
1 T. Baking Powder
1 tsp. Salt
8 T. Butter Cubed
¾ Cup Milk
½ Cup Sugar
2 T. Water

Directions:

In a large mixing bowl combine flour, sugar, salt, and baking powder. Mix well. Cut in the cubed butter until it looks like cornmeal. Add milk a little at a time making sure the milk is incorporated. Turn dough out onto a lightly floured surface and knead once or twice. Roll or pat dough to a half inch thick. Cut with a biscuit cutter. Place biscuits on top of the bubbling blackberries and place in a 400-degree oven and bake for 15 to 20 minutes or until golden brown. In a small bowl add ¼ cup sugar and water mix well. After 15 minutes remove from oven and brush the top of the biscuits with the sugar and water mixture. Return to oven for 3 to 5 minutes. Serve warm with ice cream (optional).

Contestant, 2018

Grandma's Cobbler
Kitsy Amrhein, Springfield, Illinois

The same recipe can be used to make any flavor fruit cobbler.

When I was a kid, my parents and 5 siblings went to my grandmother's house for dinner every Sunday. Grandma lived on a lake, which is a kid's paradise. We got to swim, fish, go boating and climb trees. She would often let us spend the night at her house. Spending the night also meant playing board games like Chinese checkers, Pollyanna or Mill. Or maybe card games like Go Fish, FanTan or Gin Rummy. It also meant cooking lessons. Grandma was a fantastic cook. Making cut out sugar cookies was always fun. In the summer, in addition to her teaching us to make cookies, she also let us "help" her bake pies and my favorite, cobbler. She had over an acre of land. On that land was a small backyard orchard. She had cherries, apples, pears, walnuts, mulberries and peaches. We would go out, climb the trees and pick whichever fruit was in season. Grandma would then make a pie or cobbler with our harvest. With only a handful of ingredients, this was a simple recipe to teach a kid. Grandma would measure

Photo by Barbara Kuck

everything out and if cutting up fruit with a sharp knife was involved, she took care of that. She would hand us the measuring cup with the ingredients measured out and we would add it to the mixing bowl. We got to stir and pour the mix into the baking dish. Of course, we would lick the spoon when we were done. As the house filled with the aroma of the cobbler, we would wait with anticipation for it to be done so we could sink our teeth into our creation.

> Of course, we would lick the spoon when we were done.

My grandma had committed many of her recipes to memory and unfortunately, she never wrote them down so many were lost when we lost her. This is one that survived and is cherished because we all learned to make it on a summer sleepover in paradise. It's as unforgettable as she is. Every time I make a cobbler, my mind drifts back to those cherished days of climbing trees, licking spoons and playing games with a fantastic lady that just happened to be MY grandmother. I was a lucky kid!

Peaches are in season right now, so I made the cobbler with peaches. The same recipe can be used to make any other fruit cobbler as well. Sitting down to play cards with a plate of warm cobbler and ice cream is one of my fondest memories as a kid.

Grandma's Cobbler
Kitsy Amrhein, Springfield, Illinois

Ingredients:

1 stick of butter
1 cup sugar
1 cup milk
1 teaspoon baking powder
Pinch of salt
1 quart of fruit (peaches)

Directions:

Preheat oven to 350 degrees. Peal and remove pits from peaches. Melt butter. Pour in to an 8x10 baking pan.

Mix the sugar, milk, baking powder and salt in a medium size mixing bowl. Pour into the baking pan over the butter. Lightly swirl the mix into the butter. Add the peaches. Bake 1 hour. Serve warm with whip cream or ice cream on top.

If making ahead, this can be warmed in the microwave for a few seconds before serving.

Contestant, 2011

My Family's Recipe for Date Nut Pudding
Paul L. Smith, Grandfather
Grace Meadows, Kincaid, Illinois

An English Christmas

My Grandmother came over from Scotland when she was 3 years old in 1881, my Grandfather came over from England sometime prior to the turn of the century. They met and were married here in central Illinois in the year 1900.

As far as we can learn this recipe came over with my Grandfathers family from England and my Grandmother prepared it as a Christmas dish all her adult life. The recipe was passed onto my father as it was a favorite dish for him as a child.

My father prepared this dish every Christmas as far back as I can remember and did so until his death in 2003. Attached is the recipe written in his own hand. It is not a difficult recipe, but getting the consistency of the pudding is, as getting the moisture in the pudding is critical and I have never been able to make it quite like my father did.

Paul L. Smith
December 27, 1915 - October 9, 2003

Photo by Peter Engler

My Family's Recipe for Date Nut Pudding
Paul L. Smith, Grandfather
Grace Meadows, Kincaid, Illinois

Ingredients:

½ lb. dates
½ lb. suet
3 cups bread crumbs
¾ cup sugar
½ cup chopped nuts
1 egg beaten
½ cup milk
4 T. flour
2 tsp baking powder

Directions:

Grind dates and suet very fine. Mix with dried bread crumbs and sugar. Add the other ingredients and mix thoroughly. If pudding seems dry when mixed up add more milk. Pudding should be very moist.

Fill greased metal pudding mold ⅔ full. Cover tightly with aluminum foil and seal top with string. Steam 2½ to 3 hrs. (Note: can be cooked 45 minutes to one hour after pressure comes up in pressure cooker instead.)

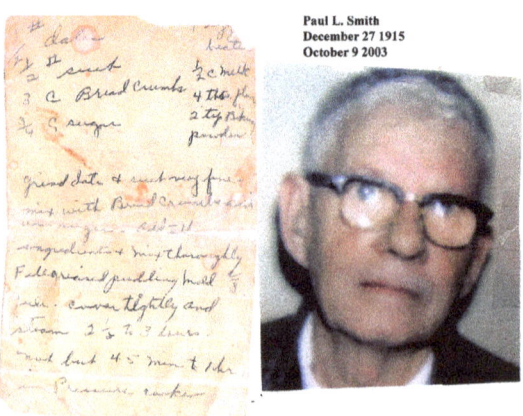

Paul L. Smith
December 27 1915
October 9 2003

Second Prize, 2016

Grandmother's Raspberry Sauce
Grandmother's Meringue Shells
Grandmommy's (My) Fudge Tarts
Jone Schumacher, Chapin, Illinois

The "family secret sauce."

My Grandmother Nickel (1898 – 1995) was a very inventive "home chef" and gardener. Even though my grandparents lived in town, she had a very large lot reserved for her grand garden. As a child, I recall seeing her adorned in her large straw hat, an apron over her house-dress and her basket in hand walking toward her garden. I remember seeing her return from the garden with her basket full and even some harvested fruit and vegetables being carried in her apron. My aunts tell me Grandmother would offer them the option of gardening or working in the house, and it was quite agreeable to all that they would choose the household chores and Grandmother would enjoy her quiet time in her garden. Besides her garden, Grandmother's joy

Photo by Peter Engler

was her large in-town raspberry patch. She would bake delicious raspberry pies and cobblers, but most popular was her sweet raspberry sauce. She would crush the very ripe berries, strain out the seeds and mix the resulting precious raspberry pulp with equal amounts of granulated sugar. Being very frugal after experiencing the Great Depression, Grandmother did not purchase special jars to store her sauce in, but rather reused various sizes of clean empty glass salad dressing bottles that she saved for this purpose.

> She would bake delicious raspberry pies and cobblers, but most popular was her sweet raspberry sauce.

One of my most precious memories of Grandmother in her later years, is the sight of her slowly walking up to my front door carrying a brown bag twisted at the top containing a highly valued dressing jar of raspberry sauce. This was her special very appreciated contribution to my children's birthday celebrations. Years prior, Grandmother was one of the first in her day to own an electric freezer and she froze her raspberry sauce to have ready to share and to serve to her family and other privileged guests. I still marvel about how elegantly my grandmother set her table. Even when my siblings and I were served our evening meal at Grandmother's, she always had a freshly washed and ironed table cloth on her table. One of our very favorite deserts was this delicious sweet raspberry sauce swirling down over a dip of vanilla ice cream nestled in a meringue shell. Grandmother's raspberry sauce recipe was never really written down formally on a recipe card as far as I know but was just known and passed down through the generations as a treasured "family Secret."

Although growing raspberries was my grandmother's joy, my husband has the same love of gardening and berry growing and is now tending around 250 raspberry bushes as well as 2,000 blueberry and 200 blackberry bushes on our farm. I would have loved for my grandmother to have seen his berry patches and I would have cherished picking berries with her, all dressed up with her straw hat and apron. My husband patiently picks the berries and helps make Grandmother's sauce, and we freeze various amounts in glass jelly jars. I have created several recipes featuring the raspberry sauce and share the "family secret sauce" as it is just too special not to share. My family's favorite way to enjoy this sauce is on ice cream served in a chocolate tart-shaped cake. My grandchildren call them "volcanoes" as they think the raspberry sauce resembles red lava flowing over their ice cream. Recently, I have introduced my grandchildren to Grandmother's meringue shells and they love this "new" old-time sugary treat as well. I am pleased to share all three recipes. Pictured is my grandmother at her own birthday party in front of her birthday cake which I made and decorated with a variety of her favorite "icing" fruits. I have so many memories of my grandmother and her delicious food and I truly enjoy making these yummy foods and creating great memories for my grandchildren. I realize someday my recipes will be heirloom and I hope they will be used and cherished as I do my grandmother's.

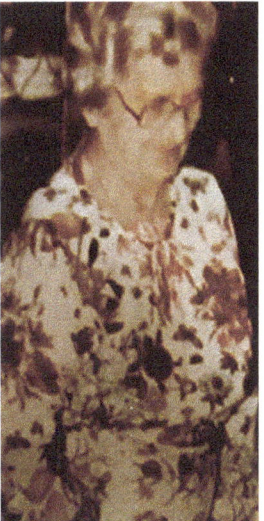

Grandmother's Raspberry Sauce
Grandmother's Meringue Shells
Grandmommy's (My) Fudge Tarts

Jone Schumacher, Chapin, Illinois

GRANDMOTHER'S RASPBERRY SAUCE

Ingredients:

3 cups fresh or frozen (thawed) raspberries
1 cup granulated sugar

Directions:

Crush raspberries in blender and then strain to remove seeds. Stir together the sugar with the raspberries. (Since berries may vary in amount, always measure and mix equal parts of the strained berry pulp with equal parts of sugar.) This amount should yield around 1⅔ cups sweetened sauce.

Refrigerate until serving. Freeze in glass jars.

GRANDMOTHER'S MERINGUE SHELLS

Ingredients:

3 egg whites, at room temperature
¼ teaspoon cream of tartar
Dash of salt
1 teaspoon vanilla
1 cup granulated sugar, preferably extra fine

Directions:

Preheat oven to 275 degrees. Cover cookie sheet with plain ungreased brown paper. Draw nine 3-inch circles. In a medium mixing bowl, beat egg whites on low speed of mixer until foamy. Add the cream of tartar, salt and then the vanilla. Continue beating until the egg whites begin to hold their shape and become opaque. Increase the speed to medium-high and gradually add the sugar in a slow stream. Beat until the whites thicken and form stiff peaks and sugar is dissolved; do not over beat. Spread approximate ⅓ cup meringue; shape with spoon to make shells, shallow in the center with higher edges around the center.

Bake in pre-heated oven for 1 hour. For crisper meringue shells turn off heat and let cool and dry with door closed for about one hour. Store in tightly sealed container until serving.

GRANDMOMMY'S (MY) FUDGE TARTS

Measure into large mixing bowl and mix until blended:

2 cups all-purpose flour
1 cup dark brown sugar
1 cup granulated sugar
1 teaspoon baking soda
½ teaspoon salt

Measure into a medium sauce pan:

½ cup salted butter
½ cup butter shortening
3 tablespoons cocoa
3 tablespoons special dark cocoa
1 cup double chocolate low fat milk

Bring fat mixture to boil, blend into flour-sugar mixture. Blend in:

2 extra large eggs
½ cup buttermilk
1 teaspoon vanilla

Pour into prepared individual tart pans and bake in pre-heated 350 degree oven for 13 to 15 minutes. Invert pans onto wire racks, remove pans and use another wire rack to turn right-side-up. Allow to cool.

Glaze:

Ingredients:

2 tablespoons melted salted butter
3 tablespoons unsweetened cocoa
3 tablespoons special dark cocoa
4 cups powdered sugar
1 teaspoon vanilla
½ to ⅔ cup double chocolate milk

Directions:

Blend until smooth and to a "drizzle thick consistency." Using a pastry brush cover top center and sides of tarts with glaze; allow to dry.

Yield: 24 to 26 tarts.

Freeze in tightly sealed plastic containers if desired.

Serve tarts or meringue shells with a dip of ice cream and top with generous amount of the raspberry sauce.

Third Prize, 2017

Grandma's Rhubarb Dessert
Amy Wendling, Pleasant Plains, Illinois

Best served with a dip of vanilla ice cream on the still warm rhubarb.

I grew up on the family farm that had been in my father's family for three generations, and he was actually born in the farmhouse along with his four other siblings. When my dad took over the day-to-day operation of the farm, he built a house for my grandma on a plot of land adjacent to our farmhouse, so we could run across our vast yard and visit her daily to see what treats she was whipping up to spoil me and my four siblings. We also took turns spending the night at her house and she would let us pick what she made for our special breakfast the next morning. Each night before we fell asleep, she would tell us stories about her childhood. It was better than watching a movie!

Growing up on our family farm, there were many flavorful fresh fruits and vegetables that I looked forward to each summer: Mom's special "peaches 'n cream" sweetcorn, big ripe tomatoes, carrots, cucumbers, strawberries and other fresh produce. Of all the wonderful flavors of the season, my absolute favorite was Grandma Miller's rhubarb and her special rhubarb dessert. As a young girl, rhubarb was an odd plant in my opinion. The rhubarb patch was tucked away in the back of the garden by Grandma Miller's white broad board fence, and it looked more like a type of lettuce, than the

Photo by Barbara Kuck

highlight of my favorite summer dessert. My grandma's rhubarb patch was famous throughout the county. I remember cars and trucks pulling up to her house and people asking if they could get a bag full of her rhubarb. She always said yes and never accepted any payment. As the rhubarb started getting redder as the season progressed, my siblings and I would pester grandma almost daily to ask when the rhubarb would be ready. She insisted that if it was picked too early, the stalks would be too stringy and sour.

We waited with patience limited by our youth, until the day each year when we ran through her back door with the screen door slamming behind us, and we would melt in anticipation as the house filled with the luscious smells of the tangy rhubarb and the sweet toppings mingled together in the oven. We hovered around the cooling pan and finally she would serve up a portion of her rhubarb dessert and sometimes even serve a dip of vanilla ice cream with the still warm rhubarb.

> ... we would melt in anticipation as the house filled with the luscious smells of the tangy rhubarb and the sweet toppings ...

My grandma passed away over 40 years ago, but I can still remember exactly where the rhubarb patch was located in her back yard, and fondly remember the wonderful childhood memories of farm fresh flavors adorning our summer table. But one of the most prominent memories is sitting at my grandma's kitchen table playing games with a serving of rhubarb crisp. This recipe and these memories are deeply cherished by me and my family - my grandmother was a treasure to me and is always in my heart.

Grandma's Rhubarb Dessert

Amy Wendling, Pleasant Plains, Illinois

Ingredients:

2 cups flour
3 tsp. baking powder
3 tbsp. sugar
¼ tsp. salt
2 eggs
¼ cup milk
6 cups rhubarb - cut into small chunks
2 pkgs. strawberry gelatin
1½ cups sugar
4 tbsp. flour

Directions:

Mix together and put in a 9"x13"x2" can pan.

Cover with the following:

1 cup flour
1½ cup sugar
½ cup oleo

Mix and spread over mixture.

Bake at 350° until rhubarb is done.

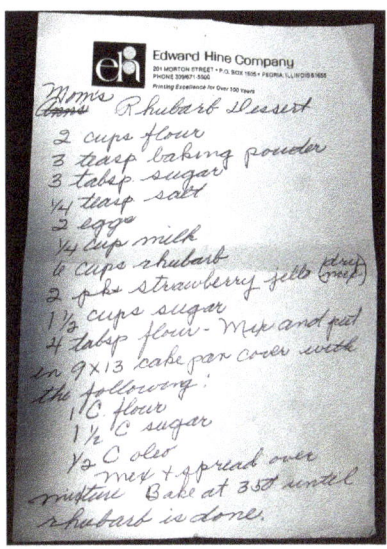

Contestant, 2009

Rhubarb Roll Up
Liz Drake, Springfield, Illinois

City Girl Meets Rhubarb

A long time ago, in times not so different from our own, when I was a little girl growing up in the city, I was always amazed when we would visit family and friends in the country. Country Grandma's seemed like they not only could, but often did accomplish the impossible task of making something wonderful out of next to nothing.

The recipe I have chosen to submit for family Heirloom Recipes Contest belongs to one such country grandma. Even though she is not my grandma, she was always "Granny" to me and a very close friend of mine. When I asked Granny for the recipe, she just laughed and said there wasn't one. When I asked how she learned to make the rhubarb roll-up she said, "Same way you're gonna." As she headed out to the kitchen she muttered, "My

Photo by Peter Engler

granny taught me and I'm gonna teach you. Mommas are just too busy being mommas, Grannies have time to pass things on." So, not being too slow to notice I had a golden opportunity, I took a pencil, a piece of paper and wrote things down as we went along.

It usually happened on the first really hot day of the summer. Granny would go out to the back garden a pick a handful of what appeared to me to be a bunch of weeds. (Rhubarb looks a lot like cockleburs) With a well-practiced hand, she would take them into the kitchen, wash them, cut up the stems and throwaway the leaves. The country version of throwaway the leaves anyway, they would go in the scrap bowl under the sink to be taken out to the chickens on the next trip out.

> "... Mommas are just too busy being mommas, Grannies have time to pass things on."

Because Granny was a wise woman who understood the impatience of youth, she would hand each of us a rhubarb stalk and a little bowl of sugar. While we were busy with our country version of dipping sticks, she would make the crust for her "famous" rhubarb roll up. She would take a handful or two of flour, throw it in a bowl, mix in some magic and some lard, roll everything together and before you knew it-delicious smells were coming from the oven.

Rhubarb Roll Up
Liz Drake, Springfield, Illinois

Ingredients:

1 cup sugar
1½ cups water-boil together till sugar is dissolved and let cool

3 cups flour
3 tsp baking powder
¾ cup shortening
¼ cup Sugar
1 tsp salt
½ cup cold milk

3 cups cut up rhubarb-mix with
½ cup sugar just before putting on dough.

Directions:

Cut together flour, baking powder, shortening, sugar and salt like pie dough and stir in ½ cup cold milk to make dough. Roll to ¼-inch-thick rectangle. (I roll onto a sheet of waxed paper to make rolling up around the rhubarb easier.)

Put rhubarb and sugar on top of dough and roll up like a jelly roll. Slice into ¾-inch slices and lay in a baking pan (I used a deep 10-inch round cake pan) and gently pour syrup over the slices.

Bake at 400 degrees for 45 minutes. Top will be lightly browned when done. Invert onto serving plate after cooling for 20 minutes.

"Dress it up with garnishes if you want, tastes just the same either way."

Contestant, 2011

Old Fashioned Baked Rice Pudding
Betty Moser, Decatur, Illinois

Our Old Cook Stove

When I was a child my mother cooked on an old-fashioned cook stove – I remember the delicious warmth it provided on a cold winter day – and in the summer seeing my mother's face and hair wet with perspiration as she worked in the very hot kitchen.

I cannot imagine cooking on a stove like this now – but I remember soups and meat loaves and cakes being prepared using this stove. My parents experienced the depression years – both their families lost ranches to the harsh financial times. The foods that my mother prepared were simple, using ingredients at hand from our pantry, from produce in the garden and milk products from our dairy cows.

A special dish that was prepared on the cook stove was a delicious rice pudding that was a family favorite – almost a staple. Mother would mix the simple ingredients in a pot and bake the pudding for several hours. This dish did not need any attention during its baking while we all worked at tasks on the farm.

For me the rice pudding had such a special flavor and texture. I still associate this dish with memories of OUR OLD COOK STOVE. OLD FASHIONED BAKED RICE PUDDING.

Photo by Peter Engler

Old Fashioned Baked Rice Pudding
Betty Moser, Decatur, Illinois

Ingredients:

4 cups milk
½ cup rice
½ teaspoon salt
⅔ cup sugar

Directions:

Wash the rice and mix the ingredients.

Pour into a buttered dish and bake 3 hours in a slow (325 degree) oven, stirring 3 times during the first hour of baking to prevent the rice from settling.

Greater Midwest Foodways Alliance
FAMILY HEIRLOOM RECIPES

Illinois State Fair
2018

2018 Winners

2018 1st Prize Winner

More Good Food

Nanny's Mother's Applesauce

Barbecue Sauce

Houby (Mushrooms)

Grandma's Mint Drink

Fried Sage – or Nature's "Potato Chips"

Contestant, 2012

Nanny's Mother's Applesauce
Kitsy Amrhein, Springfield, Illinois

Never again buy a can or jar of applesauce.

Six generations of my family have made or currently make some form of the family applesauce recipe. It's been tweaked through the years with each generation experimenting with a few changes to the basic recipe. However, had it not been for the Illinois State Fair, this family heirloom recipe might have been lost to the ages …

But I'm getting ahead of myself. Let's start at the beginning. Nanny was my great grandmother. She died when I was 7 years old so my actual memories of her are few. But her daughter Clara, (my grandma) loved to tell stories about her. That's how I learned about her making applesauce, or rather teaching my grandma and her sister Edna how to make applesauce. According to the oral history passed down by my grandma, Nanny was a true pioneer woman of the 19th century. Everything she did was done by hand. No modem conveniences for Nanny. She worked hard from sunup to sundown.

Photo by Victoria Moré

One of her favorite treats was apples. Apple pie, apple butter, apple cider, and apple anything was often on her table. One of those apple dishes was applesauce. It didn't come from a can or a jar in those days. If you wanted applesauce you needed to make it yourself. She learned to make it from her mother, my great-great-grandmother.

She would core the apples and cut them into pieces and cook them over the fire. Then the fun part started. After the apples were soft and mushy, they needed to be put through a sieve. That could take quite a while to do. Back and forth– forcing the apple pulp through the sieve with the back of a wooden spoon. But once, it was completed, you had a very tasty treat. When my grandma and her sister Edna were old enough, they were the ones that got to do the fun part. The part involving the sieve. Nanny would supervise the girls. My grandma would talk about what a mess it was and how sore her hands and arms were from making applesauce. She liked to eat it but she hated to make it. Besides, it was now the 20th century and you could buy it in the store already made. It didn't taste nearly as good though.

> Grandma started buying her applesauce instead of making it at home. That was until a little invention called the food mill.

Grandma started buying her applesauce instead of making it at home. That was until a little invention called the food mill. The food mill was invented by Jean Mantelet in Minneapolis, Minn. The invention was patented on Aug. 8, 1933. The first food mills were produced by a company named Foley. Though this was its first kitchenware product, Foley later produced other useful kitchen items, including shredders and juicers.

Now you are probably wondering how the Illinois State Fair saved the recipe. Well, there was no fair during World War II and in 1946 the fair was back in full swing. In 1946 my grandmother went to the Illinois State Fair again. Grandma walked into the Exposition building which from the way she described it was not much different than it is today. People were demonstrating all the latest modem conveniences that no housewife could live without. She saw somebody demonstrating a Foley Mill. She remembered Nanny's applesauce recipe and thought she could make it again using the Foley Mill instead of the sieve. She bought one on the spot. On the way home from the fair, she picked up a bushel of apples. That night, grandpa had his first taste of homemade applesauce with his dinner. Never again would store bought canned applesauce be served in their home.

My grandma gave my mother a Foley Mill as one of her wedding gifts. She also handed down the recipe that she had grown up hating to make. My mother learned to make the delicious treat and did so often. Once the fall would roll around and apples were in season, she made it almost daily. The only time I ever had canned applesauce was on a school lunch tray. Yuck!

Mom changed the recipe a small amount by adding cinnamon red hots to it because she loved cinnamon, and everyone knows that cinnamon and apples go together. Grandma usually made clear applesauce using green apples, but Mom always used red apples, which produces red applesauce unless you peel them, which you don't have to do.

At my sister's wedding shower, Grandma gave her a brand-new Foley Mill and told her she would need it to make her husband homemade applesauce. My sister put it away in her attic and forgot all about it.

My mother got me a Foley Mill at a garage sale. She then coached me through my first batch of applesauce. It was the easiest thing I ever made. I make it all the time in the fall when those apples are in season.

Last October, my mother was temporarily in a nursing home recovering from a fall. My niece and nephew were in town to visit their grandma. She was complaining about how horrible the food was. I had just finished making a double batch of applesauce, so I took her some. Actually, I took her about a quart of it. I also gave some to my niece and nephew. They loved it and wondered why their mom never made it. I told them she had a Foley Mill in which to make it because I saw her open the one Grandma gave her at her wedding shower almost 35 years ago.

Mom called me the next day and told me I had to bring more applesauce up to the nursing home. Now I know the food there was bad but there was no way she had consumed the entire quart already. She said she was sharing it with everyone else and they had never had homemade applesauce. All the nursing home patients were raving about how good it was and they wanted more. So, I continued the family tradition by teaching my niece and nephew how to make it while we made another batch to take up to Mom.

> A recipe saved by that cool invention first introduced to my Grandmother at the Illinois State Fair.

My niece and nephew returned home and asked their mother why she never made applesauce. She said she remembered getting the Foley Mill from Grandma but couldn't remember what she did with it. My nephew went on a mission to find it. He did. Now they are the sixth generation to make this family heirloom recipe. A recipe saved by that cool invention first introduced to my Grandmother at the Illinois State Fair. Now that they know how to make it, they will never again buy a can or jar of applesauce. It's too easy to make it yourself and a whole lot better tasting. They will be sure to pass it on to a seventh generation when their kids are old enough to learn how to make it.

I think I'll head over to the Exposition Building after the contest today and see what cool gadget is being demonstrated. You never know …. I might find something that will save another heirloom recipe for generations to come.

Nanny's Mother's Applesauce
Kitsy Amrhein, Springfield, Illinois

Ingredients:

3 pounds fresh apples
⅔ cups sugar
¼ cup water
2 teaspoon lemon juice
15 red hot candies
⅛ teaspoon ground cinnamon

Directions:

Core apples and slice into wedges. Do not peel apples.

In 2-quart pan combine water, lemon juice and apples. Cook over low heat stirring occasionally until apples are soft and mushy.

Push cooked apples through a sieve or food mill.

Fold in sugar. Stir in red hots until dissolved.

Garnish with ground cinnamon.

Chill in refrigerator or "ice box" as my Grandma called it.

Will keep up to a month in the refrigerator.

Yields 1 quart

Contestant, 2009

Barbecue Sauce
Carol Meadows, Springfield, Illinois

 riginal Recipe: is from my husband's Great Grandma Meader. This recipe has been in his family for over 100 years.

Use with: Beef, Chicken, or Pork

Sauce:

Ingredients:

1 Can Tomato Sauce
1 Large Clove Garlic Mashed
½ Cup Tomato Catsup
⅓ Teaspoon Salt
¼ Teaspoon Cumin
2 Large Bay Leaves
2 Tablespoons Worcestershire Sauce
½ Cups Firmly Packed Brown Sugar
⅔ Cups Finely Chopped Onion
⅔ Cup Finely Chopped Bell Pepper
¼ Teaspoon Oregano
1 Tablespoon White Vinegar
¼ Teaspoon Paprika

Photo by Peter Engler

Directions:

Combine all ingredients in a large saucepan over medium to low heat and cook for 20 minutes. Remove bay leaf before sauce is basted or poured over meat.

You can use with chicken, roast, pork and browned hamburger. This recipe is good to baste meat cooked on a grill or poured over meat that is baked in the oven.

First Prize, 2014

Houby (Mushrooms)
Linda D. Cifuentes, Mahomet, Illinois

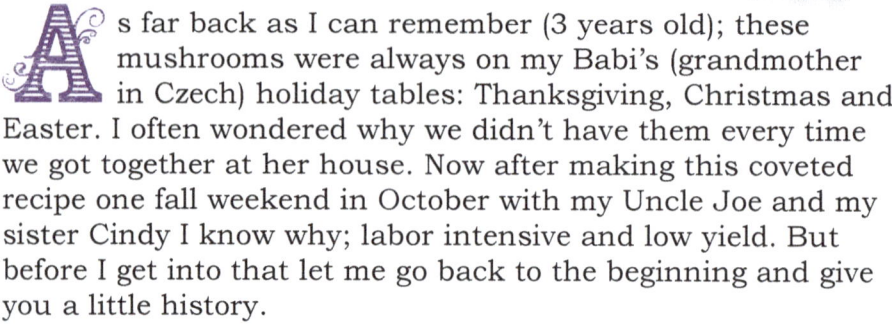

*An acquired taste.
I like them I don't love them.*

As far back as I can remember (3 years old); these mushrooms were always on my Babi's (grandmother in Czech) holiday tables: Thanksgiving, Christmas and Easter. I often wondered why we didn't have them every time we got together at her house. Now after making this coveted recipe one fall weekend in October with my Uncle Joe and my sister Cindy I know why; labor intensive and low yield. But before I get into that let me go back to the beginning and give you a little history.

My Babi; Agnes Chudaba Holas came to this country with her sister Marie and their husbands Anton (my Deda is grandfather in Czech) and Cyril Holas. Yes, you got it two sisters married two brothers. In 1898 Agnes was born near Belgrade which actually became part of Yugoslavia but she and my Deda spoke Czech. Back then the area was part of the Austro-Hungarian Empire. My Babi and Deda were married when they came to this country in 1920 after the end of World War 1.

They entered through Ellis Island and along with Marie and Cyril and many other Czechs they settled in Berwyn, Illinois. This was a large Czech community where most of the business's shopkeepers spoke Czech. The Couple settled in and started they family which soon grew to seven: Bessie, Agnes, Anton (my Dad) Frank, John, Joseph and Robert. My Deda did masonry work and my Babi had the tough task of handling the Holas brood which she did with both love and an iron hand. And with five boys I'm told her task was not easy.

Babi pretty much made everything from scratch mostly out of necessity because there were so many mouths to feed and therefor it was cheaper. She was an Excellent cook and as most cooks in that era did not have a recipe-just picked up ingredients by the handful and through them in. She canned anything she could but of all the things she canned the mushrooms was the most special in the family because it was truly a family affair. Before you could can them, you had to hunt them, so every last child was manned with a bag and often times a stick and set out to the local woods or forest preserve to fill their bags. It was a bit of hard work but since they were all together it became a fun family outing that could last for hours depending on how many mushrooms the boss (Babi) wanted.

Before the tedious job of cleaning the mushrooms commenced, which also everyone participated, each mushroom was inspected by Babi to make sure it was ok and not poisonous. Her children would all ask how she knew they were ok, and I was told she always answered, "Because I Know!"

When I was a little girl my parents tried a couple of times to take my brothers, sister and out to the local forest preserve on a mushroom hunting expedition but we didn't even find enough to make a half-pint, so my dad gave up and left the task to the experts. It was fun though while it lasted because we were all

Photo by Catherine Lambrecht

together hiking around the woods.

My Uncles John, Joe and Bob remained bachelors and eventually moved to a wooded house on a lake in north western Wisconsin. You know what woods means; MUSHROOMS! Even in her later years (she lived to be 90) Babi was still running the mushroom show. My Uncles would drive down to Berwyn and pick her up and bring her to the north. They would pick the mushrooms and she still inspected every last one. Just like when they were little, they all cleaned the mushrooms and "put them up" together.

> The word Houby is Czech for mushroom

The word Houby is Czech for mushroom and since the mushroom was the object of a hunting tradition and a significant part of the Czech diet. The Houby Parade was born in Berwyn and Cicero in 1968 until present. It was established to honor the families who settled in this area and continued the time-honored tradition.

Now sadly my Uncle Joe is the last survivor of the Holas children, but he has continued with the tradition of hunting mushrooms and canning them by himself in true Babi fashion. Last year I guess he thought it was time he better passes the tradition on, so he called my sister Cindy and me mid-October. Now, you have to understand that when he called, he said you need to come within the next two weeks or the mushrooms will be gone so Cindy and I juggled our work schedules and away we went.

We drove 400 miles north to Wisconsin and no sooner pulled into the driveway and Uncle Joe opened the doors and shoved bags in our hands and directed us to the next -door neighbor's lawn which was covered with mushrooms. We just stared at him and he said, "start picking." So, we broke the mushrooms off at the base from the ground and started filling our bags. Of course, Me and Cindy asked the million-dollar question: "Uncle Joe, how do you know they are not poisonous?" And of course, we got the million-dollar answer was "Because I know."

After two hours and many full bags of mushrooms Uncle Joe deemed the hunting session over. I must say me and Cindy did have fun under the watchful eye of Uncle Joe. Now the real work begins. We all sat down at the newspaper-covered table and began to clean each and every mushroom by throwing the debris on the floor. I can't even imagine what a mess this was when my dad and uncle were little and there were seven of them plus Babi. This task took us several hours and Uncle Joe inspected each mushroom so "quality control" was maintained. The clean mushrooms were thrown into a large cast iron pot that was then filled with water and placed in the refrigerator overnight. The next day the mushrooms were rinsed and then placed back in the refrigerator. We did not start cooking them until Sunday afternoon. After all that we got 5 pints and 2 half pints-it took us all weekend, but it was one of the best weekends I have spent with my Uncle Joe (who has always been my favorite Uncle!)

> Uncle Joe inspected each mushroom so "quality control" was maintained.

I think the mushrooms are an acquired taste-I like them I don't love them. This past Thanksgiving at my nephew's house my sister and I proudly put out a pint of "our" mushrooms and announced to everyone they should try them. My brothers who both love the mushrooms and used to fight over them when we were little wouldn't touch them until we finally told them that they were Uncle Joe supervised and approved.

Uncle Joe is battling cancer but so far has survived 2½ years we already have a date set for mid-October for another round of mushroom hunting and canning. This time we are bringing my 4-year-old great-niece Carolyn to get another generation indoctrinated in the tradition. It is on this trip I have to learn the answer to that all-important question; how do you know their ok? I NEED TO KNOW!!!

These mushrooms would go great popped in a picnic basket because the whole idea of them like picnics is family oriented.

I think they would go great with sandwiches or cold fried chicken. And while you are picnicking you could discuss mushroom hunting strategies.

P.S. I forgot to add this is how the mushrooms were always served – right in the jar with a fork; never in a bowl!

> Editor's Note:
>
> Learning mushroom identification can be achieved by joining and participating at a mushroom club. The North American Mycological Association's website has a list of regional clubs at www.namyco.org. In Illinois, there is the Illinois Mycological Association at IllinoisMyco.org.
>
> Deadly poisonous mushrooms can be found throughout Illinois and Midwest in all seasons, even in winter. Wild foragers must learn to recognize toxic fungi before harvesting edible species. A good regional guide is *Mushrooms of the Midwest* by Michael Kuo and Andrew Methven. This book paired with *Edible Wild Mushrooms of Illinois and Surrounding States: A Field-to-Kitchen Guide* by Gregory Mueller and Joe McFarland.
>
> If there is any shadow of doubt on your identification efforts, please take a pass. There are plenty of Asian markets with exotic cultivated mushrooms to satisfy your curiosity. It is best to be safe, alive and healthy.

> Editor's Note:
>
> Preservation methods are stated as-is to preserve the integrity of this family history. We consulted National Center for Home Food Preservation website (https://nchfp.uga.edu/) for research-based recommendations. Unfortunately, this recipe would require substantial adaptation to correct pH for water bath processing. If you prepare this recipe as-is, it is recommended it be refrigerated and consumed within two weeks.

Houby (Mushrooms)
Linda D. Cifuentes, Mahomet, Illinois

MUSHROOMS HOUBY

1- Pick mushrooms in the grass & woods
2- Clean all mushrooms
3- Wash mushrooms in cold water
4- Salt washed mushrooms & put in refrigerator over night
5- Relax and watch a movie
6- Next day take out of refrigerator and wash them real good
7- Strain them in a colander & put in pot on the stove pour water on top of mushrooms
8- Cook mushrooms until done (some people save water for soup)
9- Strain them under cold water
10- Put strained mushrooms into large pot
11- Cut up onion to have about the same as cooked mushrooms
12- Mix in onions with cooked mushrooms to start set-up to jar in pt. Bottles
13- Wash bottles & place in oven set oven at 225 degrees
14- Put pot on stove and put 1 pint of vinegar into pot and bring to a boil stirring constantly
15- Mix ¾ pt of sugar (more or less to your taste) into boiling vinegar mix stirring constantly
16- Take 1 pt. (A little more) mushroom & onion mix put in pot of boiling sugar & vinegar let boil for a few minutes stirring constantly
17- When mix has been boiling for a few minutes bring bottle out of the oven and put into another pot with cloth on bottom
18- Spoon mushrooms & onion mix into pint bottle
19- Then fill pint bottle with liquid mixture to top
20- Put lid & ring on bottle and tighten ring
21- Turn bottle over & place on towel
22- Take remaining mixture & pour into bowl
23- Start all over again

Contestant, 2012

Grandma's Mint Drink
Rob Dunbar, Emden, Illinois

A labor of love for someone important.

As a young boy, I always knew when someone important was coming to visit my Grandma during the summer. Usually it meant that my cousins from up north were coming down south to visit. Or, an important friend of Grandma's was in town to see her. Grandma would go out to the back of the house and gather up handfuls of mint leaves from her garden. She did this in order to make her mint drink. I always considered this drink a wonderful treat whenever it was made and whenever I was lucky enough to be around to have some.

Now, I'm grown and married. My wife and I have our own place in the country that allows us to grow our own mint leaves. We can make Grandma's mint drink as much as we want when the weather is hot. Looking back, I realize that it was a labor of love when Grandma made her drink. Squeezing six lemons and two oranges to get the right amount of juice for the drink make my hands very sore. But when we each have a glass filled with icy cold mint drink on a hot August day, it's all worthwhile.

I was told, Grandma had been making this wonderful drink since she was young. Grandma always added the homemade mint concentrate to water. My wife and I have found that the mint concentrate is also very refreshing when added to iced tea. Grandma passed away at the age of 102 in 1991, and I'm proud to carry on the tradition of this wonderful, refreshing drink.

Photo by Victoria Moré

Grandma's Mint Drink
Rob Dunbar, Emden, Illinois

(This recipe is grandmas only I have explained some steps that my grandma would have assumed the cook already knew)

Ingredients:

2 cups of sugar
2½ cups of water
6 lemons
2 oranges
A nice-sized handful of mint leaves

Directions:

Grate and juice lemons and oranges into a large bowl, then set aside.

Mix sugar and water together in a sauce pan on the stove. Bring the mixture to a boil.

Simmer for 10 minutes. Add grated mixture so that it also simmers for the 10 min. Remove from heat. Add mint leaves. Let stand for one hour. Strain and place in jar in refrigerator. To serve, mix one cup concentrate with one cup water in glass with ice. Enjoy.

** For the purpose of this competition I have already mixed the concentrate to water so that it is ready to serve.

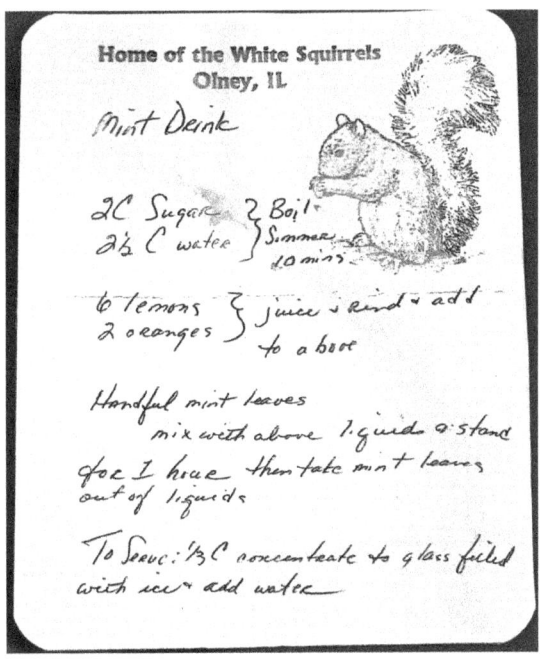

Third Place, 2012

Fried Sage – or Nature's "Potato Chips"
Amy Wertheim, Atlanta, Illinois

*History of Fried Sage Leaves
or as we call them ... Nature's "Potato Chips"*

The highlight of my week was Saturday. On Saturday mornings I ALWAYS went to my grandparent's house. Usually I would get to stay for lunch, and sometimes I was allowed to stay until supper, but on the really special days, I was allowed to go with my grandpa while he drove around the countryside checking the crops or as my grandma would say, "Getting lost so he wouldn't have to do her list of chores she had for him."

What made the driving around so wonderful were the snacks that my grandpa kept in his Fiat; there was candy bars, and walnuts, and these funny potato chips that were really weird colored, kinda greenish gray, but super crunchy and salty! They were my favorite, especially the pointy ones, but they broke really easy and there were never very many of them!!! But grandpa was strange about letting you snack on his "potato chips" .... It seemed like when school was let out for summer, we could eat as many as we wanted .... But when school started back, he didn't want to share .... and when it began to get colder out, he wouldn't even let us know where he had them hidden. Little did we know, the 'potato chips' we were eating were seasonal!

You see, those weird-colored, super crunchy, salty chips weren't potato chips at all. They were fried sage leaves. And when the summer vacation started, there were plenty of sage leaves in the garden because it was the beginning of the summer growing season. So, it would only make sense, that once the frost and colds came ... no more sage leaves. Also, the different shapes of the chips were different varieties or flavors of sage leaves.

Now, you would think being at my grandparent's house every Saturday I would have been able to figure out what in the world these "potato chips" really were, especially since my grandma was the one who was frying them up for grandpa to snack on, but I never did. They were just one of the wonderful snacks grandpa always had.

And so, here we were, just a few years ago, sitting around the table after Thanksgiving sharing memories and stories from our childhood that I asked if anyone remember those weird colored "potato chips" grandpa also had ... "What I wouldn't give to just eat one more of those they were so good. I wonder who made them?" Well, my mom just turned and looked at me and said, "Your grandma made them, and if you really wanted some all you had to do is go out to your herb garden and pick some sage leaves." I was so confused ... what? "Those were just fried sage leaves – what did you think they were?" Obviously, I had no idea, but that spring, the moment the sage came up and there were some nice leaves on them I cut them, I fried them, I salted them (oh, how I salted them!) and I ate them ... ALL! Didn't share a one 'em!!!

Of course, my family was curious about my strange behavior, so I made another batch. And they disappeared as quickly as the first

Photo by Victoria Moré

batch! So, I cooked up some more ... actually we cooked up all the sage we had. And a few weeks later, we did it again. And we continued to cook them right up until the frost came.

Now I have 3 different patches of sage: Purple Sage, Pineapple Sage and Muskmelon Sage. The Pineapple Sage are the pointy ones and they are super delicate, but oh so yummy! The Muskmelon Sage is my son's favorite and he took the whole patch of leaves with him to college to fry up; and the Purple Sage leaves are the smaller ones.

Some people, like me, like to eat them plain, enjoying the crunch and the salty goodness. Others, like my sister and brother-in-law, like to dip them in Ranch or Cajun Ranch Dressing. But no matter how they like them, everyone in our family knows that as soon as the soil starts to warm that it's just a matter of time before Fried Sage leaves are back.

As to the Age of recipe – it's anyone's guess ... my dad remembers eating them when he was a boy, and he's 71 so apparently this has been a long standing tradition in our family for at least 4 generations; although for about 10 years after my grandpa passed it was "lost" ... just waiting in the herb garden to be found and be a part of our family history of food again.

Fried Sage – or Nature's "Potato Chips"
Amy Wertheim, Atlanta, Illinois

Ingredients:

50 –100 sage leaves – any variety of sage will work
3 cups flour
Vegetable oil
Seasoning Salt, to taste

Possible dipping sauces:
Ranch dressing or Cajun Ranch dressing

Directions:

Pick 50 –100 sage leaves. Be sure to pick only the ones that are whole leaves – holes mean buggies have already been snacking on that one! Rinse thoroughly with water, leave damp.

Place about 3 cups of flour (you may need more depending on how many leaves you picked) and coat both sides of the leaves.

Heat the vegetable oil- we use a Fry Daddy, but you can cook the leaves in a skillet; use enough oil in a skillet to have a 2-inch pool. Drop a few sprinkles of flour in the hot oil, if it sizzles, you're ready to cook!

Drop sage into the hot oil – don't over fill the Fry Daddy or skillet. The sage leaves are finished cooking when they suddenly stop bubbling or sizzling …. About 30 seconds.

Remove and allow to drain on paper towel; sprinkle with seasoning salt to taste.

Once cool, enjoy. Some people like them plain, some like dipping sauce. Please try without sauce first. Enjoy!

Recipe Index
(In most cases the original recipe titles are maintained.)

Appetizers
  Fried Sage Leaves (Fried Sage – or Nature's "Potato Chips," Amy Wertheim), 295
  Mushrooms (Houby, Linda D. Cifuentes), 289

Beans
  Baked Beans (Grandma Cook's Disappearing Baked Beans, Crystal R. Smith), 159
  Baked Beans (Beans N'Such, Mary Gillespie), 162
  Kidney Beans (Kidney Bean Salad, Linda D. Cifuentes), 63
  Lima Beans (Lima Beans in Tomato Sauce, Marilyn Okon), 177

Beef
  Beef and Noodles (Grandma's Beef and Noodles, Carmen Arnberger), 92
  Beef and Noodles (Old Version – Beef 'n Noodles, from *Mrs. Peterson's Simplified Cooking*, Amy Wertheim), 100
  Beef and Noodles (Updated Version Beef & Noodles, Amy Wertheim), 98
  Meatloaf (Grandma Delong's Meatloaf, Janie Saner), 128
  Meatloaf (Great-Grandma's Meatloaf Cake, Amy Wertheim), 132
  Ox Tail Soup (Linda D. Cifuentes), 46
  Pasties (Great Grandma's Pasties, Dianna M. Wara), 140
  Polenta with Meat Sauce (Michael Marchizza), 148
  Rolled Round Steak (Ptacki, Linda D. Cifuentes), 151
  Round Steak, Potato Dumplings and Gravy (Kluski [Potato Dumplings] with Round Steak and Gravy, Caroline M. Becker), 124
  Stuffed Cabbage (Grandma Guth's Stuffed Cabbage Rolls with Sauerkraut, Denise Bollman), 103
  Stuffed Peppers (Linda D. Cifuentes), 155

Beverages
  Mint Drink (Grandma's Mint Drink, Rob Dunbar), 291

Breads
  Breakfast Bread (Potica, Dianna M. Wara), 12
  Irish Soda Bread (The Kenny Family's Irish Soda Bread, Margaret Baucom), 9

Breakfast
  Blackberry Dumplings (Grandma Bushon's Blackberry Dumplings, Carol Meadows), 28
  Breakfast Bread (Potica, Dianna M. Wara), 12
  Breakfast Casserole (Bacon, Potato, Cheese Casserole, Dennis Kirby), 18
  Coffeecake (Bublanina, Linda D. Cifuentes), 21
  Cottage Cheese Pie (Cottage Cheese Breakfast Pie/Dessert, Dennis Kirby), 32
  Donuts (Grandmother Nickel's Donuts, Jone Schumacher), 24
  Irish Soda Bread (The Kenny Family's Irish Soda Bread, Margaret Baucom), 9

Cakes
  Cherry Cake (Grandma's Birthday Cherry Cake, Linda D. Cifuentas), 189
  Cherry Walnut Cake (1-2-3-4 Cake, Marilyn Okon), 187
  Fruit Cake (Sarah Leonard's Family Fruit Cake, Brazilla Leonard), 194
  Gingerbread Cake (Grandmother's Gingerbread Cake, Gail Long), 196
  Pound Cake (Chocolate Sour Cream Pound Cake, Pamela Lynn Sage), 191
  Prune Cake (Barbara [Luchtefeld] Hopgood), 198
  Rhubarb Cake (Grandma's Rhubarb Dessert, Amy Wendling), 269
  Rhubarb Cake (Rhubarb Roll Up, Liz Drake), 272
  Upside Down Cake (Mary Joan Miller), 201

Candies
  Peanut Brittle (Amy Wertheim), 211
  Fudge (Grandma's Black Walnut Fudge, Nancy Bathurst), 207

Condiments
  Apple Sauce (Nanny's Mother's Applesauce, Kitsy Amrheim), 282
  Barbecue Sauce (Carol Meadows), 283

Cookies
  Brown Sugar Cookies (Great-Great Grandma Rouch's Brown Sugar Cookies, Elizabeth Carter), 213
  Molasses Cookies (Molasses Cut-Out Cookies, Jone Schumacher), 218
  Pfeffernusse Cookies (Betty Moser), 221
  Sugar Cookies (Grandma Rouch's Sweet Legacy Sugar Cookies, Darlene Crider), 223

Desserts
  (see All, Cakes, Candies, Cookies, Pies, Desserts Varied)

Desserts (All)
  Apple Dumplings (Darlene Crider), 252
  Blackberry Bubble (Grandma's Old Fashioned Blackberry Bubble, Earl Meadows), 254
  Blackberry Dumplings (Grandma Bushon's Blackberry Dumplings, Carol Meadows), 28
  Brown Sugar Cookies (Great-Great Grandma Rouch's Brown Sugar Cookies, Elizabeth Carter), 213
  Butterscotch Pie (Amy Wertheim), 228
  Cherry Cake (Grandma's Birthday Cherry Cake, Linda D. Cifuentas), 189
  Cherry Walnut Cake (1-2-3-4 Cake, Marilyn Okon), 187
  Coffeecake (Bublanina, Linda D. Cifuentes), 21
  Cottage Cheese Pie (Cottage Cheese Breakfast Pie/Dessert, Dennis Kirby), 32
  Date Nut Pudding (My Family's Recipe for Date Nut Pudding, Grace Meadows), 260
  French Pastry (Religieuse, Michael Marchizza), 234
  Fruit Cake (Sarah Leonard's Family Fruit Cake, Brazilla Leonard), 194
  Fruit Cobbler (Grandma's Cobbler, Kitsy Amrheim), 258
  Fudge (Grandma's Black Walnut Fudge, Nancy Bathurst), 207
  Fudge Tarts (Grandmommy's [My] Fudge Tarts, Jone Schumacher), 265
  Gingerbread Cake (Grandmother's Gingerbread Cake, Gail Long), 196
  Meringue Shells (Grandmother's Meringue Shells, Jone Schumacher), 264
  Molasses Cookies (Molasses Cut-Out Cookies, Jone Schumacher), 218
  Peach Pie (Grandma Daniel's Spicy Peach Pie, Carol Meadows), 231
  Peanut Brittle (Amy Wertheim), 211
  Pfeffernusse Cookies (Betty Moser), 221
  Pound Cake (Chocolate Sour Cream Pound Cake, Pamela Lynn Sage), 191
  Prune Cake (Barbara [Luchtefeld] Hopgood), 198
  Raspberry Sauce (Grandmother's Raspberry Sauce, Jone Schumacher), 264
  Rhubarb Cake (Grandma's Rhubarb Dessert, Amy Wendling), 269
  Rhubarb Roll Up (Liz Drake), 272
  Rice Pudding (Old Fashioned Baked Rice Pudding, Betty Moser), 274
  Strawberry Pie (Best Strawberry Pie Ever, Kitsy Amrheim), 238
  Sugar Cookies (Grandma Rouch's Sweet Legacy Sugar Cookies, Darlene Crider), 223
  Sugar Pie (Dianna M. Wara), 244
  Upside Down Cake (Mary Joan Miller), 201
  Zwieback Pie (Kitsy Amrheim), 246
Desserts (Varied)
  Apple Dumplings (Darlene Crider), 252
  Blackberry Dumplings (Grandma Bushon's Blackberry Dumplings, Carol Meadows), 28

Blackberry Bubble (Grandma's Old Fashioned Blackberry Bubble, Earl Meadows), 254
Coffeecake (Bublanina, Linda D. Cifuentes), 21
Date Nut Pudding (My Family's Recipe for Date Nut Pudding, Grace Meadows), 260
French Pastry (Religieuse, Michael Marchizza), 234
Fruit Cobbler (Grandma's Cobbler, Kitsy Amrheim), 258
Fudge Tarts (Grandmommy's [My] Fudge Tarts, Jone Schumacher), 265
Meringue Shells (Grandmother's Meringue Shells, Jone Schumacher), 264
Raspberry Sauce (Grandmother's Raspberry Sauce, Jone Schumacher), 264
Rhubarb Dessert (Grandma's Rhubarb Dessert, Amy Wendling), 269
Rhubarb Roll Up (Liz Drake), 272
Rice Pudding (Old Fashioned Baked Rice Pudding, Betty Moser), 274

Main Dishes
Breakfast Casserole (Bacon, Potato, Cheese Casserole, Dennis Kirby), 18
Beef and Noodles (Grandma's Beef and Noodles, Carmen Arnberger), 92
Beef and Noodles (Updated Version Beef and Noodles, Amy Wertheim), 98
Beef and Noodles (Old Version – Beef 'n Noodles, from *Mrs. Peterson's Simplified Cooking*, Amy Wertheim), 100
Chicken and Dumplings (Aunt Pearl's Chicken and Dumplings, Carol Meadows), 106
Chicken and Noodles, (Rouch Family Chicken and Noodles, Darlene Crider), 110
Chicken Salad (Beulah's Chicken Salad, Jone Schumacher), 58
Fruit Dumplings (Svestkove Knedlicky, Linda D. Cifuentes), 121
Meatloaf (Grandma Delong's Meatloaf, Janie Saner), 128
Meatloaf (Great-Grandma's Meatloaf Cake, Amy Wertheim), 132
Oven Fried Chicken (Old Fashion Oven Fried Chicken, Jone Schumacher), 116
Oyster Dressing (Original Oyster Dressing, Amy Wertheim), 136
Oyster Dressing (Today's Oyster Dressing, Amy Wertheim), 137
Pasties (Great Grandma's Pasties, Dianna M. Wara), 140
Polenta with Meat Sauce (Michael Marchizza), 148
Rolled Round Steak (Ptacki, Linda D. Cifuentes), 151
Round Steak, Potato Dumplings and Gravy (Kluski [Potato Dumplings] with Round Steak and Gravy, Caroline M. Becker), 125
Stew of Shrimp and Rice (Peixe a Lumbo [African Shrimp and Rice Stew], Amy Wertheim), 144
Stuffed Cabbage (Stuffed Cabbage Rolls with Sauerkraut, Grandma Guth's), Denise Bollman), 103
Stuffed Peppers (Linda D. Cifuentes), 155

Pies
  Butterscotch Pie (Amy Wertheim), 228
  Cottage Cheese Pie (Cottage Cheese Breakfast Pie/Dessert, Dennis Kirby), 32
  French Pastry (Religieuse, Michael Marchizza), 234
  Peach Pie (Grandma Daniel's Spicy Peach Pie, Carol Meadows), 231
  Strawberry Pie (Best Strawberry Pie Ever, Kitsy Amrheim), 238
  Sugar Pie (Dianna M. Wara), 244
  Zwieback Pie (Kitsy Amrheim), 246

Pork (including Bacon)
  Breakfast Casserole (Bacon, Potato, Cheese Casserole, Dennis Kirby), 18
  Baked Beans (Grandma Cook's Disappearing Baked Beans, Crystal R. Smith), 159
  Baked Beans (Beans N'Such, Mary Gillespie), 162
  Beef and Noodles (Old Version – Beef 'n Noodles, from *Mrs. Peterson's Simplified Cooking*, Amy Wertheim), 100
  Greens (Spring Wild Greens, Kimberli Yount Goodner), 181
  Lima Beans in Tomato Sauce (Marilyn Okon), 177
  Meatloaf (Great-Grandma's Meatloaf Cake, Amy Wertheim), 132
  Polenta with Meat Sauce (Michael Marchizza), 148
  Potato Salad (Great-Grandma's German Potato Salad, Jill Jackson), 77
  Rolled Round Steak (Ptacki, Linda D. Cifuentes), 151
  Round Steak, Potato Dumplings and Gravy (Kluski [Potato Dumplings] with Round Steak and Gravy, Caroline M. Becker), 125
  Stuffed Cabbage (Grandma Guth's Stuffed Cabbage Rolls with Sauerkraut, Denise Bollman), 103

Poultry
  Chicken and Dumplings (Aunt Pearl's Chicken and Dumplings, Carol Meadows), 106
  Chicken and Noodles (Rouch Family Chicken and Noodles, Darlene Crider), 110
  Chicken Salad (Beulah's Chicken Salad, Jone Schumacher), 58
  Oven Fried Chicken (Old Fashion Oven Fried Chicken, Jone Schumacher), 116

Salads
  Chicken Salad (Beulah's Chicken Salad, Jone Schumacher), 58
  Gelatin Salad (Mother's Day Strawberry Rhubarb Salad, Jone Schumacher), 85
  Kidney Bean Salad (Linda D. Cifuentes), 63
  Pasta Salad (Grandma Mohr's Pasta Salad, Kitsy Amrheim), 66
  Pasta Salad (Ruth's Pasta Salad, Jackie Bales), 70

Potato Salad (Dueling Potato Salads, Pam Elliott), 72
Potato Salad (Great-Grandma's German Potato Salad, Jill Jackson), 77
Potato Salad (Grandmother Wierman's Mashed Potato Salad, Christine Beckman), 80

Side Dishes
  Baked Beans (Beans N'Such, Mary Gillespie), 162
  Baked Beans (Grandma Cook's Disappearing Baked Beans, Crystal R. Smith), 159
  Carrot Souffle (Souffle de Zanahoria, Linda D. Cifuentes), 167
  Corn Pudding (Aunt Lynd's Infamous Corn Pudding, Amy Wertheim), 175
  Greens (Spring Wild Greens, Kimberli Yount Goodner), 181
  Lima Beans in Tomato Sauce (Marilyn Okon), 177
  Mashed Potatoes (Darlene Crider), 111
  Mushrooms (Houby, Linda D. Cifuentes), 289
  Oyster Dressing (Original Oyster Dressing, Amy Wertheim), 136
  Oyster Dressing (Today's Oyster Dressing, Amy Wertheim), 137
  Potato Dumplings (Kluski [Potato Dumplings], Caroline M. Becker), 124
  Stewed Cabbage with Tomatoes (Tomato Cabbage, Cindy Petriw), 183

Soups
  Asparagus Soup (Simple Asparagus Soup, Amy Wertheim), 42
  Beet Soup (Saltibarsciai, Deborah Steele), 51
  Ox Tail Soup (Linda D. Cifuentes), 46
  Potato Soup with Dumplings (Potato Soup with Rivels, Darlene Crider), 48
  Tomato Soup (Carlene Carter), 53
  White Asparagus Soup (Spargelsuppe, Amy Wertheim), 41

Vegetables
  Asparagus Soup (Simple Asparagus Soup, Amy Wertheim), 42
  Baked Beans (Grandma Cook's Disappearing Baked Beans, Crystal R. Smith), 159
  Baked Beans (Beans N'Such, Mary Gillespie), 162
  Beet Soup (Saltibarsciai, Deborah Steele), 51
  Carrot Souffle (Souffle de Zanahoria, Linda D. Cifuentes), 167
  Corn Pudding (Aunt Lynd's Infamous Corn Pudding, Amy Wertheim), 175
  Fried Sage Leaves (Fried Sage - or Nature's "Potato Chips," Amy Wertheim), 295
  Greens (Spring Wild Greens, Kimberli Yount Goodner), 181
  Kidney Bean Salad (Linda D. Cifuentes), 63
  Lima Beans in Tomato Sauce (Marilyn Okon), 177
  Mashed Potatoes (Darlene Crider), 111

Mushrooms (Houby, Linda D. Cifuentes), 289
Potato Salad (Dueling Potato Salads, Pam Elliott), 72
Potato Salad (Great-Grandma's German Potato Salad, Jill Jackson), 77
Potato Salad (Grandmother Wierman's Mashed Potato Salad, Christine Beckman), 80
Potato Soup with Dumplings (Potato Soup with Rivels, Darlene Crider), 48
Stewed Cabbage with Tomatoes (Tomato Cabbage, Cindy Petriw), 183
Stuffed Peppers (Linda D. Cifuentes), 155
Stuffed Cabbage (Grandma Guth's Stuffed Cabbage Rolls with Sauerkraut, Denise Bollman), 103
Sweet Corn (Family Sweet Corn, Jone Schumacher), 173
Tomato Soup (Carlene Carter), 53
White Asparagus Soup (Spargelsuppe, Amy Wertheim), 41

www.ingramcontent.com/pod-product-compliance
Lightning Source LLC
Chambersburg PA
CBHW041315110526
44591CB00021B/2795